SMITHSONIAN CONTRIBUTIONS TO KNOWLEDGE   Vol 2.

(pub. 15)

# ABORIGINAL MONUMENTS

1 72

## OF

# THE STATE OF NEW-YORK.

### COMPRISING THE RESULTS OF

## ORIGINAL SURVEYS AND EXPLORATIONS;

## WITH AN ILLUSTRATIVE APPENDIX,

BY

## E G. SQUIER, A M

FOREIGN MEMBER OF THE BRITISH ARCHÆOLOGICAL ASSOCIATION, MEMBER OF THE AMERICAN
ETHNOLOGICAL SOCIETY, THE PHILADELPHIA ACADEMY OF NATURAL SCIENCES, THE
NEW-YORK HISTORICAL SOCIETY, THE MASSACHUSETTS HISTORICAL SOCIETY, THE
HISTORICAL AND ANTIQUARIAN SOCIETY OF TENNESSEE, ETC ETC

ACCEPTED FOR PUBLICATION

BY THE SMITHSONIAN INSTITUTION,

OCTOBER 20TH, 1849

VOL II

COMMISSION

TO WHICH THE MEMOIR HAS BEEN REFERRED

BRANTZ MAYER, ESQ ,      *Of Baltimore*

WM W TURNER,      . *Union Theol. Sem , N Y.*

JOSEPH HENRY,

*Secretary of the Smithsonian Institution*

WASHINGTON, D C

*July,* 1850

PRINTED BY EDWARD O JENKINS

114 Nassau street, New York

# CONTENTS.

# ABORIGINAL MONUMENTS

OF THE

# STATE OF NEW YORK.

## CHAPTER I

### INTRODUCTORY OBSERVATIONS

THE Indian tribes found in possession of the country now embraced within the limits of New England and the Middle States have left few monuments to attest their former presence   The fragile structures which they erected for protection and defence have long ago crumbled to the earth , and the sites of their ancient towns and villages are indicated only by the ashes of their long-extinguished fires, and by the few rude relics which the plough of the invader exposes to his curious gaze   Their cemeteries, marked in very rare instances by enduring monuments, are now undistinguishable, except where the hand of modern improvement encroaches upon the sanctity of the grave.   The forest-trees, upon the smooth bark of which the Indian hunter commemorated his exploits in war, or success in the chase—the first rude efforts towards a written language—have withered in the lapse of time, or fallen beneath the inexorable axe.   The rock upon which the same primitive historian laboriously wrought out his rude, but to him significant picture, alone resists the corrosion of years.   Perhaps no people equally numerous have passed away without leaving more decided memorials of their former existence.   Excepting the significant names of their sonorous language, which still attach to our mountains, lakes, and streams, little remains to recall the memory of the departed race

But notwithstanding the almost entire absence of monuments of art clearly referable to the Indian tribes discovered in the actual possession of the region above indicated, it has long been known that many evidences of ancient labor and skill are to be found in the western parts of New York and Pennsylvania, upon the upper tributaries of the Ohio, and along the shores of Lakes Erie and Ontario. Here we find a series of ancient earth-works, entrenched hills, and occasional mounds, or tumuli, concerning which history is mute, and the origin of which has been regarded as involved in impenetrable mystery.   These remains became a

2

subject of frequent remark, as the tide of emigration flowed westward, and various detached notices of their existence were, from time to time, made public   No connected view of their extent or character was, however, given to the world, until 1817, when De Witt Clinton, whose energetic mind neglected no department of inquiry, read a brief memoir upon the subject before the "Literary and Philoso- phical Society of New York," which was published in pamphlet form, at Albany, in 1818   Mr Clinton in this memoir did not profess to give a complete view of the matter, his aim being, in his own language, "to awaken the public mind to a subject of great importance, before the means of investigation were entirely lost." It consequently contains but little more than notices of such ancient earth-works, and other interesting remains of antiquity, as had at that time fallen under his notice, or of which he had received some distinct information   Its publication was, how- ever, without any immediate effect, for few individuals, at that period, felt the interest requisite, or possessed the opportunities necessary, to the continuance of the investigations thus worthily commenced.   Nothing further, it is believed, appeared upon the subject, until the publication of McCauley's History of New York, in 1828   This work contained a chapter upon the antiquities of the State, embodying the essential parts of Mr. Clinton's memoir, together with some facts of considerable interest, which had fallen under the observation of the author him- self   Within a few years, public attention has again been directed to the subject by Mr Schoolcraft, in his "Notes on the Iroquois."   Some detached facts have also been presented in local histories and publications, but usually in so loose and vague a manner as to be of little value for purposes of comparison and research

The observations of all these authorities were merely incidental, and were limited in their range.   By none were presented plans, from actual surveys, of any of the ancient works of the State, a deficiency which, it is evident, could not be supplied by descriptions, however full and accurate, and without which it has been found impossible to institute the comparisons requisite to correct conclusions as to the date, origin, and probable connections of these remains   It has all along been represented that some of the enclosures were of regular outlines, true circles and ellipses and accurate squares—features which would imply a common origin with the vast system of ancient earth-works of the Mississippi Valley   Submitted to the test of actual survey, I have found that the works which were esteemed entirely regular are the very reverse, and that the builders, instead of constructing them upon geometrical principles, regulated their forms entirely by the nature of the ground upon which they were built   And I may here mention, that none of the ancient works of this State, of which traces remain displaying any considerable degree of regularity, can lay claim to high antiquity.   All of them may be referred, with certainty, to the period succeeding the commencement of European inter- course

Mr Clinton was unable to learn of the occurrence of any remains upon the first terrace back from the lakes, and, upon the basis of the assumed fact of their non- existence, advanced the opinion that the subsidence of the lakes and the formation of this terrace had taken place since these works were erected—a chronological period which I shall not attempt to measure by years   This deduction has been received, I believe, by every succeeding writer upon the subject of our antiquities, without any attempt to verify the assumption upon which it rests. I have, however, found that the works occur indiscriminately upon the first and upon the superior terraces, as also upon the islands of the lakes and rivers.

Misled by statements which no opportunity was afforded of verifying, I have elsewhere, though in a guarded manner, ventured the opinion that the ancient remains of western New York belonged to the same system with those of Ohio and the West generally. Under this hypothesis, the question whether they were the weaker efforts of a colony, starting from the southwestern centres, or the ruder beginnings of a people just emerging from a nomadic state, becoming fixed in their habits, and subsequently migrating southward, next suggested itself, and I gladly availed myself of the joint liberality of the Smithsonian Institution and the Historical Society of New York, to undertake its investigation. The results of my observations are briefly presented in the following pages. These observations extended from the county of St. Lawrence on the north, to Chautauque on the south, embracing the counties of Jefferson, Oswego, Onondaga, Oneida, Cayuga, Seneca, Ontario, Wayne, Monroe, Livingston, Orleans, Niagara, Erie, Genesee, and Wyoming. Throughout this entire region ancient remains are found in considerable abundance; they are also occasionally found in the counties adjoining those above named, upon the principal tributaries of the Delaware, Susquehanna, and Alleghany. They are known to extend down the Susquehanna, as far as the valley of the Wyoming; and a single one was discovered as far east as Montgomery county, in the neighborhood of Fort Plain. Some, it is said, are to be found in Canada, but no definite information was received of their localities. It is to be observed that they are most numerous in sections remarkable for their fertility of soil, their proximity to favorable hunting and fishing grounds—in short, possessing the greatest number of requisites to easy subsistence. They are particularly numerous in Jefferson county, in the vicinity of the central lakes, in the southern part of Monroe, in Livingston, Genesee, and Erie counties. Many are said to exist in Chautauque, but the lateness of the season, and the unsuspected number of remains elsewhere claiming attention, prevented me from examining them.

In respect to the number of these remains, some estimate may be formed from the fact that, in Jefferson county alone, *fifteen* enclosures were found, sufficiently well preserved to admit of being traced throughout. This is exclusive of those (probably a greater number) which have been wholly or in part destroyed, or of which no information could be obtained, in the limited time allotted to the investigation of that county. It is safe to estimate the whole number which originally existed here at between thirty and forty—a greater number than was before known to exist in the State. Erie county probably contained nearly as many. In the short period of eight weeks devoted to the search, I was enabled to ascertain the localities of not less than one hundred ancient works, and to visit and make surveys of half that number. From the facts which have fallen under my notice, I feel warranted in estimating the number which originally existed in the State at from two hundred to two hundred and fifty. Probably one half of these have been obliterated by the plough, or so much encroached upon as to be no longer satisfactorily traced.

Were these works of the general large dimensions of those of the Western States their numbers would be a just ground of astonishment  They are, however, for the most part, comparatively small, varying from one to four acres,—the largest not exceeding sixteen acres in area.  The embankments, too, are slight, and the ditches shallow ; the former seldom more than four feet in height, and the latter of corresponding proportions.  The work most distinctly marked exists in the town of Oakfield, Genesee county, it measures, in some places, between seven and eight feet from the bottom of the ditch to the top of the wall  In some cases the embankment is not more than a foot in height, and the trench of the same depth. Lest it should be doubted whether works so slight can be satisfactorily traced, it may be observed, that a regular and continuous elevation of six inches may always be followed without difficulty.

In respect of position, a very great uniformity is to be observed throughout. Most occupy high and commanding sites near the bluff edges of the broad terraces by which the country rises from the level of the lakes  From the brows of the limestone ledges, where some of these works occur, in Jefferson and Erie counties, most extensive prospects may be obtained, often terminating in the blue belt of the lakes, distant from ten to forty miles, the intervening country presenting a beautiful variety of cleared and forest lands, dotted with houses, churches, and villages When found upon lower grounds, it is usually upon some dry knoll or little hill, or where banks of streams serve to lend security to the position  A few have been found upon slight elevations in the midst of swamps, where dense forests and almost impassable marshes protected them from discovery and attack.  In nearly all cases they are placed in close proximity to some unfailing supply of water, near copious springs or running streams.  Gateways, opening toward these, are always to be observed, and in some cases guarded passages are also visible  These circumstances, in connection with others not less unequivocal, indicate, with great precision, the purposes for which these structures were erected

It has already been mentioned that Messrs Clinton, Yates, and Moulton, and others, have concluded, upon the assumption that none of these works occur upon the first and second terraces above the lakes, that the latter have subsided to their present level since their erection  This conclusion does not necessarily follow from the premises  Few positions susceptible of defence, under the system practised by all rude people, are to be found upon either of these terraces ; the builders, consequently, availed themselves of the numerous headlands and other defensible positions which border the supposed ancient shores of the lakes, simply because they afforded the most effectual protection, with the least expenditure of labor

I found an entire uniformity in the indications of occupancy, and in the character of the remains of art discovered within these enclosures, throughout the whole range of their occurrence  The first feature which attracts notice, upon entering them, is a number of pits or excavations in the earth, usually at the points which are most elevated and dry  These pits are occasionally of considerable size, and are popularly called " wells," although nothing is more obvious than that they never could have been designed for any such purpose  They are usually from three to four, but sometimes from six to eight feet in depth, and of proportionate size at the top.  Their purposes become sufficiently evident upon excavation  They were the *caches* in which the former occupants of these works deposited their stores  Parched corn, now completely carbonized by long exposure, is to be discovered in considerable abundance in many of them  Instances fell under my notice where it had been found untouched to the amount of bushels, in these primitive depositories  Traces of the bark and thin slips of wood, by which the deposits were surrounded, are also frequently to be found  In many of these enclosures the sites of the ancient lodges, or cabins, are still to be traced.  These are marked by considerable accumulations of decomposed and carbonaceous matter—stones much burned, charcoal and ashes mingled with the bones of animals, with numerous fragments of pottery, broken pipes, and occasionally rude ornaments, such as beads of stone, bone, and shell  The pottery, I may observe incidentally, is of very good material, and appears to have been worked and ornamented with considerable taste and skill  It is found in great abundance; and, in many of the enclosures now under cultivation, bushels of fragments might, if desirable, be collected without difficulty  The material, in common with that of all the aboriginal pottery of the North, is composed of clay tempered (if I may use the term) with pounded quartz and shells, or with fine sand, so as to prevent shrinkage, and resist the action of fire  Most of it is well burned, but none exhibits any appearance of glazing.  The pipes are mostly composed of clay, regularly and often fancifully moulded, and ornamented in various ways  Some bear the form of animals, the distinctive features of which are well preserved , others are moulded in the shape of the human head, or are variously fluted and dotted with regular figures  They are generally of very good material, the clay of fine quality, and well burned. Some, indeed, are so hard, smooth, and symmetrical, as almost to induce doubts of their aboriginal origin  Some of the terra cottas, other than pipes, are really very creditable specimens of art, and compare favorably with any of the productions of the aborigines which have fallen under my notice  They are, with few exceptions, representations of animals ; with the minutest features, as well as the peculiar habits of which, the American Indians had, from long observation, a thorough acquaintance

# CHAPTER II.

## EARTH-WORKS, ENCLOSURES, ETC.

For the sake of convenience and easy reference, the enclosures of earth are arranged according to counties, and so described   Works which were constructed of palisades simply, without embankments or ditches, do not fall within this arrangement, but will be described collectively in a separate chapter, under the head of "PALISADED ENCLOSURES "

# ST. LAWRENCE COUNTY.

A few aboriginal monuments are said to have existed in this county. One or two of these occurred near Pottsdam; but it is probable they are now nearly, if not quite, obliterated

A mound, eight feet in height, still exists on St. Regis Island, in the St Lawrence River  It is crossed by the boundary line separating the territories of the United States and Great Britain  It was excavated by Col. Hawkins, of the United States Boundary Commission, in 1818.  Near the surface were human bones in considerable numbers, and in good preservation, but at the base were found traces of fire, charcoal, burned bones, and fragments of pottery, together with some stone implements and ornaments.

Upon the Canada shore of the St Lawrence River, opposite Morrisville in this county, a singular aboriginal deposit was discovered some years ago. in making the excavations for the St Lawrence Canal  The principal facts concerning them were communicated to the author by Dr T Reynolds, of Brockville, C. W , and are embodied in Vol. I. of the "Smithsonian Contributions to Knowledge," pp. 201, 202  Amongst the relics of copper and other materials discovered at this spot and described as above, was a small *terra cotta* mask of very good workman-

Fig 1

ship.  An engraving of the size of the original is herewith presented (Fig. 1)  Mr Reynolds, who has the relic in his possession, describes it as follows  "It is of clay, and represents the contour of the Indian head, after which it appears to have been moulded  It corresponds very nearly in shape with the skulls discovered at the same place, and the *foramina* or holes found in the skull, are well represented,—showing that it was modelled to resemble the bony structure of the head, not the flesh or living subject  It seems to have been broken off from some idol or image "

# JEFFERSON COUNTY.

THIS county is bounded on one side by Lake Ontario, and upon the other by the wild, mountainous region which separates the waters of the Hudson River from those of the St. Lawrence. It is intersected by the Black River, one of the most picturesque streams of the State. Its surface is diversified: for about ten miles back from the shores of the lake, it is nearly level; we then reach the ledges of the Trenton limestone, and the entire country becomes more elevated and irregular. These natural features, implying an abundance of fish and game, joined to great fertility of soil and easy cultivation, fitted this county for sustaining a large aboriginal population. We are not surprised, therefore, at finding here numerous traces of former occupancy. These consist chiefly of enclosures of irregular outlines, situated, for the most part, upon the borders of the high table-land or terrace formed by the abrupt termination of the great limestone deposit of the Trenton group, the base of which, it is supposed, was formerly washed by the waters of Lake Ontario. Quite a number of these works, however, occur upon the lower terrace, in places where the natural features of the ground were favorable to their construction and objects. Works were examined in this county, in the townships of Watertown, Le Ray, Rutland, Rodman, Adams, and Ellisburgh.

The following examples are presented in the order in which they were surveyed.

———

## PLATE I

### ANCIENT WORK, ADAMS TOWNSHIP, JEFFERSON COUNTY, NEW YORK

THIS work occupies a commanding position upon the brow of the second terrace, which is here some hundreds of feet in height, and very abrupt. The ground immediately back of the site of the work is considerably depressed and swampy. It is drained by a little stream (*a*), which, falling over the cliff, forms a small but picturesque cascade. The narrow channel of this stream was formerly obstructed by a beaver-dam, which converted the marsh into a deep and impassable pond. The elevation upon which this work is situated, it will thus be seen, was well fitted by nature for defensive purposes,—possessing the two primary requisites, difficult approach and an unfailing supply of water.

The artificial defences consist of an embankment of earth, with an exterior

3

ditch. The forest covers the greater part of the work, and here the lines are still well preserved. The embankment has an average height of perhaps three feet, by ten feet in width at the base, the ditch is of corresponding dimensions  There are not less than seven gateways, varying from eight to thirty feet in width  Upon the right of the work, towards the swamp already mentioned, there is an abrupt bank not far from thirty feet in height, where the defences are interrupted  At the point indicated by the letter *b*, a large bass-wood (linden) tree is standing upon the embankment  It measures twelve feet in circumference, three feet above the ground. The trees within the enclosure are of the usual size.

Upon the northeastern slope of the eminence, within the walls of the enclosure, and where the soil is sandy and dry, are a great number of small pits and depressions in the earth. They are now nearly filled by accumulations of leaves, but they must at first have been from four to six feet in depth. Upon excavating some of them, it was found that they were the *caches* in which the former occupants of the work had placed their stores *  And although it seems probable the original deposits had been removed, considerable quantities of parched corn, now carbonized by long exposure, were still to be found within them. There were, perhaps, forty or fifty of these excavations within the walls, and several upon the crown of the eminence at *c*

Upon removing the leaves at various points within the work, carbonaceous accumulations, bones of animals, fragments of pottery, and other evidences of occupation were discovered. A small portion of the work, indicated on the map, has been cleared and put under cultivation. Here, just exterior to the wall, upon the brow of the natural bank, at the spot marked *d*, several skeletons have been exhumed by the plough  They had been buried in a sitting posture, and were very well preserved

By the operation of diluvial causes, the drift has been deposited, in a very singu-

---

* The term *cache*, literally *a hide* or place of concealment, is of French origin, and has become current amongst all the traders and trappers on the frontiers  The practice of *caching* or hiding goods or provisions on outward marches, to be used upon returning, or by parties following, was derived from the Indians, among whom it was general  A *cache* is made by digging a hole in the ground, which is lined with sticks, grass, or any material which will protect the contents from the dampness of the earth  After the goods or provisions have been deposited, the earth is carefully covered over, so as to best prevent the penetration of water from above  ' It is often, in fact always necessary, at the West, to leave no signs by means of which rival parties or the cunning savages may discover the place of deposit  To this end the excavated earth is carried to a distance, and carefully concealed, or thrown into a stream, if one is near  The place selected is usually some rolling point, sufficiently elevated to be secure from inundations  If it be well set with grass, a solid piece of the turf of the size of the proposed excavation is cut out  It is afterwards laid back, and taking root in a short time, no signs remain of its ever having been molested  However, as every locality does not afford a turfy spot, the camp fire is sometimes built upon the place, or the animals are penned over it, which effectually destroys all trace of the disturbance "—(*Gregg's Commerce of the Prairies*, vol 1 p 69 )  Father Hennepin, in his account of his passage down the Mississippi River, in 1680, describes an operation of this kind in the following terms  " We took up the green sod, and laid it by, and digged a hole in the earth, where we put our goods, and covered them with pieces of timber and earth, and then put in again the green turf  so that it was impossible to suspect that any hole had been digged under it, for we flung the earth into the river "

lar manner, upon the table-land upon which the above work is situated. In some places it occurs in long, narrow ridges, conforming to the general course of the terrace bank; in others it forms amphitheatres of various sizes, and in a few instances it assumes a conical shape, resembling artificial tumuli. A short distance to the right of the work under notice is a small natural amphitheatre, rising in the midst of the marshy grounds, which has been supposed by some to be artificial Its relative position is indicated by the letter *e*

About one and a half miles southeast of the above work, was formerly another of perhaps larger size. It occupied a high, oval-shaped hill, one side of which is very steep, while the other subsides gently to the general level The embankment extended in a semicircular form around that part of the hill not protected by nature; and, previous to the cultivation of the ground, was upwards of six feet in height from the bottom of the trench A very slight depression, and the greater luxuriance of the verdure, resulting from the filling of the trench with surface loam, are all that now indicate the original lines It is said that there was an avenue leading off, for some distance, to the westward, but it is no longer traceable. At the base of this hill is a boulder, in which are several artificial depressions, doubtless intended for mortars, and a variety of grooves, in which the stone axes and other implements of the aborigines were rubbed, in order to reduce them to the required shape

## PLATE II  No. 1

### ANCIENT WORK ON "DRY HILL," FIVE MILES SOUTHEAST OF WATERTOWN, JEFFERSON COUNTY, NEW YORK

FOLLOWING the brow of the terrace northward from the work first described, for about two miles, we come to another work of somewhat more regular figure, and of larger dimensions Most of it is under cultivation, and the outlines are very much defaced. The embankment, upon one side, runs into the forest land, where it is well preserved, measuring, perhaps, three feet in height. The darker lines of the engraving show what parts are still distinctly marked; the dotted lines those which have been ploughed down, and which are no longer distinguishable from the general level, except by the deeper green and more luxuriant growth of the grass on the line of the ancient trench. The position of the work, it will be seen, corresponds very nearly with that of the one previously described There is, however, no water near at hand, except a limited supply from a small spring. Neverthe-less, this seems to have been the site of a very populous aboriginal town. The entire area of the work is covered with accumulations of carbonaceous matter, burned stones, fragments of bones, pottery, etc. Indeed, these indications are visible for some distance exterior to the walls, upon the adjacent level. These artificial accumulations have rendered the soil within the enclosure extremely fer-tile, and it sustains most luxuriant crops. In cultivating the area, many fragments of human bones, some of them burned, have been observed,—suggesting the pos-sibility that the ancient village was destroyed by enemies, and that these are the bones of its occupants, who fell in defence of their kindred, and were burned in the fires which consumed their lodges  A little to the northward of the work, there seems to have been an aboriginal cemetery. Here the plough frequently exposes skeletons, buried according to the Indian mode, and accompanied by various rude relics of stone and bone.  Within and around the work are also found stone axes, flint arrow-heads, and other remnants of savage art  Fragments of pottery and broken pipes of clay are, however, most abundant.  Of these bushels might be collected without much difficulty.

It is clear that this work was not intended as a place of last resort, but was occupied by a considerable population for a long period.  It was undoubtedly a forti-fied town  It should be remarked, that although now nearly or quite filled up, here were originally a number of pits (popularly known as *wells*) of considerable size, the *caches* of the ancient occupants.

———

### PLATE II  No. 2

STILL continuing along the brow of the terrace northward, for two and a half or three miles, we reach a third work, the greater part of which is covered with for-est, and is consequently well preserved.  It is much smaller than any of those be-fore described, and is bounded by a series of right lines, slightly rounded at the angles, which gives it something of the appearance of a modern field-work.  The slope of the terrace bank is here comparatively gentle, and there is a *step* or table about midway from the brow to the base.  Here a number of springs start out, below the stratum of rock  Formerly the walls of the work were continued down the slope, towards the springs, as indicated by the dotted lines in the plan.  They are not now to be traced further than the edge of the terrace.  The position of this work is remarkably fine, and was selected with taste and skill  The table-land immediately around it is level; the soil gravelly and dry  There seems to have been a burial-place in this vicinity, and pipes and fragments of pottery are of common occurrence   It is to be hoped that the remaining portion of this work will be preserved from the encroachments of the plough.

---

## PLATE III  No. 1

### ANCIENT WORK HALF A MILE WEST OF BURRVILLE, NEAR WATERTOWN, JEFFERSON COUNTY, NEW YORK

A WORK, differing somewhat from those before described, is situated two miles north of the enclosure last noticed, upon a high promontory or headland, half a mile west of the little village of Burrville.  The northern base of this promontory is washed by a small and rapid stream, a branch of the east fork of Sandy Creek. Deep ravines lend strength to the position on the remaining sides, except towards the west, where it joins the highlands.  Here, extending across the neck of the promontory, (the only direction from which access is easy,) was formerly an artificial defence, consisting of an embankment of earth and a trench.  The plough has filled the one and levelled the other, but the lines can still be accurately traced by attending to the various circumstances already repeatedly mentioned   At the part marked *a*, was formerly a large deep pit, resembling the cellar of a dwelling-house   At *b*, was also an accumulation of large stones, bearing traces of fire, and which the early settlers, indulging in vague notions of the mineral wealth of the country, called "*the Furnace.*"

Most of these stones were used to fill the pit near by ; but enough still remain to mark the site of the supposed "furnace."  Whenever the land of this work is ploughed over, many relics of art are disclosed, fragments of pottery, broken pipes, implements of stone and bone, beads of similar materials, etc., etc.

About a mile northeast of this place, upon a fine level tract of ground, are the traces of an aboriginal village.  Rude fireplaces, constructed of rough stones huddled together, and surrounded by carbonaceous accumulations, sometimes two feet deep, mark the site of the ancient lodges   These indications are numerous   Here, too, are to be found relics, entirely corresponding with those already noticed, as occurring within and around the ancient enclosures.

## PLATE III. No 2.

### ANCIENT WORK, RUTLAND TOWNSHIP, JEFFERSON COUNTY, NEW YORK.

THE slightest and much the rudest structure discovered in Jefferson county, is the one here delineated. It is situated about a hundred rods back from the brow of the terrace, already so often referred to, and which here rises abruptly from the interior level, presenting a bold, and in some places, a precipitous bank.

Notwithstanding its elevation, this terrace has numberless depressions or basins, which are wet and marshy. Upon a slight elevation, in the midst of one of these, and still covered with a primitive forest, is the work in question. It will be observed that it is exceedingly irregular, and that the lines are interrupted by several wide openings, which are quite too broad to be regarded as gateways

The embankment is not of uniform dimensions   In some places it is elevated but a foot or eighteen inches, by four or five feet base, while in others it is perhaps three feet in height   The ditch is also irregular,—in sections scarcely exceeding a large plough furrow in depth and width   In fact, the work seems imperfect, and to have been constructed in haste for temporary purposes.   Within the area, which is quite uneven, are several small accumulations of stones, which bear the marks of fire   Upon removing some of them, the proprietor of the ground found ashes and other burnt matter, amongst which was a carbonized ear of maize   A small but entire vessel of pottery, of considerable symmetry of shape, was also found here some years since

Human bones have been discovered beneath the leaves ; and in nearly every part of the trench skeletons of adults of both sexes, of children, and infants, have been found, covered only by the vegetable accumulations   They seem to have been thrown together promiscuously.   They have also been found in a narrow depression resembling an artificial trench, indicated by a dotted line in the plan, and caused by the subsidence of the earth in a cleft of the limestone substratum   These skeletons, from all accounts, do not seem to have been much decayed, and no difficulty was experienced in recovering them entire.   The skulls were in some cases fractured, as if by a blow from a hatchet or club   These circumstances would seem to imply, not only that the work is of comparatively late construction, but also that this was the scene of one of those indiscriminate massacres so common in the history of savage warfare

From the bank of the terrace, near this work, a very extensive and beautiful prospect is commanded

## PLATE III  No. 3.

### ANCIENT WORK HALF A MILE WEST OF LOCKPORT, JEFFERSON COUNTY, NEW YORK.

THE remaining works of Jefferson county, so far as investigated, are situated on lower grounds, generally near streams, which are made subservient to art for purposes of defence  The work here presented is a good example  It is situated on Black River (*Kā-me-hārgo*), in Le Ray township, half a mile below the little manufacturing town of Lockport  The banks of the river are here very high, and quite inaccessible.  The character of the work is well shown in the engraving, and needs little explanation beyond what that affords  It will be seen that the ends of the embankment extend for a short distance down the slope of the river bank, and then curve slightly inwards, as though designed to prevent the flanks being turned by an enemy.  The lines, where they cross the road, and between the road and the river, are very distinct, and the embankment is between three and four feet in height  The rest of the work may be traced without much difficulty, although it has long been under cultivation.  Upon the wall, at the point indicated by the letter *c*, is still standing a pine stump, upwards of three feet in diameter, probably having an age of not less than four hundred years  The usual relics are found within the area of the enclosure, and in the natural bank at *d*, a number of skeletons have been disclosed by the plough.  They are much decayed, but in respect of position correspond with those found elsewhere in Indian cemeteries.

---

## PLATE IV  No 1

### ANCIENT WORK, LE RAY TOWNSHIP, SIX MILES NORTHEAST OF WATERTOWN.

IN the same township with the foregoing work, and about four miles distant, in a northwest direction, is the work here represented  It occupies a small sandy elevation, situated in the midst of low grounds.  It is lozenge-shaped, and is the most regular of any ancient structure which has fallen under notice of the author in the State.  Where the lines are intercepted on the north, the ground is considerably elevated, and subsides abruptly, precluding the necessity of an embankment for defensive purposes.  The sites of the ancient lodges, indicated by heaps of burned stones, calcined shells, fragments of pottery, etc, are yet to be traced, notwithstanding that the land has been for a considerable time under cultivation.  Near this work skeletons have been frequently exhumed

## PLATE IV  No  2

### ANCIENT WORK, LE RAY TOWNSHIP, JEFFERSON COUNTY, NEW YORK

THREE miles to the westward of the enclosure last described, near " Sandford's Corners," was formerly another work of similar character, but larger size.  Only a small portion of the embankment is yet visible , the dotted lines, however, show the original outlines, according to the recollection of those who were acquainted with the work before it was disturbed.  The walls then measured not less than six feet in height, measuring from the bottom of the trench.

Within the area are found great numbers of the shells of the fresh-water molluscas, accumulations of burnt matter, quantities of pottery in fragments, with broken pipes, etc.  Some of the pipes are of good workmanship and fine finish. In this vicinity, also, have skeletons been found ; all buried in a sitting posture.

Several other works formerly existed in this township, but they have been either entirely or in great part obliterated   One is spoken of near Felt's Mills, but no opportunity was afforded of examining it.

———

## PLATE IV  Nos  3  AND  4.

### ANCIENT WORKS IN ELLISBURGH TOWNSHIP, JEFFERSON COUNTY, NEW YORK.

A NUMBER of ancient works formerly existed in Ellisburgh, one of the southern towns of the county.  Plate IV., No. 3, is one of those which are yet perfect.  It presents no novel features, is protected in the usual manner, and has the usual relics and traces of occupancy within its walls.  Three quarters of a mile to the eastward is another similar, but larger work (Plate IV., No. 4), which has been very nearly obliterated by the plough.  The sections indicated in the engraving are yet quite distinct, nor can the parts supplied differ very materially from the original lines.  Perhaps no work in the State has more decided evidences of aboriginal occupation   The entire area is covered with traces of ancient habitations, and with relics of art,—pottery, ornaments, and implements.  Exterior to the walls, in all directions, but particularly on the level grounds between the two works, the same indications are abundant   Indeed, the artificial accumulations are so great as materially to augment the fertility of the soil.  *Caches* have been observed here, in some of which the present proprietor of the grounds has found a number of bushels of parched corn, carbonized by long exposure   It is scattered over the surface, and may after rains be collected in considerable quantities. Here, too, have been found skeletons buried according to the usual custom

The aboriginal population must have been very large at this spot, which, both in aspect of soil and the close proximity of springs and pure streams, affords a most beautiful site for an Indian village

About a mile to the southward of this group, upon the land of Mr. Mendall, was another work, of which no trace now remains    Another occurred at a place called Clark's Settlement, still another at Ellis Settlement, and others in various parts of the township, concerning which no definite information can now be obtained

Near the neat and pretty village of Pierrepoint's Manor, is also the site of an ancient town, undistinguishable from the fortified village already described, except by the absence of an embankment and trench    Large quantities of relics have been recovered here    A work of considerable size was visible until within a few years, half or three fourths of a mile northwest of the village of Adams, on the lands of Mr. W Benton    It is described by Mr. Justus Eddy, in a letter to the author, as having been semicircular in form, five hundred feet in diameter, and the open segment facing or rather opening towards a marshy piece of ground, through which flowed a small stream.    There were two or three breaks, or passage-ways, in the embankments    At the time of the settlement of this part of the country by the whites, about fifty years ago, trees two and three feet in diameter were growing upon the wall, and within the area.    The embankment was then between three and four feet in height    Within the work were found quantities of pottery, pipes, and beads, covered with ornamental figures.    A silver star-shaped ornament, bearing the initials P. H., was also found    It was quite thin, not exceeding the common sixpence in thickness

Upon an island, outside of Sackett's Harbor, known as Snow-shoe Island, it is said, there are traces of an ancient work    So far as could be gathered, it was a palisaded structure, unaccompanied by an embankment.

Besides the various earth-works above described, there are a number of other interesting objects of antiquarian interest in this county.    Among them may be mentioned the " *bone-pits*," or deposits of human bones    One is found near the village of Brownsville, on Black River    It is described as a pit, ten or twelve feet square, by perhaps four feet deep, in which are promiscuously heaped together a large number of human skeletons    It will be seen ultimately, that these accumulations owe their origin to a remarkable custom, common to many of the Indian tribes, of collecting and depositing together the bones of their dead, at stated intervals. Another pit, very unlike this, however, exists about three miles east of Watertown. It is situated upon the slope of a hill, and was originally marked by a number of large stones heaped over it.    Upon removing these and excavating beneath them, a pit about six feet square, and four deep, was discovered, filled with human bones, all well preserved, but in fragments.    Upwards of *forty* pairs of the *patella* were counted, showing that at least that number of skeletons had been deposited in the pit.    It is said that the bones, when first exhumed, exhibited marks such as would result from the gnawing of wild animals ; and from this circumstance, and the fact that they were so much broken up, it has been very plausibly supposed

4

that these are the bones of some party which had been cut off by enemies, and whose remains were subsequently collected and buried by their friends    All the bones are those of adults    Many of the fragments have been removed and scattered, but several bushels yet remain    No relics of any kind were found with them.

A large mound is said to occur "about one mile from Washingtonville, and eleven from Adams, on a cross-road from the 'ridge road,' leading from Lamb's tavern to Washingtonville    It is conical in shape, and thirty feet high"    It is questionable whether this is artificial

# OSWEGO COUNTY.

A GREAT part of this county is low and wet, and it is not generally so well adapted to sustain an aboriginal population as the adjoining counties of Jefferson and Onondaga.    Few ancient monuments occur within its limits, and concerning these, little was ascertained in the course of these investigations.    The following facts were chiefly derived from J V H Clark, Esq., of Manlius, Onondaga county, whose attention was especially called thereto in the preparation of his forthcoming History of the Onondaga and Oswego Country.    Two enclosures, circular in form, existed in Granby township, in the southern part of the county.    One of these occurred on State's Hundred, lot 24.    Each contained about two acres, and both had gateways opening to the east    Another formerly existed near Phillipsville, of which no traces now remain, and still another is said to occur in Granby township, near "Little Utica," in a bend of Ox Creek    Near the town of Fulton, on the west side of Oswego River, is a mound of small size, which seems to be made up of human bones promiscuously heaped together.    They are much decayed    Intermixed with them were found a number of flint arrow-heads.    It is probable that none of these remains possessed features differing essentially from those of other parts of the State.

# ONONDAGA COUNTY.

Probably no county in the State had originally a greater number of aboriginal monuments within its boundaries, than the county of Onondaga  It has, however, been so long settled, and so generally brought under cultivation, that nearly all vestiges of its ancient remains have disappeared  The sites of many are, however, still remembered, but even these will soon be forgotten  It is a fortunate circumstance that the antiquities of this county were the first to attract the attention of observers, and our accounts relating to them are more complete than concerning those of the other parts of the State  Still we have to regret that we have not a single plan from actual survey,—a deficiency which no mere description can supply  Our principal source of information respecting their numbers, localities, and character, is the memoir of De Witt Clinton, already several times alluded to  Mr. Schoolcraft and Mr. J V H Clark, of Manlius, have presented additional information, and from these authorities we derive most of the facts which follow.

Ancient works occurred in the towns of Fabius, De Witt, Lafayette, Camillus, Onondaga. Manlius, Elbridge, and Pompey ; but of many of them we know nothing beyond the simple fact of their former existence  It should be mentioned that some of the townships here named have been erected within the last few years, and since the date of Mr. Clinton's Memoir.

Those in Elbridge, according to Mr Clinton, occurred near the village of that name, about four miles from Seneca River, upon lands then (1817) occupied by Judge Munro  They were two in number  "One was on a very high hill, and covered three acres.  It had a gateway opening towards the east, and upon the west was another, communicating with a spring about ten rods from the fort  It was elliptical in shape : the ditch deep, and the eastern wall eight feet high  The stump of a black oak-tree, certainly one hundred years old, stood upon the embankment  The second work was about half a mile distant, upon lower grounds  It was constructed like the first, but was only half as large  *  *  *  *  The early settlers observed, in this vicinity, the shells of testaceous animals accumulated, in several places, in considerable masses, together with numerous fragments of pottery.  Judge Munro found, in digging the cellar of his house, several pieces of burned clay ; and, in various places, large spots of deep black mould, demonstrating the former existence of buildings or erections of some kind  At one place he observed what appeared to be a well, viz , a hole ten feet deep, and the earth much caved in  Upon digging to the depth of three and a half feet, he came to a quantity of flints, below which he found a great number of human bones "  This disposition of the dead, Mr Clinton conjectures, was made by an enemy, but we shall soon see that it probably owed its existence to the practice of gathering the bones of the dead at stated intervals, and depositing them in pits,—a practice common among the Hurons and other Indians around the great lakes

" In the town of Pompey," continues Mr Clinton, " is the highest ground in that county, which separates the waters flowing into the Chesapeake and the Gulf of St Lawrence. The most elevated portions of the town exhibit the remains of ancient settlements, and in various places the traces of a numerous population appear. About two miles south from Manlius Square, in this township, I examined the remains of a large town, which were obviously indicated by large spots of black mould, at intervals of a few paces asunder, in which I observed bones of animals, ashes, carbonized grains of corn, etc., denoting the residence of human beings This town must have extended at least half a mile from east to west, and three-quarters of a mile from north to south. On the east side of this old town there is a perpendicular descent of one hundred feet, into a deep ravine, through which flows a fine stream of water   Upon the north side is a similar ravine   Here there are graves, on each side of the ravine, close to the precipice. Some of the graves contain five or six skeletons, promiscuously thrown together. On the south bank of the ravine, gun-barrels, bullets, pieces of lead, and a skull perforated by a bullet have been found   Indeed, relics of this kind are scattered all over these grounds. A mile to the eastward of this town, there is a cemetery, containing three or four acres; and to the westward of it is still another.

" There are, in this vicinity, three old forts. placed in a triangular position, and within eight miles of each other   One is about a mile south of Jamesville [in the present town of De Witt], the second in a northeastern, and the third in a south-eastern direction   They are circular or elliptical in form, bones are found scattered over their areas, and standing on a heap of mouldering ashes, within one of them, I saw a white pine-tree, eight and a half feet in diameter, and at least one hundred and thirty years old."

Mr. Clinton expresses the opinion that the three " forts " were designed to protect the " town," the vestiges of which attracted his attention; and he even goes so far as to conjecture, from the occurrence of bones upon the brows of the northern ravine, that the attack by which the town was destroyed was made from this direction ! Of course this is wholly supposititious. The relics of European art, scattered over the site, show clearly enough that this was an Indian village, occupied by the savages subsequent to the commencement of intercourse with the whites. The traces which Mr Clinton describes are precisely those which mark the site of every abandoned Indian settlement throughout the country. This county possessed a very heavy aboriginal population, probably greater than any equal extent of territory north of the Floridas, and it is not surprising, therefore, that the traces of ancient occupancy are so abundant *   Mr. Clinton states that it was

---

* Mr Schoolcraft states, on the authority of Le Fort, late chief of the Onondagas, that Ondiaka, the great chronicler of his tribe, informed him  on his last journey to Oneida, that in ancient times, before they

estimated there were not less than eighty cemeteries in Pompey township alone. McCauley states that one of the three works, mentioned above by Mr. Clinton, was triangular in form, and contained about six acres

Mr. J V H Clark has described a work situated in part of lot 33 in this township ; but whether or not it is one of the three mentioned by Mr Clinton, it is impossible to determine. "It is about four miles southeast from Manlius village, situated on a slight eminence, which is nearly surrounded by a deep ravine, the banks of which are quite steep and somewhat rocky. The ravine is in shape somewhat like an ox-bow, made by two streams which pass nearly around and then unite. Across this isthmus of this peninsula, if we may so call it, was a wall of earth running from northeast to southwest When first discovered by the early settlers, the embankment was straight, four or five feet high, with an exterior ditch from two to three feet deep. The area thus enclosed is from ten to twelve acres A portion of the area was free from trees, and was called the *Prairie*, and is still noted among the old men as the spot where the first battalion military training was held in the county of Onondaga But that portion of the work near the wall has recently been cleared of a heavy growth of black-oak timber Many of the trees were large, and probably one hundred and fifty or two hundred years old. Some were standing in the ditch and others on the embankment. The plough has defaced the lines to a considerable degree, but they may still be traced the whole extent Within the enclosure there is a burial-place. Here, too, are to be found numerous fragments of dark-brown pottery, of coarse material "[*]

Mr. Clark mentions that a great number of rude relics have been discovered here Among other things found in the vicinity were some small three-pound cannon balls There is a large rock in the ravine on the south, on which the following characters are inscribed, viz . I I I I I X They are cut nine inches long, three-quarters of an inch deep, and the same in width, and are perfectly regular

Within two miles of Jamesville, in De Witt township, upon the banks of Butternut Creek, there existed until recently the traces of an enclosure or fort, and in the vicinity many evidences of comparatively late occupation by the Indians. The fort had been rectangular, with bastions, and constructed with cedar pickets, firmly set in the ground The stumps of the palisades were struck by the plough when the land was first cultivated. It appeared that the cabins which it had enclosed had been arranged with regularity—a practice not common among the Indians before intercourse with the whites In the year 1810 an oak was felled near this fort, in cutting which a leaden bullet was found imbedded in the wood. One hun-

---

had fixed their settlements at Onondaga, and before the Five Nations were confederated, the Onondagas lived below Jamesville and in Pompey, that in consequence of continued warfare with other tribes, they removed their villages frequently, and that, after the confederation, their fortifications being no longer necessary, they were allowed to fall into decay This he believed was the origin of the ancient works at these points —*Notes on the Iroquois* p 442

[*] Schoolcraft's Notes on the Iroquois, p 469

dred and forty-three cortical layers were counted above it. It must, therefore, have been fired in 1667. Fire-arms were introduced among the Iroquois, by the French, as early as 1609—the date of Hudson's exploration of the river bearing his name. Brass crucifixes, medals of silver and other metals, dial-plates, and articles of iron are of frequent occurrence here, mingled with stone-axes, and implements and ornaments of bone, shell, and clay, the relics of an earlier period. Amongst other articles of European origin, a cross of pure gold was found some years ago, bearing the sacred monogram I H S. Not far from this spot are two high hills of great regularity, sometimes called mounds, the surfaces of which are covered with pits, and which Mr Schoolcraft conjectures were *caches*

Some investigators are of opinion that Champlain penetrated into this county in 1615. The reasons in support of this opinion are forcibly put forward by Mr O H Marshall, of Buffalo, in a paper published in the Bulletin of the New York Historical Society, for March, 1849. From this paper the subjoined account of the Indian fort attacked by Champlain is extracted. It throws light upon the modes of defence common to the Indians at that period, besides being of interest in several other particulars. Says Champlain :

"'On the 10th of October, at 3 P M, we arrived before the fort of the enemy. Some skirmishing ensued among the Indians, which frustrated our design of not discovering ourselves until the next morning. The impatience of our savages, and the desire they had of witnessing the effects of our fire-arms on the enemy, did not suffer them to wait. When I approached with my little detachment, we showed them what they had never before seen or heard. As soon as they saw us, and heard the balls whistling about their ears, they retired quietly into the fort, carrying with them their killed and wounded. We also fell back upon the main body, having five or six wounded, one of whom died'

" The Indians now retired out of sight of the fort, and refused to listen to the advice of Champlain as to the best mode of conducting the siege. He continued to aid them with his men, and, in imitation of the more ancient mode of warfare, planned a kind of movable tower, sufficiently high when advanced to the fort to overlook the palisades. It was constructed of pieces of wood placed one upon another, and was finished in one night.

"' The village,' says Champlain, ' was enclosed by four rows of large interlaced palisades, thirty feet high, near a body of unfailing water. Along these palisades the Iroquois had placed conductors to convey water to the outside, to extinguish fire. Galleries were constructed inside of the palisades, protected by a ball-proof parapet of wood, garnished with double pieces of wood

"' When the tower was finished, two hundred of the strongest men advanced it near to the palisades. I stationed four marksmen on its top, who were well protected from the stones and arrows which were discharged by the enemy'

" The French soon drove the Iroquois from the galleries, but the undisciplined Hurons, instead of setting fire to the palisades, as directed by Champlain, consumed the time in shouting at the enemy, and discharging harmless showers of arrows into the fort    Without discipline, and impatient of restraint, each one acted as his fancy pleased him    They placed the fire on the wrong side of the fort, so that it had no effect.

" ' When the fire had gone out, they began to pile wood against the palisades, but in such small quantities that it made no impression    The confusion was so great that nothing could be heard.  I called out to them, and pointed out, as well as I could, the danger they incurred by their imprudent management; but they heard nothing by reason of the great noise which they made.  Perceiving that I should break my head in calling, that my remonstrances were in vain, and that there were no means of remedying the disorder, I resolved to effect, with my own people, what could be done, and to fire upon those we could discover.

" ' In the meantime, the enemy profited by our disorder    They brought and threw water in such abundance, that it poured in streams from the conductors, and extinguished the fire in a very short time    They continued, without cessation, to discharge flights of arrows, which fell on us like hail    Those who were on the tower killed and wounded a great number

" ' The battle lasted about three hours    Two of our chiefs, some head-men, and about fifteen others were wounded.' "

Mr Marshall is of the opinion that this fort was situated upon the shores of Onondaga Lake    He arrives at this conclusion from an analysis of the courses and distances travelled by Champlain, the streams which he crossed, etc., and continues.

"Another circumstance to aid us in the location, is the description given by Champlain of the fort itself.  ' It was situated,' says he, ' on the borders of an unfailing body of water '  This he calls ' *Etang*,' a word generally applied to an artificial pond, but sometimes used for a small lake or other natural collection of water    There is nothing that will answer the terms of the description in so many particulars, as the shore of Onondaga Lake ; and it is quite probable that it is there we must look for the location of the fort which was invested by the invaders

" Three miles southeast of its outlet, on the northern bank of the lake, and near the present village of Liverpool, an ancient Indian work was discovered by the early settlers, which may have been the site of the fortification in question    There is reason to believe that the same locality was occupied by Monsieur Dupuis and the Jesuits, when they established themselves among the Onondagas in 1656.

" Mr. Clark, of Manlius, thinks that the Count de Frontenac occupied this position when he invaded the Onondaga country, in 1696, and that Col. Van Schaick encamped there while on his expedition against the Onondagas, in 1779."

In the account of Frontenac's Expedition contained in Vol. V of the Paris Documents, now deposited in the office of the Secretary of State of New York. it is stated that the principal fort of the Onondagas was burned by the Indians upon the approach of the French army    The terms of the account are as follows : " The cabins of the Indians and the triple palisade which encircled their fort were found entirely burnt    It was an oblong flanked by four regular bastions    The two rows of pickets, which touched each other, were of the thickness of an ordinary mast; and at six feet distance outside stood another palisade of much smaller dimensions, but from forty to fifty feet high." This account also states that the invaders were successful in discovering almost all of the *caches* in which the Indians had deposited their corn *

# MADISON COUNTY.

On the site of the village of Cazenova, situated in the township of the same name, which adjoins Pompey, Onondaga county, on the east, it is said an ancient earth-work once existed. No vestige of it now remains  By some it was represented to be circular, by others rectangular. Many rude relics have been found here.

In the town of Lenox there were still visible, in 1812, the traces of a work of more modern date  It occupied a position corresponding with most of the defensive structures of the aborigines, at the junction of two deep ravines, the precipitous banks of which not only afforded protection, but precluded the necessity, in great part, of artificial defences. Within the point thus cut off and defended there is a small eminence, in which there are a number of excavations, containing traces of decayed wood.

It may be suggested (though, not knowing their dimensions, the suggestion may be absurd) that the pits were originally designed for *caches*  Mr. Schoolcraft supposes that this work was erected by the French,—a supposition which finds support in the regular form of the palisaded outlines, and the circumstance that the ground within and around the work has not yet returned to a forest state.

* Documentary History of New York, Vol I, p 332

# OTSEGO COUNTY.

IT is stated, upon very good authority, that an ancient circular earth-work once existed near Unadilla, in this county. Nothing is known concerning it, further than that it was situated on low ground

.

———— — ————

# CHENANGO COUNTY.

THERE was formerly an ancient enclosure, of small size, within the limits of the village of Oxford, in the township of that name, on the banks of the Chenango River It is described by Clinton as occupying a small eminence, three or four acres in extent, which rises abruptly from the flats bordering the river. At the base of this eminence, upon the western side, flows the stream, and here the descent is precipitous. A line of embankment and a trench extended in a semicircular form from this bank, leaving narrow interruptions at the ends, for ingress and egress The area thus enclosed was about three-fourths of an acre. At the period of the first settlement, it was covered with a dense forest; yet, says Mr Clinton, "the outline of the work could be distinctly traced among the trees, and the elevation from the bottom of the trench to the top of the embankment was about four feet. The stump of a decayed pine which stood upon the wall exhibited one hundred and ninety-five cortical layers, and there were many more which could not be counted, as the heart of the tree alone remained Probably the tree was three or four hundred years old,—certainly more than two hundred. It probably stood many years after it had completed its growth, and it is reasonable to suppose that some time elapsed from the period of the construction of the work to the commencement of the growth of the tree

5

"Probably the work was encircled with palisades, but no traces of the wood were discoverable. The situation was very eligible, elevated, commanding a fine prospect, and having no eminence near from which it could be commanded. No implements or utensils have been found, except some fragments of coarse pottery, roughly ornamented. The Indians have a tradition that the family of the Antones, which is supposed to belong to the Tuscarora nation, is the seventh generation from the inhabitants of this fort, but of its origin they know nothing.

"There is also a place at Norwich in this county, on a high bank of the river, called 'the Castle,' where the Indians lived at the period of our settlement of the country, and where some vestiges of a fortification appear, but in all probability of much more modern date than those at Oxford."

In Greene township, about two miles below the village, was formerly a mound of some interest. It was situated about thirty rods back from the bank of the Chenango River, and was originally about six feet in height and forty in diameter "Until within a few years a large pine stump stood on its top, and a variety of trees covered it when first discovered    One of these showed two hundred consecutive growths    An examination of the mound was made in 1829 by excavation. Great numbers of human bones were found, and beneath them, at a greater depth, others were found which had evidently been burned    No conjecture could be formed of the number of bodies deposited here. The skeletons were found lying without order, and so much decayed as to crumble on exposure    At one point in the mound a large number, perhaps two hundred, arrow-heads were discovered, collected in a heap    They were of the usual form, and of yellow or black flint    Another pile, of sixty or more, was found in another place, in the same mound, also a silver band or ring, about two inches in diameter, wide but thin, and with what appeared to be the remains of a reed pipe within it.    A number of stone gouges or chisels, of different shapes, and a piece of mica, cut in the form of a heart, the border much decayed and the laminæ separated, were also discovered"*

It may be mentioned here, that the character of the lower deposit, and also some of the relics, coincide with some of those found in the mounds of the Mississippi Valley. The ancient mound-builders often burned their dead    The upper and principal collection of bones had probably a comparatively late date, as is shown by the silver bracelet, which, it is presumed, although not so expressly stated, was found with this deposit

---

* Annals of Binghampton

# CAYUGA COUNTY

## PLATE V No 1

### ANCIENT WORK NEAR AUBURN, NEW YORK.

ONE of the best preserved and most interesting works in the State, is that over-looking the flourishing town of Auburn  It is situated upon a commanding emi-nence, which rises abruptly from the level grounds upon which the town is built, to the height of perhaps one hundred feet  It is the most elevated spot in the vicinity, and commands a wide and very beautiful prospect.  The ground occupied by the work subsides gently from the centre of the area , but exterior to the walls are steep acclivities and deep ravines, rendering approach in nearly every direc-tion extremely difficult.  These natural features are indicated in the plan, which obviates the necessity for a detailed description.  Upon the south are several deep gulleys, separated by sharp, narrow ridges, rendering ascent at this point, in the face of determined defenders entirely impracticable  It has been conjectured by some that the walls here have been washed away , but it is clear that there was slight necessity for any defences at this point, and that none ever existed beyond what may still be traced.

The number and relative proportions of the gateways or openings are correctly shown in the plan  That upon the north is one hundred and sixty feet wide ; that upon the east sixty feet, and that upon the west thirty feet.  These wide, unpro-tected spaces would seem to conflict with the supposition so well sustained by its remaining features, that the work had a defensive origin  It is not improbable, however, that palisades extended across these openings, as well as crowned the embankments , for without such additions, as has been already observed, the best of these structures could have afforded but very slight protection.

The embankments of this work are now between two and three feet in height, and the trenches of corresponding depth.  The area of the work and the ground around it are covered with forest-trees  There are several depressions, which probably were the *caches* of the ancient occupants.*

It is said that a number of relics have been recovered here from time to time,

---

* This work has an accidental approach to regularity , but it is far from being a true ellipsis, as has been supposed by some who have visited it

and among others the head of a banner-staff of thin iron, fourteen inches long and ten broad. It is, of course, of French or English origin, and was probably lost or buried here by the Indians, into whose hands, by purchase or capture, it had fallen. We may perhaps refer it back to the days of Champlain and Frontenac, when the armies of France swept the shores of the western lakes, in the vain hope of laying the foundation of a Gallic empire in America. This relic is now in the possession of Mr J. W. Chedell, of Auburn

McCauley, in his History of New York, presents the subjoined facts bearing upon the question of the probable antiquity of this work, which may not be with-out their interest. He says · " We examined the stump of a chestnut-tree in the moat, which was three feet two inches in diameter, at a point two feet and a half above the surface of the earth    A part of the trunk of the same tree was lying by the stump. As this tree had been cut down, we endeavored to ascertain its age , and for this purpose we counted the rings or concentric circles, and found them to amount to two hundred and thirty-five. The centre of the tree was hollow, or rather decayed ; and estimating this part as equal to thirty more layers or growths, we calculated the entire age of the tree to be two hundred and fifty-five years About five years had elapsed since the tree was cut down. This was in 1825, and would carry back the date of the work to 1555.

" At the distance of three paces from this stump was another of chestnut, stand-ing in the ditch    It exceeded three feet in diameter, and the tree must have died standing, and probably remained in that position many years before it fell from decay. In our opinion, the tree dated back as far as the discovery of the conti-nent. Besides, it may be conjectured, for aught we know to the contrary, that several growths of forest intervened between the abandonment of this work and the date of the present forest."[*]

About two miles northeast of the work above described, upon elevated ground, was another similar work. It is now entirely levelled, and its site can only be ascertained by the fragments of pottery which are scattered over the ground    It was visible in 1825, when it was visited by McCauley, who says

" It enclosed about two acres, and had a rampart, ditch, and gateway. It is now nearly obliterated by the plough. In its original state, or the condition it was in thirty-five years ago, about the time the land was cleared, the rampart was seven feet high, and the ditch ten feet wide and three deep. Two persons, the one standing in the ditch, and the other within the enclosure, were unable to see each other. The gateway was on the northeastern side, in the direction of a spring which flowed close by. The work was three hundred and fifty paces in circum-ference."

---

[*] History of New York, Vol 1, p 112

## PLATE V   No. 2

ANCIENT WORK, MENTZ TOWNSHIP, CAYUGA COUNTY, NEW YORK.

Six miles northwest of Auburn, and three miles from Troopsville, in the township of Mentz, is the small but well preserved work of which a plan is here given. The country around is hilly, and the work itself is built upon the crest of a narrow ridge, which extends nearly north and south, and along which the main road passes  There is a hollow, with springs flowing into it, towards the left, in which direction, it will be observed, a gateway opens  Although the ground has been for many years under cultivation, the lines of embankment are still between two and three feet high.  A quantity of relics, some of comparatively late date, have been found here  Some skeletons, also, have been disclosed by the plough, both within and without the walls.  The plan obviates the necessity for any further description

The existence of this work does not seem to have been hitherto known, beyond the secluded vicinity in which it occurs  It is, however, probable that it is the one alluded to by McCauley in the following very indefinite terms : " On the east side of the Seneca River, near Montezuma, there are still to be seen the ruins of a small fort  A small mound occurs not far from the fort ; it is artificial "  Montezuma is situated in the same township with the work above described, and about four miles distant, in a northwestern direction  In the " New York Magazine," for 1792, mention is made of a couple of ancient works, said to occur south of Cross and Salt Lakes, east of the Seneca River, and falling probably within the limits of the present township of Brutus, in Cayuga or Elbridge, in Onondaga county  One of these was in the " form of a parallelogram, two hundred and twenty yards long and fifty-five broad, with openings on either side, one of which led to the waters  Half a mile south was another work of crescent form, large trees were growing upon both "  Quantities of well burned pottery in fragments were found there ; also a slab of stone five feet long, three and a half broad, and six inches thick, upon which were some rude tracings, specimens perhaps of the " picture writing " of the Indians

McCauley mentions an ancient work near the town of Aurora, in the southern part of this county, and near Cayuga Lake  According to this authority, it was situated " two miles from the village, in a southwesterly direction ; the area triangular, and containing two acres.  Two of its sides were defended by precipitous banks, and the third by an embankment and ditch  Fragments of earthen vessels and the bones of animals had been found there enveloped in beds of ashes."

There are traces of an ancient palisaded work of the Cayugas, in Ledyard township, about four miles southeast of Springport  In fact, the whole country has numerous vestiges, cemeteries, etc , of its former aboriginal possessors

# CHEMUNG COUNTY

THERE is a work in this county which possesses peculiar interest, from the circumstance that the embankments still retain unmistakable traces of the palisades with which it was crowned, thus demonstrating the correctness of the conjectures already indulged in, as to the probable construction of the entire system of earthworks of Western New York   The accompanying plan and description are from the note-books of Prof E. N. Horsford, of Harvard University, who visited this work in company with other gentlemen connected with the State Geological Survey, at the time that enterprise was in progress

## PLATE VI. No. 1.

### ANCIENT WORK NEAR ELMIRA, CHEMUNG COUNTY, NEW YORK.

" THIS work is situated about two and a half miles west of Elmira, upon the summit of an eminence, the base of which, upon one side, is washed by Chemung River, and upon the other by the waters of a deep and almost impassable ravine. It is, in fact, a bold headland.   The approach is by a narrow path, which in some places will admit of the passage of a single person only, and which traverses the very abrupt crown of the ridge.   Towards the top, the ascent is more gradual, and the ground continues to ascend slightly until we reach the defences   The site chosen exhibits the strongest proof of design, being such as to command a most extensive view along the course of the river, and being, except from behind, accessible only by the difficult pathway already mentioned.

" The artificial defences consist of an embankment, with an outer ditch, which extends, as shown in the plan, from the steep bank towards the river, to the brow of the ravine upon the other side.   This embankment is about two hundred feet long, fourteen feet broad at the base, and about three and a half feet high.   The rotting stump of an old pine-tree, three feet in diameter, and a yellow pine-tree, nine feet in circumference, are standing upon the wall, and indicate its high antiquity

" What appeared to be a furrow was observed extending along the summit of the embankment throughout its entire length.   Upon examination, it was found that this appearance was produced by a succession of *holes*, about a foot in depth

Just within this chain of holes is another parallel chain, not quite so distinct as the first    Still further inwards, and extending but part of the way across the area of the work, are several parallel furrows, without accompanying ridges, the design of which is hardly apparent."

It will be seen that this work corresponds entirely in position with most of the earth-works of the State, was chosen with reference to the same principles, and was defended in precisely the same manner    It is peculiar in still retaining the holes left by the decay of the palisades, which show that it was strengthened by a double line    It is rational to conclude, upon general principles, that all the works of the State were protected in like manner, although, except in this instance, all traces of the wooden superstructure have disappeared.   As already observed, this work, for the positive light which it throws upon the original character of these ancient defences, is probably the most interesting one in the State

# ONTARIO COUNTY.

## PLATE VI No 2

### ANCIENT WORK NEAR CANANDAIGUA

ONE mile east of the town of Canandaigua, upon the slope of a hill overlooking Canandaigua Lake, is the work here figured.   It is unsurpassed for the beauty of its position.   A considerable portion of the embankment has been obliterated by cultivation, and another portion by the turnpike road, from Canandaigua to Geneva, which passes through it.   The parts which may yet be traced are appropriately indicated in the plan, and enable us to make out the original form of the work with sufficient exactness.   In constructing the road, human bones in considerable quantities were disclosed on the brow of the hill, accompanied by the usual rude relics of Indian art. It is mentioned by Mr. Schoolcraft, that the Senecas deduce their descent from the remarkable eminence upon which this work is situated *

Between three and four miles west of Canandaigua, on the road to Victor, there is a long, narrow trench running nearly in a direction from N. E. to S. W. It may be traced, with occasional interruptions, for some miles, and has been erroneously, but very generally, believed to be a work of art. It marks the line of a long, narrow fissure in the limestone substratum, into which the earth has subsided. The water which accumulates in it sinks, to swell the volume of some subterraneous stream   The cause of this singular fissure is worthy of the inquiries of geologists.

Judge Porter, of Niagara, mentions another ancient enclosure, similar to that above described, in the vicinity of Canandaigua ; but its locality could not be ascertained   It is probably now completely destroyed.

---

## PLATE VII. No. 1

### ANCIENT WORK NEAR GENEVA

ONE and a half miles west of Geneva are the traces of the old Indian " Castle" of *Ganundesâga*, built by the Senecas, and destroyed by Sullivan in 1779.   Near it is a mound thickly covered over with graves.   A plan and description of this work will be given in another connection   About two miles beyond, in the same direction, in Seneca township, is another work of more ancient date, a plan of which is here presented.   It is situated upon elevated grounds, and coincides generally with those already described.   The position upon the east side is protected by a steep, natural bank, perhaps sixty feet in height, which subsides into low, marshy grounds.   At the foot of the bank is a copious and perennial spring.   Upon the west, south, and north, the ground falls off gently, and here we find the artificial defences.   Although the whole has been for some time under cultivation, the lines of entrenchment may be followed throughout nearly their entire extent, without difficulty   The usual evidences of ancient occupancy are found within the area.

Half a mile further to the westward, upon a corresponding site, are the traces of an ancient palisaded work, which will be described in its appropriate place.

---

* Notes on the Iroquois p 196

# MONROE COUNTY.

A NUMBER of aboriginal monuments formerly existed in this county; but, with the exception of a few small mounds, they have been wholly obliterated or so much defaced that they can no longer be made out. Two mounds occupy the high, sandy grounds to the westward of Irondequoit Bay, where it connects with Lake Ontario. The point is a remarkable one. The position of the mounds in respect to the natural features around is indicated in the accompanying sketch, Plate VII. No 2

They are small, the largest not exceeding five feet in height. It was found upon excavation that they had been previously disturbed, and their examination proved fruitless. Some bits of charcoal and a few small fragments of bones were observed mingled with the sand. At various places, upon the elevations around them, were scattered fragments of pottery, and arrow-heads and other rude relics are also of frequent occurrence here

The spot was evidently a favorite one with the Indians, the vicinity abounding in fish and game.

The waves of the lake have thrown up a narrow bar or bank of sand, called the "*Spit*," which extends nearly across the mouth of the bay, leaving but a small opening. Upon this bar, a few scattered trees are standing, and it was here that the Marquis De Nonville landed with his troops, at the time of his expedition against the Senecas, in 1687. He constructed a stockade at or near this point.

Upon the eastern shore of the bay, and occupying a position corresponding with that of the mounds already described, it is said there is another mound of considerable size. It was opened many years ago, and was found to contain human bones.

Some eight or ten miles to the southeastward, and half a mile east of the village of Penfield, on the banks of Irondequoit Creek, is still another mound, situated upon a headland, which now projects into an artificial pond. It must have been originally eight or nine feet in height, by perhaps forty feet base. It is a favorite haunt of "money-diggers," by whom it has been pretty thoroughly excavated. A shaft had been sunk in it but a short time before it was visited by the author, and at that period many fragments of human bones, much decayed, which had been thrown up from near the base, were bleaching upon the surface. The soil is here light and sandy, and a depression is still visible near by, marking the spot whence the material composing the mound was procured. It could not be ascertained that any relics of art were obtained here. See Plate VII Fig 3

As already observed, most, if not all, of the ancient works which existed in this county are now obliterated. We can consequently do but little more than indi-

6

cate the sites which they occupied according to the best information obtained from the early settlers  It is asserted that an enclosure of considerable size exists in the town of Irondequoit, west of Irondequoit Bay, and near the Genesee River, about five miles north of Rochester.  A day was spent in search of it, but without success  Its discovery may reward the perseverance of some future explorer *

A fine work once occupied a commanding site at the point known as "Hand-ford's Landing," three miles north of Rochester.  It consisted of a semicircular embankment, the ends of which extended to the very edge of the immense ravine which shuts in the Genesee River below the falls at Rochester.  It had three narrow gateways placed at irregular intervals

There is a locality in the town of Parma, about seven miles west of Rochester, where the earth has subsided into the fissures of the sand rock, forming what has generally been supposed to be a line of entrenchments  From some distance the apparent ditch has all the regularity of a work of art, but still it is hard to under-stand how it came to be regarded as an "Indian Fort," by which name it is currently known in the neighborhood  It would seem incredible that errors of this kind should become general, had not a large experience shown that upon no class of subjects do the mass of men exercise so little sound judgment, as upon those which relate to the history and monuments of the past

In the town of Ogden, which adjoins Parma on the south, it is reputed that some ancient works are to be found; but from the best information which could be obtained, it seems probable that the report has no better foundation than hun-dreds of similar ones, and originated it is very likely, in the discovery of an Indian cemetery, or of the traces of an Indian village

Ascending the valley of the Genesee for twenty miles, we come to a section of country which is very rich in evidences of aboriginal occupancy, but chiefly such as may be referred to a comparatively late date.  In the town of Wheatland, and a short distance to the westward of the village of Scottsville, there formerly existed two very interesting earth-works.  There is scarcely a trace of them now to be seen  They were visited by Kirkland in 1788  He found the first work "about two miles west of Allen's residence, which was an extensive flat, at a deserted Indian village near the junction of a creek (Allen's Creek) with the Genesee, eight miles north of the old Indian village of *Kanawageas*, and five miles north of the *Magic Spring* (Caledonia Springs), so called by the Indians, who believed its waters had the power of petrifying all things subjected to its influence  This work enclosed about six acres, and had six gates.  The ditch was about eight feet wide, and in some places six feet deep, and drawn in a circular form on three sides  The fourth side was defended by nature with a high bank, at the foot of which was a fine stream of water  The bank had probably been secured by a stockade, as there appeared to have been a deep covered way in the middle of it,

---

* McCauley states that there is an ancient work on Irondequoit Bay, in Penfield township on the north side of the "ridge"  No information could be obtained concerning it

down to the water    Some of the trees on the work appeared to be two or three hundred years old."

The usual variety of relics, fragments of pottery, stone chippings, etc , have been found upon the site of this work    About half a mile south of this, and upon a greater eminence, Mr. Kirkland traced another work, "of less dimensions than the first, but with a deeper ditch, and in a situation more lofty and defensible "  Although it is well remembered by the older settlers in the neighborhood, nothing now remains to indicate that it ever existed, except the greater abundance of stones on the line of the former embankment    The position is such as the builders of these works usually selected for their defences    Upon one side is a high and precipitous bank, at the base of which flows Allen's Creek , and in every other direction the ground slopes gently.    It is altogether a well chosen and very beautiful site    About three miles south of these works, on the bank of the Genesee River, and probably falling in Caledonia township, Livingston county, are to be observed the traces of a mound.    It was originally about eight feet high, and was filled with human bones heaped promiscuously together.    Still another mound is said to occur a few miles N  W. of Scottsville, in the town of Chili

Near the village of West Rush, in the town of Rush, upon the banks of Honeoye Creek, were formerly two considerable enclosures    One of these was situated immediately upon the bank of the creek, which defended it upon one side , while the other occupied higher ground a hundred rods to the southward    Each contained about four acres, and the embankments were originally four feet in height.    A few slight depressions indicating the ancient *caches*, with fragments of pottery scattered around, alone remain to mark the sites of these structures

The whole of this country was occupied by the Senecas , and their cemeteries, and the traces of their ancient forts and towns, are particularly numerous along the Genesee River, and on the banks of the Honeoye    We shall refer to these in another place

# LIVINGSTON COUNTY.

This county, which adjoins Monroe on the south, was also a favorite ground with the Senecas    It is unsurpassed in beauty and fertility by any territory of equal extent in the State, and abounds with mementoes of its aboriginal possessors, who yielded it reluctantly into the hands of the invading whites    Here, too, once existed a considerable number of ancient earth-works, but the levelling plough has passed over most of them ; and though their sites are still remembered by the early

settlers, but few are sufficiently well preserved to admit of exact survey and measurement.

"In 1798," says the venerable Judge Augustus Porter, of Niagara, in a letter to
O H. Marshall, Esq, of Buffalo, "I surveyed the Indian Reservation of *Kanawageas*. There were then in the open flats of the Reservation the embankments of
an old fort, which included very nearly two acres. It corresponded in situation and
appearance with many others which I have seen in this part of the country, and
which seem to bear a high antiquity" The Kanawageas Reservation embraced
the township of York in this county.

Judge Porter also mentions that he knew of two other works on the "Smith and
Jones's Flat," near Mount Morris, (also in Livingston county,) all of which had the
same appearance.

A work also occurs in the town of Avon, not far from the beautiful village of
Avon Springs, upon the flats of the Genesee River It is described by W H. C.
Hosmer, Esq, in the notes to his poem of "YONONDIO"

Another and very similar work once existed in the northeastern part of Avon
township, about two and a half miles from the village of Lima. Some portions of
the lines may yet be traced, but with difficulty

---

## PLATE VIII. No. 1.

### ANCIENT WORK, LIVONIA TOWNSHIP, LIVINGSTON COUNTY, NEW YORK.

THE work here represented occurs in the township of Livonia, three miles N. E
of the village of that name It is situated upon the summit of a commanding
hill, and is the largest enclosure which fell under the notice of the author, within
the limits of the State. It has an area of not less than *sixteen acres*. Where the
lines of the entrenchment were crossed by fences, and consequently preserved
from the encroachments of the plough, the embankment and ditch are distinctly
visible. Elsewhere, however, the outlines can only be traced by a very gentle
undulation of the ground, and by the denser verdure on the course of the ancient
trench With the assistance of Mr Haddock, the proprietor of the estate, who
knew the work before it had been materially impaired, the original form was made
out with entire satisfaction. General Adams, who had often been over the grounds
before the removal of the forest, states that the ditch was breast deep, and the
embankment of corresponding height. *Caches* were formerly discovered here, and
fragments of pottery are now abundant.

The enclosure had four gateways, one of which, at the northwestern extremity,
opened directly towards a copious spring of water, as shown in the plan. It was
thought by General Adams, from certain indications (which might have been

caused by the decay of palisades), that slight parallel embankments extended down the slope of the hill, and enclosed the spring here referred to     Be that as it may, the position was well chosen for defence, for which purpose the work was doubtless constructed.

A mile and a half to the southward are remains of some old fortified towns of the powerful tribe of the Senecas, for plans and descriptions of which the reader is referred to the chapter on " Palisaded Works "

It is said that a mound, containing a large number of human bones, occurs near the head of Hemlock Lake, in the township of Springwater, but no opportunity was afforded of visiting it     At various places in the county large cemeteries are found; but most, if not all, of them may be with safety referred to the Senecas. Indeed, many articles of European origin accompany the skeletons.   A cemetery of large size, and, from the character of the relics found in the graves, of high antiquity, is now in part covered by the village of Lima     Pipes, pottery, etc , are discovered here in great abundance , and it is worthy of remark, they are identical with those found within the ancient enclosures.

A number of ancient works are reported to exist higher up the Genesee River, in the southern part of Livingston and in Alleghany counties ; but this entire region has been brought so thoroughly under cultivation, that it was esteemed hopeless to look for them with a view to their survey or measurement.   The only information of any authentic kind which was received in addition to what is here presented, relates to a remarkable work upon a high hill, not far from the falls of the Genesee, in Alleghany county     Says Judge Porter, in a private letter dated Niagara Falls, November 18th, 1848 : " Upon the west side of Genesee River, a mile or two above the falls, there is a hill, the base of which may perhaps cover two acres of ground, circular in form, and shaped like a sugar-loaf, with a truncated summit a fourth of an acre in area     Upon this summit is a breastwork     The height of the hill is between eighty and one hundred feet     I visited it in 1798, before any settlements were made by the whites nearer than Mount Morris."

Mr Moses Long, of Rochester, describes a work which is substantially the same, as follows .   " About four miles above the village of Portage, in Alleghany county, is a circular mound or hill, which rises probably a hundred feet above the surrounding interval or ' bottom ' lands.   The acclivity is steep on all sides     The Genesee River curves around its base, describing nearly a semicircle, and then sweeps on in a tortuous course to the cascades or cataracts below the village of Portage.   The top of the hill is quite level, covered thinly with small forest-trees, and its area may comprise an acre.   There are appearances of an entrenchment around that part of the summit unprotected by the river

" My guide informed me that he had been acquainted with *Shongo*, an aged chief, and several other Indians of the Caneadea Reservation, who all concurred in saying, that they had no knowledge nor any tradition in relation to this work. *Shongo* remembered the invasion of Sullivan, when the Indians cut up their corn and threw it into the river, and then retreated with their movable effects a few miles up the stream to the top of an elevated bluff, where they determined to await the attack of their enemy.  I came to the conclusion that the entrenchment might have been made by an advanced detachment from Sullivan's army "

# GENESEE COUNTY.

A NUMBLR of very interesting remains formerly existed in this county ; but few of them are sufficiently well preserved to be satisfactorily traced.

In the town of Alabama, in the extreme northwest of the county, were once three of these works, all of small size.  The plough has completely defaced them.  This town adjoins the town of Shelby, in Orleans county, on the south, and touches Newsted, in Erie county, on the west  It will ultimately be seen that its ancient works constitute part of a chain extending from the "Lake Ridge" on the north to Buffalo Creek on the southwest, a distance of fifty miles.  Not less than twenty ancient works are known to occur within this range

## PLATE VIII  No  2

### ANCIENT WORK, OAKFIELD, GENESEE COUNTY, NEW YORK.

In the town of Oakfield, half a mile west of the little village of Caryville, is found the ancient enclosure, a plan of which is here given  It is remarkable as being the best preserved and most distinct of any in the State which fell under the notice of the author  It is situated upon the western slope of one of the billowy hills which characterize the rolling lands of the West, and between which the streams find their way to the rivers and lakes.  The banks of the little stream which washes the work upon the north are steep, but not more than ten feet in height.  Upon the brow of the bank, where the stream approaches nearest the work, the entrenchment is interrupted, and the slope towards the water is more gentle than elsewhere,—indicating an artificial grade.  The plan obviates the necessity for a detailed description.  The embankments will now probably measure six feet in average height measuring from the bottom of the trench.  In the part of the work under cultivation, it is easy to trace the ancient lodges.  Here, too, is to be found the unfailing supply of broken pottery  At the sides of the principal gateway (*a*), leading into the enclosure from the east, according to the statement of an intelligent aged gentleman, who was among the earliest settlers in this region, traces of oaken palisades were found, upon excavation, some thirty years ago. They were, of course, almost entirely decayed. A part of the area is still covered with the original forest, in which are trees of the largest dimensions. An oaken stump upwards of two feet in diameter stands upon the embankment at the point *b*.

About one mile northeast of this work was originally a large enclosure, but which is now entirely destroyed. It was called the "*Bone Fort*," from the circumstance that the early settlers found within it a mound, six feet in height by thirty at the base, which was entirely made up of human bones slightly covered with earth. A few fragments of these bones, scattered over the surface, alone mark the site of the aboriginal sepulchre. The popular opinion concerning this accumulation is, that it contained the bones of the slain, thus heaped together after some severe battle. It will, however, be seen that it probably owed its origin to the same practice to which we are to attribute the "*bone pits*" found elsewhere, that of collecting together at stated intervals the bones of the dead—a practice very prevalent among the northwestern Indians.

There is no doubt but this is one of the works visited by Rev. Samuel Kirkland, Missionary to the Senecas, in 1788. His MS Journal was in the possession of Messrs. Yates and Moulton, who have given a synopsis of the part relating to this group of remains in the subjoined passages.

"Having examined the works (already referred to, in Monroe county) on the Genesee, he returned to *Kanawageas*, and resumed his journey west, encamping for the night at a place called *Joaika*, i e Raccoon (Batavia), on the river *Tonawande*, about twenty-six miles from *Kanawageas*. Six miles from this place of encampment, he rode to the open fields, and arrived at a place called by the Senecas *Tegataineaaghgue*, which imports a '*double-fortified town*,' or a town with a fort at each end. Here he walked about half a mile with one of the Seneca chiefs, to view the vestiges of this double-fortified town. They consisted of the remains of two forts: the first contained four acres of ground, the other, distant about two miles, at the other extremity of the ancient town, enclosed about eight acres. The ditch around the first was about five or six feet deep. A small stream of water and a high bank circumscribed nearly one third of the enclosed ground. There were traces of six gates or openings, and near the centre a way was dug to the water. The ground on the opposite side of the water was in some places nearly as high as that on which the fort was built, which might render this covered way to the water necessary. A considerable number of large thrifty oaks had grown up within the enclosed ground, both in the ditch and upon the wall, some of which appeared to be two hundred years old or more. The ground is of a hard, gravelly kind, intermixed with loam, and more plentifully at the brow of the hill. At some places at the bottom of the ditch, Mr. Kirkland ran his cane a foot or more in the soil, from which circumstance he concludes that the ditch was much deeper originally.

"Near the western fortification, which was situated on high ground, he found the remains of a funeral pile, where the slain were buried after a great battle,

which will be spoken of hereafter.  The mound was about six feet in height by
thirty feet diameter at the base.  The bones appeared at the surface, projecting
at many places at the sides.

"Pursuing his course towards Buffalo Creek, (his ultimate destination,) Mr.
Kirkland discovered the vestiges of another fortified town    He does not delineate
it in his MSS., but says: 'On these heights, near the ancient fortified town, the
roads part, we left the path leading to Niagara on our right, and went a course
nearly southwest for Buffalo Creek    After leaving these heights, which afforded
an extensive prospect, we travelled over a fine tract of land for about six or seven
miles, then came to a barren white-oak shrub plain    We passed a steep hill on
our right, in some places fifty feet perpendicular, at the bottom of which is a small
lake, affording another instance of pagan superstition.  The old Indians affirm
that formerly a demon, in the form of a dragon, resided in this lake, which frequently disgorged balls of liquid fire    To appease him, many sacrifices of tobacco
had been made by the Indians.  At the extremity of the barren plain, we came
again to Tonawande River, and forded it about two miles above the Indian town
of that name.  At a short distance on the south side of the same stream, is
another fortification '"

## FIG  II.

### ANCIENT WORK, LE ROY, GENESEE COUNTY, NEW YORK

REMNANTS of another ancient work occur in the town of Le Roy, three miles
north of the village of the same name, in the southeastern part of this county.

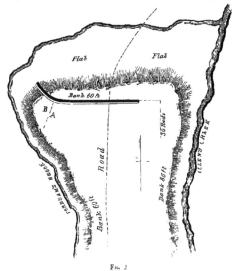

FIG. 2

The accompanying sketch, by L. H Morgan, Esq, of Rochester, although not from an exact instrumental survey, is sufficiently accurate for all essential purposes.

The position which the work occupies is a portion of a high plain or table-land, nearly surrounded by deep ravines, bounded by Fordham's Brook and Allen's Creek, which effect a juncture at this point   These streams have worn their beds through the various strata of lime and sandstone to the depth of from seventy to one hundred feet, leaving abrupt banks difficult of ascent.   These natural features are best illustrated by the plan, which precludes the necessity for a minute description.

The peninsula measures about 1300 feet from north to south, by 2000 feet at its broadest part, and  1000 feet across the neck connecting it with the general table Positions similar to this were often selected by the aborigines for defensive purposes, but in such cases have usually an embankment and trench extending across the isthmus   In this instance, however, the only trace of art is an embankment and ditch, about 1500 feet in length, and running nearly east and west across the broadest part of the peninsula, and not very far back from the edge of the ravine The part which is laid down in the plan is said to be still very distinct , the embankment being between three and four feet in height, and the ditch of corresponding depth   The western extremity of the line curves gently outwards, and extends some distance down the bank, which is at this point less abrupt than elsewhere It is said that formerly trenches existed on the courses indicated by dotted lines on the plan; but the statement is not confirmed by any remaining traces

A number of skeletons have been found here, together with many fragments of pottery.   There have also been discovered some heaps of small stones; which have been supposed to be the missiles of the ancient occupants of the hill, thus got together to be used in case of attack.   Various relics of art, pipes, beads, stone

hatchets, arrow-heads, etc , have been disclosed here by the operations of agriculture   One of the pipes composed of baked clay is now in the possession of Rev. C. Dewey, of Rochester. It is represented of half size in the accompanying engraving, Fig. 3.   The material is very fine, and the workmanship good , so good indeed, as to induce some doubt of its aboriginal origin   Another pipe carved from granular limestone was found here, as were also a number of beads, long and coarse, made of clay and burned

According to Mr Dewey, " the trench was estimated by the early observers at from eight to ten feet deep and as many wide.   The earth in making it had been thrown either way, but much of it inwards   The road formerly crossed it by a bridge.   When first known, forest-trees were standing both in

Fig. 3.

the trench and on its sides   In size and growth they corresponded with the forests around them   Prostrate upon the ground were numerous trunks of the heart-wood of black cherry trees of larger size, which, it is conjectured, were the remains of more

7

antique forests, preceding the growth of beech and maple. They were in such a
state of soundness as to be employed for timber by the early settlers."*

From all that remains of this work, it is impossible to conjecture for what purposes it was constructed. Indeed it bears so few evidences of design, that we are
led to distrust its artificial origin, a distrust which is strengthened by the circumstance, that in a number of instances, elevations and depressions bearing some
degree of regularity, but resulting from fissures in a rock substratum or other natural causes, have been very generally mistaken for works of art. The fact that the
trench in this instance has a course so nearly parallel with the edge of the ravine,
is also a suspicious circumstance. The spot was not visited by the author, but he
is authorized in saying that Prof. Dewey, who gave the first and most complete
account of the supposed work, is now inclined to the opinion that it may be the
result of natural causes.

On what is called the " Knowlton Farm," about one mile south of the town of
Batavia, is a small natural elevation which was used as a burial-place by the
Indians. It has been mistaken for a mound. Various relics have been discovered
in ploughing over it.

---

# ORLEANS COUNTY.

It is not known that many ancient remains occur in this county. There is, however, an interesting work in Shelby township, one and a half miles west of Shelby
Centre. The following account of it was communicated by Dr S M. Burroughs,
of Medina, to O. Turner, Esq., of Buffalo, by whom it was presented to the author.

" It consists of a ditch and embankment, enclosing, in a form nearly circular,
about three acres of ground. The ditch is still well defined and several feet in
depth. Adjoining this fortification on the south is a swamp, about one mile in
width by two in length; which was once, if not a lake, an impassable morass.
There is a passage-way through the lines of the entrenchment towards the swamp,
and this is the sole gateway discoverable. Large quantities of small stones, of a
size to be thrown with the hand, are accumulated in piles within and near the
work. Here, too, are many arrow-heads of flint (silex), stone axes, and fragments
of pottery, exhibiting ornaments in relief. Human skeletons almost entire have
been exhumed here. Half a mile west of the fort on a sand-hill, an immense number of skeletons have been found in a very perfect state. Many seem to have been
deposited in the same grave. As some of the skulls appear to have been broken by
clubs or tomahawks, is it not probable that this was the site of some great battle ?"

---

* Schoolcraft's Notes on the Iroquois p 203

# ERIE COUNTY.

ERIE county ranks next to Jefferson in the number of its ascertained aboriginal monuments  The topographical features of the two counties are much the same, although the former is by far the least elevated.  Along the shores of Lake Erie and bordering Buffalo Creek are low and fertile alluvials; back of these we come to the limestone formation, and the country rises, forming a second grand terrace, along the brow of which most of the ancient works are situated.  Within the limits of the late Seneca Reservation, which has been only in part brought under cultivation, there are a number of ancient works, which are unimpaired except by the operation of natural causes  It is extremely difficult, howevei, to find them, in consequence of the forest and the thick undergrowth.  As the Reservation is cleared up, no doubt new ones will be discovered, and it is to be hoped sufficient interest in these matters may be found to exist among the citizens of Buffalo, to secure their prompt and careful investigation.

----

## PLATE IX  No. 1.

### ANCIENT WORK NEAR BUFFALO

ONE of the most interesting works in this county is that here represented  It derives much of its interest from the associations connected with it.  The site which it occupies was a favorite spot with the Senecas, and one of their largest cemeteries occurs within its walls.  Here is buried an Indian chief whose name is inseparably interwoven with the history of the Five Nations.  He was a man who possessed a rare combination of talents, which, developed under different circumstances, would have secured for him a high position among the greatest statesmen and proudest orators of the world.  This is hardly a proper place to speak of his character; but his devoted patriotism, his inflexible integrity. the unwavering firmness, calm and lofty dignity, and powerful eloquence with which he opposed the encroachments of the whites, notwithstanding that he knew all resistance was vain and hopeless—command an involuntary tribute to the memory of the last and noblest of the proud and politic Iroquois. the haughty and unbending Red Jacket, who died exulting that the Great Spirit had made him an Indian! Here, too, is buried Mary Jemison, " the white woman," who, taken a prisoner by the Indians when a child, conformed to their habits, became the wife of one of their chiefs, and remained with them until her death  The story of her life is one of the most eventful of those connected with our border history, filled as it is with thrilling adventures and startling incidents.

The work under notice is situated upon the edge of the second terrace, which is here moderately elevated above the fertile alluvials bordering Buffalo Creek. The particular spot which it occupies is considerably higher than any other near it, and the soil is sandy and dry  It will be seen that the terrace bank upon one side is made to subserve the purposes for which the trench and embankment were erected upon the others. There is now no direct evidence to that effect; but no doubt can be entertained that, in common with all the other works of the State, the wall was crowned with palisades, which were also carried along the brow of the terrace. The greater portion of this work has been for some time under cultivation ; and the original lines are so much defaced, that they would probably escape the notice of the careless observer  They may, nevertheless, be distinctly traced throughout their extent  At the point nearest the Indian cemetery, a portion of which is still spared by the plough, the embankment is very distinct, and cannot fail to attract attention. At a short distance to the northward of the work is a low spot of ground or marsh, towards which opens a gateway  From this was probably obtained a portion of the supply of water required by the ancient occupants of the work  A number of springs start from the foot of the terrace where the ground is also marshy. Within the walls of this work are to be found the various traces of occupancy which I have already mentioned, sites of old lodges, fragments of pottery, etc

Tradition fixes upon this spot as the scene of the final and most bloody conflict between the Iroquois and the " Gah-kwas " or Eries,—a tradition which has been supposed to derive some sanction from the number of fragments of decayed human bones which are scattered over the area

The old mission-house and church stand in close proximity to this work.  The position of the former is indicated in the plan  Red Jacket's house stood above a third of a mile to the southward upon the same elevation ; and the abandoned council-house is still standing, perhaps a mile distant, in the direction of Buffalo  A little distance beyond in the same direction and near the public road, is a small mound called " Dah-do-sot " artificial hill, by the Indians, who it is said were accustomed to regard it with much veneration, supposing that it covered the victims slain in some bloody conflict in the olden time  A genuine representative of the Celtic stock had selected it as the site of his cabin, and his worthy but somewhat superstitious spouse was much horrified at the intimation that it probably contained the bones of the unsanctified heathen  A shaft was sunk near the foundation of the cabin to the base of the mound, but nothing of interest was disclosed  A few half-formed arrow-heads, some chippings of hewn stone, and some small bits of charcoal were discovered, intermingled with the soil thrown from the excavation  Whatever deposits are contained in the mound, if any, probably occur

immediately beneath the apex which is occupied by the cabin of the Celt aforesaid Its investigation is therefore reserved for the hands of some future explorer.
It was originally between five and six feet in height by thirty-five or forty feet
base, and is composed of the adjacent loam A depression still exists upon one
side, marking the spot whence the material was obtained

---

## PLATE IX No 2.

### ANCIENT WORK, LANCASTER, ERIE COUNTY, NEW YORK

It is not known that any ancient remains occur nearer the work last described
than the one here presented, which is situated upon lot No 2, of the late Reservation, about four miles southeast of the village of Lancaster, near Little Buffalo
Creek It occurs upon the summit of a small eminence, in the midst of a dense
and tangled forest, and is reached by a bridle path which passes through it It
approaches more nearly to the form of a true circle than any work which fell
under the observation of the author in Western New York. It is small, containing less than an acre The embankment is however very distinct, being not less
than three feet in height, and the ditch of equal depth Trees, corresponding in
all respects with those of the surrounding forest, are standing within the area and
upon the wall. The ground is here gravelly and dry. A number of *caches* of considerable size were observed within the enclosure

---

## PLATE IX No. 3.

### ANCIENT WORK, LANCASTER, ERIE COUNTY, NEW YORK

Half a mile to the southeast of the above work, and as nearly as could be
ascertained on lot No 6, is a work of larger size and more irregular outline It
occupies a beautiful level spot of ground not far from the edge of the second terrace back from the creek. The embankment is somewhat higher than that of the
previous work, and, with a single exception, quite as well defined as any observed
within the State It is very slightly reduced from its original height, which may
be estimated as having been between seven and nine feet, measuring from the bottom of the ditch. At the point indicated by the letter *a* upon the embankment is

standing the stump of a withered pine-tree, which is sixteen feet in circumference six feet above the roots    A few rods to the southward of the work is a narrow ravine leading off towards Little Buffalo Creek.    Within this is a spring from which flows a small stream    It will be observed that two of the gateways of the work placed not far apart open in this direction—leading to the inference that it was here that the water used by the ancient occupants was obtained    A number of large *caches* also occur within this work.

---

## PLATE X  No. 1

### ANCIENT WORK ON LATE INDIAN RESERVATION, ERIE COUNTY, NEW YORK.

Upon the opposite bank of the creek already named, and probably on lot No 3 of the Reservation, is the singular work here presented.  The land upon this side of the creek rises abruptly to the height of 150 or 200 feet, forming a high bluff. The edge of this bluff is cut by ravines into spurs or head-lands ; and upon one of these the work under notice is situated    It is not large, and is singular only in having wide interruptions in the embankment—so wide indeed, that were it not from the perfect condition of the lines where they exist, it might be conjectured that the structure was never completed.  *Caches* were noticed here    The ground is covered with a dense forest, which obscures all parts of the work

To the southwestward of this, on lot 29 of the same range and on the south side of "Big Buffalo Creek," is still another similar work, which is described by Mr. Junius Clark, in a private communication, as about eight hundred feet in circumference, having three gateways and an open space ten rods wide at the southwestern corner    A gateway on the north opens towards a spring of water, distant about a dozen rods.   Other works, probably differing in no essential respect from these, are said to occur at various places upon the southern border of the Reservation.

---

## PLATE X   No. 2.

### ANCIENT WORK, CLARENCE TOWNSHIP, ERIE COUNTY, NEW YORK.

Passing northward from the localities last mentioned to the distance of five or six miles, keeping upon the limestone plateau, we find another series of remains, composed of a succession of works placed a mile or two apart, and extending quite through the town of Clarence. The first of these (No. 2) is two and a half miles south of the little village of " Clarence Hollow " It has been under cultivation for a number of years, and its outlines can now be traced only by carefully observing the stronger vegetable growth upon the course of the ancient trench. Where fence lines crossed the wall, short sections of the embankment are yet visible Fragments of pottery are scattered over the area If any of the usual pits ever existed, they have been filled up by the operations of agriculture.

## PLATE X No 3.

### ANCIENT WORK, CLARENCE TOWNSHIP, ERIE COUNTY, NEW YORK

A MILE northward of the work last described, and occupying a position in no respect well adapted for defence, is the enclosure here presented It is now much defaced, the part, however, which has never been cultivated is very distinct, and one or two other short sections may yet with some difficulty be traced Flint chippings, fragments of pottery, and a number of deep *caches* occur within the area. A large Indian cemetery is said to exist somewhere between this work and the one just noticed. However true this may be, about half a mile to the northwest on the land of a Mr Fillmore there is a large deposit of bones, a "*bone pit,*" some fourteen feet square and four or five in depth, filled with crumbling human skeletons The spot was marked by a very slight elevation of the earth a foot or too in height

A couple of miles distant, still following the brow of the terrace, and not far back of the village of Clarence, was formerly another similar work now completely destroyed. Still a mile beyond is another, (Plate XI. No 1,) which, although upon grounds which have been cleared, is yet perfect. It is situated upon a sandy, slightly elevated peninsula, which projects into a low tangled swamp A narrow strip of dry ground connects it with the higher lands, which border the swamp on the south It is small, containing less than an acre The embankment does not preserve uniform dimensions, but has perhaps an average height of three feet The ditch too is irregular, both in width and depth. owing probably in some degree to the rocky substratum, which in some places comes nearly or quite to the surface of the ground. The stumps of immense pine-trees are standing within the work, as also upon its walls Here, too, are to be found *caches*, fragments of pottery, etc. The position, for purposes of concealment and defence, is admirably chosen, and recalls to mind the famous stronghold of the Narragansetts in Rhode Island, destroyed in 1676 by the New England colonists under Winthrop and Church.

A short distance from this work, upon the brow of a neighboring elevation, a number of human skeletons have been exposed by the plough. They probably mark the site of an Indian cemetery   A mile to the eastward, upon a dry sandy spot, is another of the "bone-pits" already several times referred to, which is estimated, by those who excavated it originally, to have contained *four hundred* skeletons heaped promiscuously together.   They were of individuals of every age and sex.   In the same field are found a great variety of Indian relics, also brass cap and belt plates, and other remains of European origin   Not far distant, some lime burners discovered, a year or two since, a skeleton surrounded by a quantity of rude ornaments.   It had been placed in a cleft of the rock, the mouth of which was covered by a large flint stone

Passing onward in the same direction which we have been pursuing, we come to the Batavia and Buffalo road, the great thoroughfare over which, previous to the construction of the railroad and canal, passed the entire western trade and travel.   Here, at a point a few miles from Clarence, known as the "Vandewater Farm," are the traces of another work   A few sections alone remain, barely sufficient to indicate that it was of considerable size   The road passes through its centre.

———

## PLATE XI  No. 2

ANCIENT WORK, FISHER'S FALLS, NEWSTED TOWNSHIP, ERIE COUNTY, NEW YORK.

The sole remaining work in this county which was personally examined by the author is the one here presented.   It is situated five miles eastward of the locality last noticed, at a place known as "Fisher's Falls," in the town of Newsted, upon the banks of a creek, at present barbarously designated "Murder Creek"   The creek here plunges down into a deep, narrow gorge with precipitate banks, which continues to the edge of the terrace a fourth of a mile distant.   The relative position of the work, which is of large size, is correctly designated on the plan   It is now under cultivation, and is much reduced from its original elevation, but can be traced without difficulty throughout its extent   The older inhabitants affirm that the walls were originally five feet in height, and the ditch of corresponding proportions.   Traces of the ancient *caches* are yet to be observed, and without the enclosure is a rock, the surface of which bears a number of artificial depressions hollowed out by the Indians,—the rude mortars in which they pounded their corn.

This work occurs upon the old Indian trail, which extended from the Genesee River to Batavia, and thence to Buffalo and Niagara.   A branch of this trail, after striking the limestone ledge at Tonawanda Creek, followed along its brow to Buffalo Creek. It diverged inwardly at the point under notice, so as to escape the impassable ravine already mentioned Kirkland, missionary to the Senecas in 1787, passed along this trail on his way to Buffalo, and incidentally refers to a work which he encountered after crossing Tonawanda Creek, and which is probably the one here figured

Besides the ancient remains here noticed. there are no doubt many others of which no information has yet been obtained It is not probable, however, that they possess any novel features, or differ materially in any respect from those already described Some "bone-pits" in addition to those already mentioned occur in Clarence township, and will be noticed in another connection

This county abounds in traces of recent Indian occupancy, in fact the rude cabins of the aborigines have scarcely crumbled away, since they deserted their favorite haunts upon the banks of the Buffalo Creek and its tributaries. A small band are at bay upon the borders of the Tonawanda, sullenly defying the grasping cupidity of those who Shylock-like, sustained by fraudulent contracts, are impatient to anticipate the certain doom which impends over this scanty remnant, and would deny these the poor boon of laying their bones beside those of their fathers.

# CHAUTAUQUE COUNTY.

THIS county abounds in ancient monuments, but no opportunity was afforded of examining them during the progress of the investigations here recorded. It is probable they are but a continuation of the series extending through Erie county, (which adjoins Chautauque on the northeast,) and it is not likely they present any new features.

One of the most remarkable occupies an eminence in Sheridan township, four miles east of Fredonia, on the banks of Beaver Creek. It corresponds in all respects with the hill-works already described Another of like character occurs in the southern part of the same township.

# MONTGOMERY COUNTY

## PLATE XII.

THE work here figured is in many respects the most remarkable in the State It is the only one known which is situated upon waters flowing into the Hudson River. Its nearest neighbors upon the west are the ancient works in Onondaga county, a hundred miles distant Between it and the Atlantic, we are not aware of the existence of a single monument of like character

It occurs upon the banks of the Otstungo Creek, a branch of the Otsquago,— itself a tributary of the Mohawk, about four miles in a southwestern direction from Fort Plain, in the town of Minden. It is known in the vicinity by the name of "*Indian Hill*." The position is admirably chosen, and is naturally by far the strongest and most defensible of any which fell under the observation of the author in the entire course of his explorations in this State. It is a high point of land projecting into a bend of the creek, which upon one side has cut away the slate rock, so that it presents a mural front upwards of one hundred feet in height, and entirely inaccessible. Upon the opposite side is a ravine, within which flows a small stream. Here the slope, though not precipitous, is very abrupt; and if a line of palisades were carried along its brow, it would be entirely inaccessible to a savage assailant Across the narrow isthmus which connects this head-land with the adjacent high grounds, is an embankment and ditch two hundred and forty feet in length, extending from the precipice upon the south to the brow of the ravine on the north, along which, curving inwards, it is carried for some distance, terminating at a gigantic pine six feet in diameter. It has been supposed by some that this tree has grown upon the embankment since it was erected; but it seems most likely that it was the starting point of the ancient builders. The wall is not of uniform height, but at the most elevated point rises perhaps six feet above the bottom of the ditch No gateway is apparent, but one may have existed where the "wood road" now crosses the entrenched line The plan will afford an accurate idea of the position and its natural strength. The enclosed area is about seven hundred feet long by four hundred and fifty broad at its widest part, and contains very nearly six acres. It is densely covered with immense pines throwing over it a deep gloom, and, with the murmur of the stream at the foot of the precipice, impressing the solitary visitor with feelings of awe, which the professed antiquary might deem it a weakness to acknowledge.

Fragments of pottery and a variety of rude implements, as also copper kettles and other articles of European origin, have been found upon excavation within the enclosure and in its immediate vicinity.    At *c* and *d* skeletons have been disclosed by the plough    They were well preserved, and had been buried according to the Indian custom in a sitting posture

The valley of the Mohawk in this vicinity, it is well known, was the favorite seat of the tribe whose name it bears, and has been made classical ground by the stirring incidents of our early history    It was here the Indians maintained themselves until the period of the Revolution, and it seems probable that it was they who erected the work in question at an earlier or later date in their history *    It corresponds in position and character with the works of the other parts of the State, and is precisely such a structure as we might expect to find erected by a very rude people    It could not be ascertained that there are any traditions connected with it; in fact, its existence is scarcely known beyond its immediate vicinity    The first intimation concerning it was derived from O Morris, Esq., of the New York Institution for the Deaf and Dumb, to whom the author would convey his acknowledgments

---

* In the London Documents preserved in the Office of the Secretary of State is a paper containing the observations of Wentworth Greenhalgh, who in 1677 made a journey from Albany among the Indians to the westward    The following notices of the towns of the Maquaes or Mohawks, are interesting in this connection

' The Maquaes have four towns, viz    Cahainaga, Canagora, Canajorha, Tionondogue, besides one small village about 110 miles from Albany

" Cahainaga is double stockaded round, has four ports, about four foot wide apiece, conteyns about twenty four houses, and is situate upon the edge of a hill, about a bow-shot from the river side

" Canagora is only singly stockaded, has four ports like the other, contains about sixteen houses, and is situated upon a flat about a stone's throw from the water's edge

" Canajorha is also singly stockaded, with like number of houses, and a similar situation, only about two miles distant from the water

" Tionondogue is doubly stockaded round, has four ports, four foot wide apiece, contains about thirty houses, and is situated on a hill about a bow-shot from the river "—*Documentary History of New York,* Vol I, p 11

# CHAPTER III.

## PALISADED ENCLOSURES

Besides the earth-works which have already been described, and which furnish the principal objects of antiquarian interest in the State, occasional traces are found of defensive structures of a probably later date  These traces consist chiefly of a succession of small holes in the earth, caused by the decay of wooden palisades erected without the addition of an embankment and trench  These holes, which are never visible in cultivated grounds, enable us to follow the outlines and make out the forms of the structures which once existed where they are found  Some of these, as that of *Ganundesaga* near Geneva, are known to have been occupied within the historical period.  And although it seems probable that the embankments of all the enclosures already described were originally crowned with palisades, still I have thought the difference between these and simple palisaded works sufficiently marked to constitute the basis of a classification.  We may also premise what in the sequel will probably admit of no doubt in any mind, that these two classes of works are of different eras, though possessing a common origin.

———

## PLATE XIII  No  1

### " ANUNDESAGA CASTLE," NEAR GENEVA, ONTARIO COUNTY, NEW YORK

The traces of this palisaded work are very distinct, and its outline may be followed with the greatest ease  Its preservation is entirely due to the circumstance that at the time of the cession of their lands at this point, the Senecas made it a special condition that this spot should never be brought under cultivation  " Here," said they, " sleep our fathers, and they cannot rest well if they hear the plough of the white man above them "  The stipulations made by the purchasers have been religiously observed.

The site of this ancient palisade slopes gently towards a little stream, called Ganundesaga Creek, which supplied the occupants of the fort with water  The ground is covered with a close greensward, and some of the apple-trees planted by the Indians are still flourishing.  In form the work was nearly rectangular, having

small bastions at the northwestern and southeastern angles    At *a* and *b* are small
heaps of stone, bearing traces of exposure to fire, which are probably the remains
of forges or fireplaces    The holes formed by the decay of the pickets are now
about a foot deep    A fragment of one of the pickets was removed by Mr L. H.
Morgan, of Rochester, in 1847, and is now in the State Cabinet at Albany.    It is
of oak.

A few paces to the northward of the old fort is a low mound with a broad base,
and undoubtedly of artificial origin    It is now about six feet high, and is covered
with depressions marking the graves of the dead    There is a tradition current
among the Indians concerning this mound, to the effect that here in the olden
time was slain a powerful giant, above whom the earth was afterwards heaped
They believe that the bones of this giant may be found at the base.    It would be
interesting for a variety of reasons to have this mound excavated    By whatever
people erected, it is certain that it was extensively used by the Senecas for
purposes of burial

In the cultivated fields surrounding the interesting works here described, numerous relics have been discovered—chiefly however of European origin

This fort was destroyed by Sullivan in 1779.    He burned the palisade, destroyed
the crops in the adjoining fields, and cut down most of the fruit-trees which the
Indians had planted.

------

## PLATE XIII  No 2

### PALISADED WORK OF THE SENECAS, SENECA TOWNSHIP, ONTARIO COUNTY, NEW YORK

THIS work is situated about four miles to the northwest of that last described,
upon a high ridge of land extending north and south, and parallel to and not far
distant from another on which is situated an ancient earth-work figured on Plate
VII No 1.  A cross road from the " Castle Street Road " to the town of Vienna runs
along the crown of the ridge, and longitudinally through the work under notice
Upon the right of this road the ground has been cultivated, and here the outlines
of the work are obliterated    Traces of several *caches* which existed within the
lines may however yet be seen.    Upon the left, the forest still remains undisturbed ;
and here the outlines of the enclosure are quite distinct, yet not sufficiently
marked to arrest the attention of the passer    The indications are precisely the
same as in the work at Ganundesaga    Fragments of pottery, pipes, and other
relics exactly corresponding with those which are so frequent in the earth-works
described in a previous chapter, are also found in abundance upon this site    The
work does not appear to have had bastions, and is probably of more ancient date
than the one just noticed

## PLATE XIII. No 3.

### ANCIENT WORK OF THE CAYUGAS, LEDYARD TOWNSHIP, CAYUGA COUNTY, NEW YORK

THIS work is found about twelve miles southwest of Auburn, in the town of Ledyard, Cayuga county   It forms a good illustration of the character of the aboriginal defences   It is situated upon a high point of ground, formed by the junction of two immense ravines, which here sink some hundreds of feet below the table-lands   A narrow spur, hardly wide enough to permit two to walk abreast, extends down to the bottom of the ravines, starting from the extreme point of the head-land   It is still called the "Indian Path," and affords a practicable descent to the water   At every other point the banks are almost if not entirely inaccessible   At some distance inward, extending from the bank of one ravine to the other, was originally a line of palisades.   The holes left by their decay are still distinct, each about eight inches in diameter   The position is eminently a strong one, and, under the system of attack practised by the Indians, must have been impregnable   Within the enclosure are to be found *caches* and other features common to the class of works previously described, and with which this work entirely coincides, except that the embankment is wanting

So far as could be ascertained, there is no tradition current respecting this work.   Still, as it is known that the principal towns of the Cayugas existed in this vicinity until a very late date, there can be no doubt that this was one of their places of last resort   Very many traces of their former occupancy occur here and along the eastern shores of Cayuga Lake.

---

## PLATE XIV   No 1

### ANCIENT WORK OF THE SENECAS, NEAR VICTOR, ONTARIO COUNTY, NEW YORK.

THE site occupied by the work here figured and the country adjacent, derives considerable interest from its historical associations   Recent investigations have satisfactorily determined that the Marquis De Nonville penetrated here in his celebrated expedition against the Senecas, in 1687, and there is good reason to believe that the traces at present existing are those of the palisaded fort which was destroyed at that time   They occupy the summit of a high hill, so steep upon most sides as to be ascended only with the greatest difficulty   The line of the palisades can now be traced only at intervals, but from the nature of the ground and the recollection of persons familiar with the site before it was disturbed by the plough, it was found easy to restore with accuracy the parts which have been obliterated    The sole entrance which can now be made out is at the point marked by the letter *a* where the palisades were carried for some distance inwards, leaving an open rectangular space, which may have been occupied by a block-house or something equivalent    Nearly in front, and at the bottom of a deep and narrow ravine, a copious spring starts out from the hill, probably the one alluded to by De Nonville in his letter of the 25th of August, 1687

"On the next day,' says this commander, "the 14th of July, we marched to one of the large villages of the Senecas, where we encamped    We found it burned and a fort quite nigh abandoned, it was very advantageously situated on a hill. * * * We remained at the four Seneca villages for ten days    All the time was spent in destroying the corn, which was in such great abundance that the loss, including the old corn which was in *cache* which we burnt, was computed at 400,000 minots (1,200,000 bushels) of Indian corn"

The large village alluded to here is no doubt the one which was situated on the eminence now known as "Boughton's Hill," where abundant traces of Indian occupancy at this period are found    These consist of copper kettles, French hatchets, broken gun-barrels. arrow-heads, pipes, pottery, burnt corn, etc.    The iron recovered here at the time of the first settlement of the country, was suffi-ciently abundant to repay the cost of clearing the grounds    Indeed it was the source whence the early blacksmiths, for a long distance round, derived the iron for ordinary consumption, and even now the smithies in the vicinity consume large quantities of the metal which the operations of agriculture continue to bring to light.

The remains upon Boughton's Hill are mentioned by Mr Clinton as corre-sponding in all respects with those which he observed in Onondaga county, and to which he was disposed to ascribe a high antiquity    They may all be referred to the same period, and no doubt mark the sites of Onondaga and Seneca villages in the 17th century.

----

## PLATE XIV. No. 2.

### ANCIENT WORK OF THE SENECAS, LIVONIA TOWNSHIP, LIVINGSTON COUNTY, NEW YORK.

THE traces of another palisaded work, no doubt erected by the Senecas, but probably at a later period than that near Victor. may still be seen on the farm of Gen Adams, in Livonia township, Livingston county, two miles northeast of the village of Livonia

It occupied a beautiful, broad swell of land, not commanded by any adjacent heights. Upon the west side of the lines is a fine, copious spring; for which the Indians had constructed a large basin of loose stones The form and dimensions of the work are given in the accompanying plan Upon a little elevation to the left, as also in the forest to the northward, are extensive cemeteries. Many articles of comparatively late date are found in the graves. The area of the work was about ten acres.

Three miles to the eastward formerly existed the traces of a work represented to have been octangular in shape, and of considerable size It has been wholly obliterated.

In Queen's county there were, some years ago, traces of aboriginal works, which seem to have differed very slightly from a portion of those just noticed. They are thus described by Judge Samuel Jones, in a notice of the local history of Oyster Bay, written in 1812

" When this part of Long Island was first settled by the Europeans, they found two fortifications in the neighborhood of Oyster Bay, upon a neck of land ever since called, from that circumstance, 'Fort Neck.' One of them, the remains of which are very conspicuous, is on the southernmost point of land on the neck adjoining the Salt Meadow. It is nearly, if not exactly, a square, each side of which is about *one hundred feet* in length The breastwork or parapet is of earth, and there is a ditch on the outside, which appears to have been about six feet wide. The other was on the southernmost point of the Salt Meadow, adjoining the bay, and consisted of palisades set in the ground The tide has worn away the meadow where the fort stood, and the place is now part of the bay and covered with water; but my father has often told me that within his memory part of the palisades were still standing In the bay, between the Salt Meadow and the beach, are two islands of marsh, called Squaw Islands, and the uniform tradition among the Indians is, that the forts were erected by their ancestors for defence against their enemies, and that upon the approach of a foe, they sent their women and children to these islands, which were in consequence called Squaw Islands "*

Examples of this class of aboriginal remains might be greatly multiplied Those, however, which have already been presented, will serve sufficiently to illustrate their character In all are found relics corresponding in every particular with those discovered within the walls of the earth-works described in the preceding chapter, but usually with the addition of articles of later date and known European origin This circumstance is not without its importance in estimating the probable dependence between the two classes of remains

---

* Coll N Y Hist Soc, Vol III p 338

# CHAPTER IV.

Various references to mounds or tumuli, resembling those found in the Valley of the Mississippi, have been made in the preceding pages. These mounds are far from numerous, and hardly deserve a separate notice. It is nevertheless an interesting fact to know that isolated examples occur, in situations where it is clear no dependence exists between them and the grand system of earth-works of the Western States. It serves to sustain the conclusion that the savage Indian tribes occasionally constructed mounds; which are however rather to be considered as accidents than the results of a general practice. The purposes of the mounds of New York, so far as can be determined, seem uniformly to have been those of sepulture. They generally occur upon commanding or remarkable positions. Most of them have been excavated, under the impulse of an idle curiosity, or have had their contents scattered by "money-diggers," a ghostly race, of which, singularly enough, even at this day, representatives may be found in almost every village. I was fortunate enough to discover one upon Tonawanda Island, in Niagara River, which had escaped their midnight attentions. It was originally about fifteen feet in height. At the base appeared to have been a circle of stones, perhaps ten feet in diameter, within which were several small heaps of bones, each comprising three or four skeletons. The bones are of individuals of all ages, and had evidently been deposited after the removal of the flesh. Traces of fire were to be discovered upon the stones. Some chippings of flint and broken arrow-points, as also some fragments of deers' horns, which appeared to have been worked into form, were found amongst the bones. The skulls had been crushed by the superincumbent earth.

The mounds which formerly existed in Erie, Genesee, Monroe, Livingston, St Lawrence, Oswego, Chenango, and Delaware counties, all appear to have contained human bones, in greater or less quantities, deposited promiscuously, and embracing the skeletons of individuals of all ages and both sexes. They probably all owe their origin to a practice common to many of the North American tribes, of collecting together at fixed intervals the bones of their dead, and finally depositing them with many and solemn ceremonies. They were sometimes heaped together so as to constitute mounds, at others placed in pits or trenches dug in the earth, and it is probable they were in some instances buried in separate graves, but in long ranges, or deposited in caverns, either promiscuously or with regularity.

The period when this second burial took place occurred at different intervals amongst the different tribes, but was universally denominated the "Festival of the Dead." Bartram, speaking of the burial customs of the Floridian Indians, says. "After the bone-house is full, a general solemn funeral takes place. The nearest kindred and friends of the deceased, on a day appointed, repair to the bone-house, take up the respective coffins, and, following one another in the order of seniority, the nearest relations and connections attending their respective corpses and the multitude succeeding them, singing and lamenting alternately, slowly proceed to the place of general interment, when they place the coffins in order forming a pyramid Lastly, they cover all over with earth, which raises a conical hill or mount They then return to town in order of solemn procession, concluding the day with a festival which is called the 'Feast of the Dead.'"* The author here quoted adds in a note, that it was the opinion of some ingenious men with whom he had conversed, "that all those artificial pyramidal hills, usually called 'Indian Mounts,' were raised on such occasions, and are generally sepulchres ," from which opinion he takes occasion to dissent. There is no doubt a wide difference between the mounds thus formed and the great bulk of those connected with the vast ancient enclosures of the Western States.

The large cemeteries which have been discovered in Tennessee, Kentucky, Missouri, and Ohio, seem to have resulted from a similar practice In these the skeletons were generally packed in rude coffins composed of flat stones, placed in ranges of great extent The circumstance that many of these coffins were not more than two or three feet in length, gave rise to the notion of the former existence here of a pigmy race The discovery of iron and some articles of European origin in one of these cemeteries in the vicinity of Augusta, Kentucky, shows that this mode of burial existed at a late period among the Indians in that direction

The "bone-pits" which occur in some parts of Western New York, Canada, Michigan, etc , have unquestionably a corresponding origin Several of these have been described in a previous chapter. They are of various sizes, but usually contain a large number of skeletons In a few instances the bones appear to have been arranged with some degree of regularity.

One of these pits discovered some years ago, in the town of Cambria, Niagara county, was estimated to contain the bones of several thousand individuals. Another which I visited in the town of Clarence, Erie county, contained not less than four hundred skeletons A deposit of bones comprising a large number of skeletons was found not long since, in making some excavations in the town of Black Rock, situated on Niagara River, in Erie county. They were arranged in a circle, with their heads radiating from a large copper kettle, which had been placed in the centre, and filled with bones Various implements both of modern and remote date had been placed beside the skeletons

In Canada similar deposits are frequent. Accounts of their discovery and character have appeared in various English publications, among which may be named the "British Colonial Newspaper," of September 24th, 1847, and the

---

* Travels, p 514

"Edinburgh New Philosophical Journal," for July, 1848. From a communication in the latter, by Edward W Bawtree, M. D., the subjoined interesting facts are derived.

A quantity of human bones was found in one spot, in 1846, near Barrie, and also a pit containing human bones near St. Vincent's. Great numbers were found in the latter, with several copper and brass kettles, and various trinkets and ornaments in common use among the Indians This discovery led to the examination of a similar pit, about seven miles from Penetanqueshene, in the township of Giny. "This pit was accidentally noticed by a Canadian while making sugar in the neighborhood. He was struck by its appearance and the peculiar sound produced at the bottom by stamping there, and, in turning up a few spadefuls of earth, was surprised to find a quantity of human bones It was more accurately examined in September, 1847, and found to contain, besides a great number of human skeletons, of both sexes and all ages, twenty-six copper and brass kettles and boilers, three large conch-shells, pieces of beaver-skin in tolerable preservation, a fragment of a pipe; a large iron axe, evidently of French manufacture, some human hair (that of a woman), a copper bracelet, and a quantity of flat auricular beads, perforated through the centre

"The form of the pit is circular, with an elevated margin; it is about fifteen feet in diameter, and before it was opened was probably nine feet deep from the level of its margin to its centre and bottom, it was, in one word, funnel-shaped. It is situated on the top of a gentle rise, with a shallow ravine on the east side, through which, at certain seasons, runs a small stream The soil is light, free from stones, and dry. A small iron-wood tree, about two inches in diameter, is growing in the centre of the pit

"The kettles in the pit were found ranged at the bottom, resting on pieces of bark, and filled with bones They had evidently been covered with beaver-skins

The shells and the axe were found in the intervals between the kettles. The beads were in the kettles among the bones, generally in bunches of strings.

"The kettles, of which Fig. 4 is an example, resemble those in use at the present day, and appear to be formed of sheet copper, the rim being beaten out so as to cover an iron band which passes around the mouth of the vessel.

Fig 4

The iron handle by which they were suspended hooks into eyes attached to the band above mentioned The smallest holds about six gallons, the largest not far from sixteen gallons. The copper is generally very well preserved, the iron, however, is much corroded. Two of the kettles were of brass

"The largest of the conch-shells, Fig 5, weighs three pounds and a quarter, and measures fourteen inches in its longest diameter Its outer surface has lost its polish, and is quite honey-combed by age and decomposition; the inside still retains its smooth lamellated surface It

Fig. 5

has lost its color, and appears like chalk. A piece had been cut from its base, probably for making the beads that were found in it.* From the base of the columella of the smallest shell a piece had been cut, evidently for the purpose of manufacturing beads. The extreme point of the base of each shell had a perforation through it.

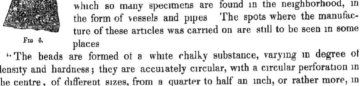

Fig. 6.

"The axe, Fig. 6, is of nearly the same model with the tomahawk now in use among the Chippeway Indians, though very much larger, measuring eleven inches in length and six inches and a half along its cutting edge   Numbers of these have been found in the neighborhood on newly cleared land

"The pipe is imperfect. It is made of the earthenware of which so many specimens are found in the neighborhood, in the form of vessels and pipes   The spots where the manufacture of these articles was carried on are still to be seen in some places

"The beads are formed of a white chalky substance, varying in degree of density and hardness; they are accurately circular, with a circular perforation in the centre, of different sizes, from a quarter to half an inch, or rather more, in diameter; but nearly all of the same thickness, not quite the eighth of an inch   They may be compared to a peppermint lozenge with a hole through the centre.   They were found in bunches or strings, and a good many were still closely strung on a fibrous woody substance.   The bracelet is a simple band of copper, an inch and a half broad, closely fitting the wrist.   The hair is long evidently that of a woman  and quite fresh in appearance.

"Another pit, about two miles from that just noticed, was also examined in September   It is considerably smaller, being not more than nine feet in diameter, by about the same original depth   It is situated on rising ground, in a light sandy soil, and there is nothing remarkable in its position.   A beech-tree, six inches thick, grew from its centre.   It contained about as many skeletons as the other pit, but had no kettles in it   The bones were of individuals of both sexes and of all ages. Among them were a few fœtal bones   Many of the skulls bore marks of violence, leading to the belief that they were broken before burial   One was pierced by a round hole, like that produced by a musket ball.   A single piece of a brass vessel was found in the pit; it had been packed in furs   A large number of shell beads, of various sizes, were also found here   Besides these, there were some cylindrical pieces of earthenware and porcelain or glass tubes, from an eighth to a quarter of an inch in diameter, and from a quarter to two inches long †   The former had the appearance of red and white tobacco-pipes, worn away by friction, the latter of red and white glass   A hexagonal body, with flat ends, about an inch and a half in diameter, and an inch thick, was also found.   It was composed of some kind of porcelain, of hard texture, nearly vitreous, and much variegated in color  with alternate layers of red, blue, and white   It was perforated through the centre.

* Dr Bern W Budd, of New York states that this shell, the *pyrula perversa*, abounds in the Gulf of Mexico and particularly in Mobile Bay   It has also been found by the officers of the U S Coast Survey as far north as Cape Fear, in North Carolina

† These were clearly the European imitations of the much prized Indian *wampum*

"The third of these pits was examined in November, 1847   It is situated in the township of Oro, on elevated ground.   The soil is a light sandy loam   It measures about fifteen feet in diameter, has the distinctly defined elevated ring, but the centre less depressed than in those before examined, which may have resulted from the greater bulk of its contents   On its margin grew formerly a large pine, the roots of which had penetrated through the pit in every direction. The bones, which were of all sizes, were scarcely covered with earth.   The skeletons amounted to several hundreds in number, and were well preserved.   On some, pieces of tendon still remained, and the joints of the small bones in some cases were unseparated.   Some of the skulls bore marks of violence.

"As in the first noticed pit, so in this, were found twenty-six kettles—four of brass and the rest of copper, one conch-shell, one iron axe, and a number of the flat perforated shell beads   The kettles were arranged in the form of a cross through the centre of the pit, and in a row around the circumference.   The points of this cross seem to have corresponded with the cardinal points of the compass. All except two of the kettles were placed with their mouths downwards   The shell was found under one of the kettles, which had been packed with beaver-skins and bark.   The kettles were very well preserved, but had all been rendered useless by blows from a tomahawk.   The holes were broken in the bases of the vessels Should any doubt exist as to the purposes of these pits, the fact that the kettles were thus rendered unserviceable would tend to increase that doubt, as it appears to have been a proceeding so very contrary to the habits and ideas of the Indians in general *

"A pipe was found in this pit, described as having been composed of blue limestone or hard clay   On one side it had a human face, the eyes of which were formed of white pearly beads.   An iron axe and sundry beads were also found here.

"A fourth pit was opened in December, 1847   It is situated on a gentle slope, in the second concession west of the Penetanqueshene road, in the township of Giny In size it corresponds very nearly with the two first described, and probably contained about the same number of skeletons.   In it were found sixteen conch-shells ; a stone and clay pipe , a number of copper bracelets and ear ornaments ; eleven beads of red pipe-stone , copper arrow-heads , a cup of iron resembling an old iron ladle ; beads of several kinds, and various fragments of furs.   The shells were

Fig 7

arranged around the bottom of the pit, not in a regular row, but in threes and fours ; the other articles were found mixed with the bones.   The bones were of all sizes, and the skulls uninjured except by time.   The accompanying sketch (Fig 7) will sufficiently indicate the character of the pipes   The arrow-heads, as they are supposed to have been, were simple folds of sheet copper, resembling a roughly-formed ferule to a walking-stick   Besides the flat circular beads, which were found

---

* Dr Bawtree is mistaken in supposing this practice uncommon   The Oregon Indians invariably render useless every article deposited with their dead, so as to remove any temptation to a desecration of the grave which might otherwise exist   A similar practice prevailed among the Floridian Indians

in great numbers, were a few cylindrical porcelain beads, etc    The red-stone beads
were five eighths of an inch broad, and three eighths thick, with small holes at one
end, uniting with each other.

" There is reason to believe that the above constitute but a very small proportion of the pits that may be found in this neighborhood.   The French Canadians,
now that their attention has been directed to the subject, say that they are of
frequent occurrence in the woods.   But besides these larger and more evident
excavations, smaller ones of the same shape and apparent character are often met
with.   They are usually called ' potato-pits '   So far as they have been examined,
they do not contain deposits.   Some appear to have been covered with bark at
the bottom.   One was examined in which were found some pieces of pottery and
one or two human bones mixed with stones and black mould ; which seemed to
strengthen the supposition previously formed, that they were Indian graves from
which the bones had been removed for interment in the large pits.

" A fifth pit has also been examined.   It occurs about eight miles from Penetanqueshene, near the centre of the town of Giny    Close by its side is another
pit, which is not circular but elongated, with a mound on each side.   At the brow
of the hill, if it may be so called, and commencing about twenty yards from the
pits, there is the appearance of a long ditch extending in a southwestern direction ;
another ditch about half the length of this meets it at right angles on the top of
the rising ground, and is continued a few yards beyond the point of junction ; a
third ditch intersects the short one, as shown in the following plan.

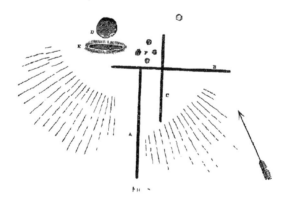

Fig.

" The two first ditches form two sides of a parallelogram ; but there is no sign of
an enclosure at the other sides, where the ground is low and nearly level.   The
long ditch is seventy-five paces in length, the other half that length    The first
terminates at a moderate sized gum-tree, the latter at the foot of a large birch.
These ditches appear to be a succession of small pits or graves, and have an
average depth of from one to two feet    Excavation disclosed no bones.   Upon
the north side of the shorter and upper ditch, several Indian graves were found,

not placed in any order, but scattered around at various distances apart. Three of these were examined and found to contain human bones In one was an entire skeleton No implements or ornaments accompanied the bones.

" The bones in the large pits were covered with three or four feet of earth, which is more than is usually found over them, and the marginal ring was in consequence less apparent. It contained very few relics besides the bones, which, from their decayed condition, seemed to indicate that burials here were made at a very remote period."

In Isle Ronde, situated near the extremity of Lake Huron, is a burial-place of the aborigines corresponding generally with those just described It was visited in 1843 by Mr. Schoolcraft, who states that the human remains appeared to have been gathered from their original place of sepulture and finally deposited here. The bones were all arranged longitudinally, from north to south, in a wide grave or trench. There is upon the same island an Indian cemetery of comparatively modern date, in which the interments were made in the ordinary way Another similar burial-place was visited by Mr. Schoolcraft, in the town of Hamilton, seventeen miles west of the head of Lake Ontario. The burials had been made on a high, dry ridge, in long trenches and rude vaults, the bones being piled upon each other longitudinally as at Isle Ronde The trenches extend over the entire ridge; and one of these examined by Mr Schoolcraft was estimated to include not less than fifteen hundred square feet. Various remains of art, pipes, shells, beads, etc., were found with the bones, and among them several brass kettles in one of which were five infant skulls

The origin of the various cemeteries above noticed admits of no doubt The same practice which Bartram described as existing among the Floridians, and which we have reason to believe prevailed among the Indians of Tennessee, Kentucky, etc, also existed in a slightly modified form among the more northern tribes They, too, had their solemn " Festival of the Dead," which is minutely described by Charlevoix, Brabeuf, Creuxius, and other early writers Says Charlevoix " This grand ceremony, the most curious and celebrated of all connected with the Indian religion, took place every eight years among some of the tribes, every ten years among the Hurons and the *Iroquois* It was called the ' *Fête des Morts*, Festival of the Dead, or ' *Festin des Ames* '

" It commenced by the appointment of a place where they should meet. They then chose a president of the feast, whose duty it was to arrange every thing and send invitations to the neighboring villages. The appointed day arrived, all the Indians assembled and went in procession, two and two, to the cemetery Among some tribes of stationary habits, the cemetery was a regular burial-ground outside the village Some buried their dead at the foot of a tree, and others suspended them on scaffolds to dry, this last was a common proceeding among them when absent from home on a hunting expedition, so that on their return they might more conveniently carry the body with them.

" Arrived at the cemetery, they proceeded to search for the bodies; they then waited for some time to consider in silence a spectacle so capable of furnishing serious reflections The women first interrupted the silence by cries of lamenta-

10

tion, which increased the feeling of grief with which each person seemed over-come    They then used to take the bodies, arrange the separate and dry bones, and place them in packets to carry on their shoulders.  If any of the bodies were not entirely decomposed, they separated the flesh, washed the bones, and wrapped them in new beaver-skins    They then returned in the same procession in which they came, and each deposited his burden in his cabin.  During the procession the women continued their lamentations, and the men testified the same marks of grief as on the death of the person whose bones they bore    This was followed by a feast in each house, in honor of the dead of the family    The succeeding days were considered as public days, and were spent in dancing, games, and combats, at which prizes were bestowed    From time to time they uttered certain cries, which were called ' *les cris des âmes* '

" They made presents to strangers, and received presents from them on behalf of the dead    These strangers sometimes came a hundred and fifty leagues    They also took advantage of these occasions to treat on public affairs or select a chief. Every thing passed with order, decency, and moderation ; and every one seemed overcome with sentiments suitable to the occasion    Even the songs and dances expressed grief in some way    After some days thus spent, all went in procession to a grand council-room fitted for the occasion.  They then suspended the bones and bodies in the same state as they had taken them from the cemetery, and placed there the presents intended for the dead    If among the skeletons there happened to be one of a chief, his successor gave a grand feast in his name.   In some cases the bodies were paraded from village to village, and every where received with great demonstrations of grief and tenderness, and every where presents were made to them.   They then took them to the spot designated as their final resting-place    All their ceremonies were accompanied with music, both instrumental and vocal, to which each marched in cadence.

" The last and common place of burial was a large pit, which was lined with the finest skins and any thing which they considered valuable.   The presents destined for the dead were placed on one side , and when the procession arrived, each family arranged itself on a sort of scaffold around the pit , and as soon as the bodies were deposited, the women began again to cry and lament    Then all the assistants descended into the pit, and each person took a handful of earth, which he carefully preserved, supposing it would serve to give them success in their undertakings.   The bodies and bones were arranged in order, and covered with furs and bark, over which were placed stones, wood, and earth    Each person then returned to his home, but the women used to go back from day to day with some *sagamatie* (pounded parched corn) "*

---

* Charlevoix, Vol II , p  194, ubi supra , Creuxii Historia Canadensis, p  97

# CHAPTER V.

## IMPLEMENTS, ORNAMENTS, ETC

MOST of the minor relics of art discovered in the State of New York are such as are known to have been common amongst the Iroquois and other tribes which once occupied its territories. The character of these is so well known as to render unnecessary any detailed notice of the various articles obtained in the course of the explorations here recorded. A brief reference to the more remarkable specimens is therefore all which will be attempted.

Upon the site of every Indian town, as also within all of the ancient enclosures, fragments of pottery occur in great abundance. It is rare, however, that any entire vessels are recovered. Those which have been found, are for the most part, gourd-shaped, with round bottoms, and having little protuberances near the rim, or oftener a deep groove, whereby they could be suspended. A few cases have been known in which this form was modified, and the bottoms made sufficiently flat to sustain the vessel in an upright position. Fragments found in Jefferson county seem to indicate that occasionally the vessels were moulded in forms nearly square, but with rounded angles. The usual size was from one to four quarts, but some must have contained not less than twelve or fourteen quarts. In general there was no attempt at ornament; but sometimes the exteriors of the pots and vases were elaborately if not tastefully ornamented with dots and lines, which seem to have been formed in a very rude manner with a pointed stick or sharpened bone. Bones which appear to have been adapted for this purpose are often found. After the commencement of European intercourse, kettles and vessels of iron, copper, brass, and tin, quickly superseded the productions of the primitive potter, whose art at once fell into disuse. Pipes and various articles of clay, which may be denominated *terra cottas*, continued, nevertheless, to be made. The pipes of native manufacture were preferred, as they still are, to those of European or American production. After the introduction of tools, and as soon as the Indians became acquainted with foreign models, great improvement was made in their manufacture. The following examples will furnish very good illustrations of the forms of the Indian pipe.

Fig 9 was found within an enclosure in Jefferson county, Plate IV. No 4. It is engraved one half the size of the original. It is of fine red clay, smoothly moulded, and two serpents rudely imitated are represented coiling around the bowl. Bushels of fragments of pipes have been found within the same enclosure. Some appear to have been worked in the form of the human head, others in representations of animals, and others still in a variety of regular forms

Fig. 10 was found within another enclosure in the same county. It differs from the first only in respect of size.

Fig. 11 was found on the site of an old Seneca town, in the town of Livonia, Livingston county. It resembles the other in shape, but is of darker color, and not so well burned. The difference to be observed between it and the others may be ascribed entirely to the difference in the clay composing it.

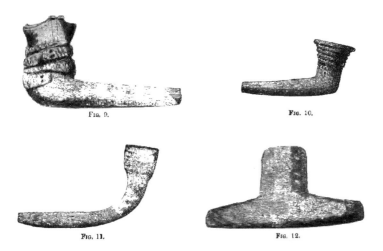

Fig. 9.                                    Fig. 10.

Fig. 11.                                    Fig. 12.

Fig. 12. This is a greatly reduced representation of an article of stone found near Mount Morris, in Livingston county, and now in the New York State Cabinet at Albany. It is composed of "soap stone," and in shape corresponds generally with the pipes of stone found in the mounds of the Mississippi Valley. If intended for a pipe, which seems most likely, it was never finished, as the cavity of the bowl is merely indicated. One or two pipes of stone of very nearly the same shape have been found in this vicinity, but in point of symmetry or finish they are in no way comparable to those of the mounds.

Some pipes of precisely the same material, and of identical workmanship with those found in the ancient enclosures, have been discovered in modern Indian graves, in Cayuga county. One of these, in the form of a bird, and having eyes made of silver inserted in the head, is now in possession of the author. Various articles of European or American manufacture were found in the same grave.

The most beautiful *terra cotta* which I found in the State, and which in point of accuracy and delicacy of finish is unsurpassed by any similar article which I have seen of aboriginal origin, is the head of a fox, of which Fig. 13 is a full-size engraving. The engraving fails in conveying the spirit of the original, which is composed of fine clay, slightly burned. It seems to have been once attached to a body, or perhaps to a vessel of some kind. It closely resembles some of the terra cottas from the mounds of the West and Southwest. It was found upon the site of an ancient enclosure in Jefferson county, in the town of Ellisburgh, near the beautiful village of Pierrepont Manor.

Fig. 13.

Fig. 14.

Fig. 15.

Figs. 14 and 15 were found upon the site of an abandoned Seneca village, in the town of Mendon, Monroe county. The spot is now known as the "Ball Farm," and is remarkable for the number and variety of its ancient relics. Vast quantities of these have been removed from time to time. Some of the miniature representations of animals found here are remarkable for their accuracy.

Fig. 16.

The stone axe or hatchet may be found from Cape Horn to Baffin's Bay. Specimens taken from the intervening localities can be distinguished from each other only by the difference of the materials of which they are composed. I have found them in Nicaragua precisely resembling those of New York. Little, therefore, need be said concerning them. Fig. 16 was obtained in the vicinity of an ancient work on the Susquehanna River, in Pennsylvania, near the New York State line. It is remarkable for its symmetry and size, and also for the manner in which it is hollowed upon the inner side. This last named feature is well indicated in the engraving.

Figs. 17 and 18 present a front and reverse view of a very fine stone axe, found in Livingston county, near Avon Springs. The material is of intense hardness,

Fig. 17.

Fig. 18.

resembling porphyry. It is, nevertheless, worked with mathematical accuracy, and highly polished. The edge is very sharp. It is as fine a specimen of the Indian stone axe as ever fell under my notice.

Fig. 19 is of a greenish colored slate, and resembles a kind of ornamental hatchet, made of delicate material, which is found at the South and West. It was obtained near Spring-port, Cayuga county. For examples of similar articles, the reader is referred to the first volume of the Smithsonian Contributions to Knowledge, p. 218.

Fig. 19.

One of the most interesting relics which has yet been dis-covered in the State is an axe of *cast copper*, of which Fig. 20 is a reduced engraving. The original is four inches long by two and a half broad on the edge, and corresponds in shape with some of those of wrought native copper, which have been found in the mounds of Ohio. From the granulations of the surface, it appears to have been cast in sand. There is no

evidence of its having been used for any purpose. Its history, beyond that it was ploughed up somewhere in the vicinity of Auburn, Cayuga county, is unknown. No opportunity has yet been afforded of analyzing any portion, so as to determine whether it has an intermixture of other metals. It appears to be pure copper. An inspection serves to satisfy the inquirer that it is of aboriginal origin; but the questions when and by whom made, are beyond our ability to answer. There is no evidence that the mound-builders understood the smelting of metals; on the contrary, there is every reason to believe that they obtained their entire supply in a native state, and worked it cold. The

Fig. 20.

Portuguese chronicler of Soto's Expedition into Florida, mentions copper hatchets, and rather vaguely refers to a "smelting of copper," in a country

which he did not visit, far to the northward, called "Chisca." The Mexicans and Peruvians made hatchets of copper alloyed with tin. It would seem that this hatchet was obtained from that direction, or made by some Indian artisan after intercourse with the whites had instructed him in the art of working metals. At present it is prudent to say that the discovery of this relic is an anomalous fact, which investigators should only bear in mind, without venturing to make it the basis of deductions or inferences of any kind.

Fig. 21 is an example of the iron axe introduced among the Indians by the French. Thousands of these are found in the western counties of the State.

Fig. 21.

Figs. 22, 23, and 24 are selected by the author from the collection of relics made in the progress of these explorations, from their resemblance to relics of common occurrence in the mounds of the Mississippi Valley. Fig. 22 is almost identical in shape and material with some of the articles from the mounds, described on page 237 of the first volume of these Contributions. The same may be observed of Fig. 23. The material is the green, variegated slate, of which so many of the above named relics are composed. The first mound was found near Scottsville, Wheatland township, Monroe county; the second, near Springport, Cayuga

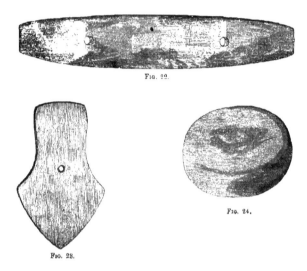

Fig. 22.

Fig. 24.

Fig. 23.

county. Near this place also was found the disk, Fig. 24. It is of green slate, and corresponds entirely with those described on page 221 of the same volume with the preceding.

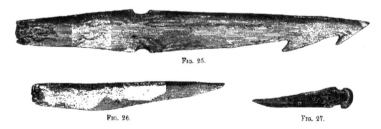

Fig. 25.

Fig. 26. Fig. 27.

Fig. 25 is the point of a fish-spear, made of the ulna of the deer; found in Livingston county. Figs. 26 and 27 are of the same material, and were used as bodkins or for working clay; found in Jefferson county.

Besides these relics, quantities of beads of stone, bone, and shell, ornaments of many kinds and of various materials, as also implements of aboriginal, or European, or American fabric, are found all over the State, but in more abundance in the western counties. They are not of sufficient importance to merit a detailed notice, and are chiefly interesting as the relics of a race fast disappearing, and whose existence will soon be known to history alone. It is to be hoped that, however insignificant they may seem, they may be carefully preserved and treasured for public inspection, in places or institutions designated for the purpose

# CHAPTER VI.

## CONCLUDING OBSERVATIONS

By whom were the aboriginal monuments of Western New York erected, and to what era may they be ascribed? The consideration of these questions has given rise to a vast amount of speculation, generally not of the most philosophical, nor yet of the most profitable kind. If the results arrived at have been erroneous, unsatisfactory, or extravagant, it may be ascribed to the circumstance that the facts heretofore collected have been too few in number and too poorly authenticated to admit of correct conclusions, not less than to the influence of preconceived notions, and to that constant leaning towards the marvellous, which is a radical defect of many minds. Rigid criticism is especially indispensable in archæological investigations, yet there is no department of human research in which so wide a range has been given to conjecture. Men seem to have indulged the belief that here nothing is fixed, nothing certain, and have turned aside into this field as one where the severer rules which elsewhere regulate philosophical research are not enforced, and where every species of extravagance may be indulged in with impunity. I might adduce numberless illustrations of this remark. The Indian who wrought the rude outlines upon the rock at Dighton, little dreamed that his work would ultimately come to be regarded as affording indubitable evidence of Hebrew, Phœnician, and Scandinavian adventure and colonization in America, and the builders of the rude defences of Western New York, as little suspected that Celt and Tartar, and even the apochryphal Madoc with his "ten ships," would, in this the nineteenth century of our faith, be vigorously invoked to yield paternity to their labors!

The probable purposes to which these works were applied are perhaps sufficiently evident from what has already been presented. Their positions, general close proximity to water, and other circumstances not less conclusive, imply a defensive origin. The unequivocal traces of long occupancy found within many of them, would further imply that they were fortified towns and villages, and were permanently occupied. Some of the smaller ones, on the other hand, seem rather designed for temporary protection,—the citadels in which the builders sought safety for their old men, women, and children, in case of alarm or attack.

In respect to date nothing positive can be affirmed. Many of them are now covered with heavy forests, a circumstance upon which too much importance has been laid, and which in itself may not necessarily be regarded as indicative of great age, for we may plausibly suppose that it was not essential to the purposes of the builders that the forests should be removed. Still I have seen trees from

11

one to three feet in diameter standing upon the embankments and in the trenches ; which would certainly carry back the date of their construction several hundred years, perhaps beyond the period of the discovery in the fifteenth century.   There is nothing, however, in this circumstance, nor in any other bearing upon the sub-ject, which would necessarily imply that they were built by tribes anterior to those found in occupation of the country by the whites   And this brings us at once to the most interesting point of our inquiry, viz: *By whom were these works erected ?*

I have already mentioned that within them are found many relics of art and many traces of occupancy.   These, I had ample opportunities of ascertaining in the course of my investigations, are absolutely *identical* with those which mark the sites of towns and forts known to have been occupied by the Indians, within the historical period.   The pottery taken from these sites and from within the supposed ancient enclosures, is alike in all respects ; the pipes and ornaments are undistinguishable , and the indications of aboriginal dwellings are precisely similar, and, so far as can be discovered, have equal claim to antiquity   Near many of these works are found cemeteries, in which well-preserved skeletons are con-tained, and which, except in the absence of remains of European art, differ in no essential respect from the cemeteries found in connection with the abandoned modern towns and "castles" of the Indians.   There are other not less important facts and coincidences, all of which go to establish that if the earth-works of Western New York are of a remote ancient date, they were not only *secondarily* but *generally* occupied by the Iroquois or neighboring and contemporary nations ; or else—and this hypothesis is most consistent and reasonable—they were erected by them.

The questions by whom were the aboriginal monuments of Western New York erected, and to what era may they be ascribed, have probably been answered to the satisfaction of every mind by the simple detail of facts in the preceding chapters

It may be objected that if the Indians constructed works of this kind, it could not have escaped the notice of the early explorers, and would have been made the subject of remark by them.   The omission is singular, but not unaccountable. They all speak of the defences of the Indians as composed of palisades firmly set in the ground.   The simple circumstance of the earth being heaped up around them, to lend them greater firmness, may have been regarded as so natural and simple an expedient, as not to be deserving of special mention, particularly as the embankment, in such a case, would be an entirely subordinate part of the struc-ture   After the introduction of European implements, enabling the Indians to plant their pickets more firmly in the ground, and to lend them a security before unattainable, the necessity for an embankment was in a great degree obviated. We may thus account for its absence in their later structures, which also under-went some modification of form, suggested by the example or instructions of the whites, or by the new modes of warfare following the introduction of fire-arms Thus in the plan of the old Seneca fort of *Ganundasaga*, we find distinct traces of the bastion—a feature observable in none of the more ancient defences

I am aware that the remnants of the Indian stock which still exist in the State, generally profess total ignorance of these works. I do not, however, attach much importance to this circumstance. When we consider the extreme likelihood of the forgetfulness of ancient practices, in the lapse of three hundred years, the lack of knowledge upon this point is the weakest of all negative evidence. Cusick, the Indian, in his so-called "History of the Six Nations," has, no doubt, correctly described the manner in which they constructed their early defences. "The manner of making a fort: First, they set fire against as many trees as it requires to make the enclosure, rubbing off the coals with their stone axes, so as to make them burn faster. When the tree falls, they put fires to it about three paces apart, and burn it into pieces. These pieces are then brought to the spot required, and set up around, according to the bigness of the fort. *The earth is then heaped on both sides.* The fort has generally two gates, one for passage and one to the water." "The people," continues Cusick, "had implements with which they made their bows and arrows. Their kettles were made of baked clay; their awls and needles of sharpened bones, their pipes of baked clay or soft stone, a small turtle-shell was used to peel the bark, and a small dry stick to make fire by boring it against seasoned wood."

Colden observes of their defences, as they were constructed in his time: "Their castles are generally a square surrounded with palisades, without any bastions or outworks, for, since the general peace, their villages all lie open."[*]

In full view of the facts before presented, I am driven to a conclusion little anticipated when I started upon my trip of exploration, that the earth-works of Western New York were erected by the Iroquois or their western neighbors, and do not possess an antiquity going very far back of the discovery. Their general occurrence upon a line parallel to and not far distant from the lakes, favors the hypothesis that they were built by frontier tribes—an hypothesis entirely conformable to aboriginal traditions. Here, according to these traditions, every foot of ground was contested between the Iroquois and the Gah-kwas and other western tribes; and here, as a consequence, where most exposed to attack, were permanent defences most necessary. It was not until after the Confederation, that the Five Nations were able to check and finally expel the warlike people which disputed with them the possession of the beautiful and fertile regions bordering the lakes, and it is not impossible that it was the pressure from this direction which led to that Confederation,—an anomaly in the history of the aborigines. Common danger, rather than a far-seeing policy, may be regarded as the impelling cause of the consolidation.

In conclusion, I may be permitted to observe, that the ancient remains of Western New York, except so far as they throw light upon the system of defence practised by the aboriginal inhabitants, and tend to show that they were to a degree fixed and agricultural in their habits, have slight bearing upon the grand ethnological

---

[*] History of the Five Nations, Vol I, p 9

and archæological questions involved in the ante-Columbian history of the continent    The resemblances which they bear to the defensive structures of other rude nations, in various parts of the world, are the result of natural causes, and cannot be taken to indicate either a close or remote connection or dependence All primitive defences, being designed to resist common modes of attack, are essentially the same in their principles, and seldom differ very much in their details. The aboriginal hunter and the semi-civilized Aztec, selected precisely similar positions for their fortresses, and defended them upon the same general plan , yet it would be palpably unsafe to found conclusions as to the relations of the respective builders, upon the narrow basis of these resemblances alone

# APPENDIX.

WITHOUT the boundaries of the State of New York, there are works composed of earth, closely resembling those described in the preceding pages. Among these may be named the small earth-works of Northern Ohio, which the author himself was at one time led to believe constituted part of the grand system of the mound builders.* The more extensive and accurate information which he has now in his possession concerning them, as also concerning those of Western New York, has led to an entire modification of his views, and to the conviction that they are all of comparatively late date, and probably of common origin.

Some similar works are said to occur in Canada, but we have no account at all satisfactory concerning them. One is mentioned by Laing (*Polynesian Nations,* p. 109) upon the authority of a third person, as situated upon the summit of a precipitous ridge, near Lake Simcoe, and consisting of an embankment of earth, enclosing a considerable extent of ground. Mr Schoolcraft also states that there are some ancient enigmatical walls of earth in the vicinity of Dundas, which extend several miles across the country, following the leading ridges of land. These are represented to be from five to eight miles in length, and not far from six feet high, with passages at intervals. as if for gates (*Oneota,* p 326). Our knowledge concerning these is too limited to permit any conjecture as to their design

In the State of Pennsylvania, there are some remains, which may be regarded as the "outliers" of those of New York. They are confined to the upper counties. Those in the Valley of Wyoming are best known. They have, however, been lately so much obliterated, that it is probable they can be no longer traced. One of the number was examined and measured in 1817 by a gentleman of Wyoming, whose account is published by Mr Miner, in his "History of Wyoming"

"It is situated in the town of Kingston, Luzerne county, upon a level plain, on the north side of Toby's Creek, about one hundred and fifty feet from its bank, and about half a mile from its confluence with the Susquehanna. It is of an oval or elliptical form, having its longest diameter from northeast to southwest, at right angles to the creek. Its diameters are respectively 337 and 272 feet. On the southwest side appears to have been a gateway, twelve feet wide, opening towards the great eddy of the river into which the creek falls It consisted of a single

---

* Ancient Monuments of the Mississippi Valley

embankment of earth, which in height and thickness appears to have been the same on all sides   Exterior to the wall is a ditch.   The bank of the creek upon the side towards the work is high and steep.   The water in the creek is ordinarily sufficiently deep to admit canoes to ascend to the fortification from the river. When the first settlers came to Wyoming, this plain was covered with its native forests, consisting principally of oak and yellow pine ; and the trees which grew upon the work are said to have been as large as those in any part of the valley. One large oak, upon being cut down, was found to be 700 years old.   The Indians have no traditions concerning these fortifications , nor do they appear to have any knowledge of the purposes for which they were erected."—(*Miner's History of Wyoming*, p. 25 )   Traces of a similar work existed on "Jacob's Plains," on the upper flats of Wilkesbarre.   "It occupied the highest point on the flats, which in the time of freshets appears like an island in the sea of waters.   In size and shape it coincides with that already described   High trees were growing upon the embankment at the period of the first settlement of the country   It is about eighty rods from the river, towards which opened a gateway ; and the old settlers concur in stating that a *well* [*cache ?*] existed in the interior near the southern line On the banks of the river is an ancient burial-place, in which the bodies were laid horizontally in regular rows   In excavating the canal through the bank bordering the flats, perhaps thirty rods south of the fort, another burial-place was disclosed, evidently more ancient, for the bones crumbled to pieces almost immediately upon exposure to the air, and the deposits were far more numerous than in that near the river.   The number of skeletons are represented to have been countless, and the dead had been buried in a sitting posture.   In this place of deposit no beads were found, while they were common in the other."—(*Miner's History*, p 28 )

Near this locality, which seems to have been a favorite one with the Indians, medals bearing the head of the First George, and other relics of European origin, are often discovered

Still further to the northwest, near the borders of New York, and forming an unbroken chain with the works of that State, are found other remains.   One of these, on the Tioga River, near Athens, was ascribed by the Duke de Rochefoucauld to the French, in the time of De Nonville !   He describes it as follows :

"Near the confines of Pennsylvania, a mountain rises from the banks of the River Tioga, in the shape of a sugar loaf, upon which are to be seen the remains of some entrenchments.   These are called by the inhabitants the ' Spanish Ramparts,' but I judge that they were thrown up against the Indians, in the time of De Nonville.   A breast-work is still remaining '—(*Travels in America*.)   A similar work, circular or elliptical in outline, is said to exist in Lycoming county. Near it are extensive cemeteries.—(*Day's Hist. Coll* , p 455 )

In the New England States few traces of works of this kind are to be found There are, however, some remains in the State of New Hampshire, which, whatever their origin, are entitled to notice.   The subjoined plan of one of these is from a sketch made in 1822 by Jacob B Moore, Esq., late Librarian of the Historical Society of New York, who has also furnished the accompanying description.

"According to your request, I send the enclosed sketch and memoranda of an ancient fortification, supposed to have been the work of the Penacook Indians, a once powerful tribe, whose chief seat was in the neighborhood of Concord, New Hampshire. The original name of the town was derived from that of the tribe. The last of the Penacooks long since disappeared, and with them have perished most of the memorials of their race. Enough has come down to us, however, in tradition, added to the brief notes of our historians, to show that the Penacooks were once a numerous, powerful, and warlike tribe. Gookin places them under the general division of the Pawtucketts, which he calls 'the fifth great sachemship of Indians.'* Under the name of Penacooks, were probably included all the Indians inhabiting the valley of the Merrimack, from the great falls at the Amoskeag to the Winnepiseogee Lake, and the great carrying-place on the Pemigewasset. That they were one and the same tribe, is rendered probable from the exact similarity of relics, which have been found at different places, and from the general resemblance of the remains of ancient fortifications, which have been traced near the lower falls of the Winnepiseogee, in Franklin and Sanbornton, and on the table-land known as the Sugar-Ball Plain, in Concord. Tradition ascribes to each the purpose of defence against a common enemy, the Maquaas or Mohawks of the west.

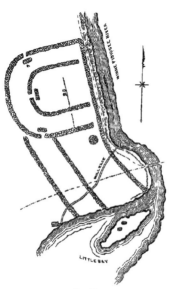

Fig 28

"The accompanying sketch was taken in pencil, on a visit to the spot, in company with the Hon. James Clark and several friends in the month of September, 1822. The remains are on the west side of the Winnepiseogee, near the head of Little Bay, in Sanbornton, New Hampshire. The traces of the walls were at that time easily discerned, although most of the stones had been removed to the mill-dam near at hand, on the river. On approaching the site, we called upon a gentleman (James Gibson) who had lived for many years near the spot, and of whom we learnt the following particulars. He had lived in Sanbornton fifty-two years, and had known the fort some time previous to settling in the place. When he came to the town to reside, the walls were two or three feet high, though in some places they had fallen down, and the whole had evidently much diminished in height, since the first erection. They were about three feet in thickness, con-

---

* Gookin, in I Mass Hist Coll, I, 149

structed of stones outwardly, and filled in with clay, shells, gravel, &c, from the bed of the river and shores of the bay.  The stones of which the walls were constructed were of no great size, and such as men in a savage state would be supposed to use for such a purpose.  They were placed together with much order and regularity, and when of their primitive height, the walls must have been very strong—at least, sufficiently strong for all the purposes of defence against an enemy to whom the use of fire-arms was unknown.

" The site of the fortification is nearly level, descending a little from the walls to the bank of the river  West, for the distance of nearly half a mile, the surface is quite even  In front or east, on the opposite side of the river, are high banks, upon which at that time stood a thick growth of wood  When the first settlers discovered the fort, there were oak trees of large size standing within the walls. Within the enclosure, and in the mound and vicinity, were found innumerable Indian ornaments, such as crystals cut into the rude shapes of diamonds, squares, pyramids, &c., with ornamental pipes of stone and clay,—coarse pottery ornamented with various figures,—arrow-heads, hatchets of stone, and other common implements of peace and war

" The small island in the bay appears to have been a burial-place, from the great quantity of bones and other remains disclosed by the plough, when settlements were commenced by the whites  Before the island was cultivated, there were several large excavations, resembling cellars or walls discovered, for what purpose constructed or used, can of course only be conjectured.  There is a tradition that the Penacooks, at the time of their destruction by the Maquaas, had three hundred birch canoes in Little Bay

" After writing thus far, I addressed a note to the Hon. James Clark, of Franklin, New Hampshire, with inquiries as to the present state of these ruins.  Mr Clark was kind enough at once to make a special visit to the site of the ruins, in company with Mr. Bamford, son of one of the first settlers.  The following is an extract from his reply .

" ' The remains of the walls are in part plainly to be traced ; but the ground since our former examination has been several years ploughed and cultivated, so as to now give a very indistinct view of what they were at our previous visit, when the foundation of the whole could be distinctly traced  No mounds or passage-ways can now be traced  A canal to convey water to a saw and grist mill occupies the place of the mound marked m.  The stones used in these walls were obtained on the ground, and were of such size as one man could lift ; they were laid as well as our good walls for fences in the north, and very regular , they were about three feet in thickness and breast high when first discovered.  The stones have been used to fill in the dam now adjoining  There were no embankments in the interior.  The distance between the outer and inner wall was about sixty feet , the distance from the north to the south wall was about 250 feet, and from the west wall to the river about 220 feet.  There were two other walls extending south to Little Bay  The general elevation of the ground was about ten feet above, and gently sloping to the river bank, which is about five feet above the water of the river  The distance between Great Bay and Little Bay is about 160 rods, with a gradual fall of fifteen feet  Here was a great fishing-place for the Indians.' Mr. Bamford states that he has heard his father and Mr Gibson say, that on their first acquaintance with this place, they have seen three hundred bark canoes here at a time  This may have been in consequence of the number of bays and lakes near this place.  Sanbornton was laid out and surveyed in 1750 , but Canterbury, adjoining the bay, was settled as early as 1727.

" The remains of a fortification, apparently of similar construction to that above described, were some years since to be seen on the bluffs east of the Merrimack River, in Concord, on what was formerly known as Sugar-ball Plain  The walls could readily be traced for some distance, though crumbled nearly to the ground, and overgrown with large trees "*

## CHARACTER OF INDIAN DEFENCES

The fortifications of the savage or hunter tribes of North America are uniformly represented to have been constructed of rows of pickets, surrounding their villages, or enclosing positions naturally strong and easy of defence  The celebrated stronghold of the Narragansetts in Rhode Island, destroyed in 1676 by the New England colonists under Winthrop and Church, was an elevation of five or six acres in extent, situated in the centre of a swamp, and strongly defended by palisades.  It was of extraordinary size, and enclosed not far from six hundred lodges.

Of like character was the fort of the Pequots, on the Mystic River, in Connecticut, destroyed by Captain Mason  According to Hackluyt, the towns of the Indians on the St. Lawrence were defended in a similar manner.  The first voyagers describe the aboriginal town of Hochelaga, now Montreal, as circular in form, and surrounded by three lines of palisades.  Through these there was but a single entrance, well secured by stakes and bars , and upon the inside of the defence, were stages or platforms, upon which were placed stones and other missiles, ready for use, in case of attack.  The town contained about fifty lodges.—(*Hackluyt*, Vol III , p 220 )

---

* " A mound 45 or 50 feet in diameter is situated on the northern shore of Ossipee Lake, New Hampshire  It is ten feet high, and was originally covered with timber  The earth is not like that of the meadow in which it stands, but of the adjacent plain  A slight excavation was made in it a number of years ago, in the course of which three entire skeletons were found, accompanied by two tomahawks and some coarse pottery  On the surrounding meadow were to be seen, when the ground was first cleared, the hills where the corn had anciently grown "—*Hist and Mis Coll of N H* Vol II p 47  *New Hampshire Gazetteer* p 207

Charlevoix observes, that "the Indians of Canada are more expert in erecting their fortifications than in building their houses." He represents that their villages were surrounded by double and frequently by triple rows of palisades, interwoven with branches of trees, and flanked by redoubts —(*Canada*, Vol. II., p 128 ) Champlain also describes a number of fortified works on the St. Lawrence, above *Trois Rivières*, which "were composed of a number of posts set very close together." He also speaks of "forts which were great enclosures, with tiers joined together like pales," within which were the dwellings of the Indians — (*Purchas*, Vol IV, pp 1612, 1644 ) Says La Hontan, "their villages were fortified with double palisades of very hard wood, which were as thick as one's thigh, fifteen feet high, with little squares about the middle of the courtines (curtains).— (Vol. II , p 6 ) The Indians on the coasts of Virginia and North Carolina are described as possessing corresponding defences "When they would be very safe," says Beverly, "they treble the pales."—(*Hist Vir.*, p. 149. See also *Amidas* and *Barlow*, in *Pink.*, Vol. XII , p. 567 , *Hariot, ib.* p 603 , *Lafitau*, Vol. III , p. 228, etc etc )

Among the Floridian tribes, the custom of fortifying their villages seems to have been more general than among the Indians of a higher latitude This may readily be accounted for from the fact that they were more fixed in their habits, considerably devoted to agriculture. and less averse to labor than those of the north. The chronicler of Soto's Expedition speaks of their towns as defended by "strong works of the height of a lance," composed of "great stakes driven deep in the ground, with poles the bigness of one's arm placed crosswise, both inside and out, and fastened with pins to knit the whole together" Herrara, in his compiled account of the same expedition, has the following confirmation. "The town of Mabila or Mavila (Mobile) consisted of eighty houses seated in a plain, enclosed by piles driven down, with timbers athwart, rammed with long straw and earth between the hollow spaces, so that it looked like a wall smoothed with a trowel, and at every eighty paces was a tower, where eight men could fight. with many loop-holes and two gates In the midst of the town was a large square "—(*Hist. America*, Vol V , p 324 ) Du Pratz also gives a corresponding account of the defences of the Natchez and neighboring tribes. "Their forts are built circularly, of two rows of large logs of wood, the logs of the inner row being opposite to the joinings of those of the outer row These logs are about fifteen feet long, five feet of which are sunk in the earth. The outer logs are about two feet thick, the inner ones half as much At every forty paces along this wall, a circular tower juts out, and at the entrance of the fort, which is always next the river, the two ends of the wall pass beyond each other, leaving a side opening In the middle of the fort stands a tree, with the branches lopped off within a short distance of the trunk, and this serves as a watch-tower —(*Hist Louisiana*, p 375.) The subjoined description and illustrative engraving, copied from De Bry, no doubt convey a correct idea of the character of the Floridian defences

"Solent Indi hac ratione sua oppida condere. Delecto aliquo loco secundum torrentis alicujus profluentem, eum quantum fieri potest complanant ; deinde sulco in orbem ducto, crassos et rotundos palos duorum hominum altitudinis conjunctim terræ infigunt, circa oppidi ingressum circulum nonnihil contrahendo cochleæ in morem, ut aditum angustiorem reddant, nec plures quam binos conjunctim admittentem, torrentis etiam alveo ad hunc aditum ducto ; ad hujus aditus caput solet ædicula rotunda extrui, altera item ad ejus sinum, singulæ rimis et foraminibus plenæ, et eleganter pro regionis ratione constructæ. In his constituuntur vigiles viri illi, qui hostium vestigia è longinquo odorantur; nam simul atque aliquorum vestigia naribus perceperunt, adversus contendunt, et iis deprehensis clamorem attollunt, quo exaudito incolæ statim ad oppidi tutelam convolant; arcubus sagittis, et clavis armati. Oppidi meditullium occupant, Regis ædes nonnihil sub terram depressæ ob solis æstum; has cingunt, nobiliorum ædes, omnes palmæ ramis leviter tectæ, quia novem mensibus dumtaxat iis utuntun, tribus aliis mensibus, ut diximus, in sylvis degentes. Unde reduces, domos repetunt; sin eas ab hostibus incendio absumptas reperiunt, novas simili materia exstruunt, adeo magnifica sunt Indorum palatia."

Fig. 29.

"The Indians build their towns in this wise. Having made choice of a spot near a running stream, they level it off as even as they can. They next draw a furrow of the size of the intended town in the form of a circle, in which they plant large round stakes, twice the height of a man, and set closely together. At the place where the entrance is to be, the circle is somewhat drawn in, after the fashion of a snail-shell, making the opening so narrow as not to admit more than two at a time. The bed of the stream is also turned into this entrance. At the head of the entrance, a small round building is usually erected; within the passage is placed another. Each of them is pierced with slits and holes for observation, and is handsomely finished off after the manner of the country. In these guard-houses are placed those sentinels who can scent the trail of enemies at a great distance. As soon as their sense of smelling tells them that some are near, they hasten out, and, having found them, raise an alarm. The inhabitants on hearing the shouting immediately fly to the defence of the town, armed with bows, arrows, and clubs

"In the middle of the town stands the king's palace, sunk somewhat below the level of the ground, on account of the heat of the sun Around it are ranged the houses of the nobles, all slightly covered with palm branches, for they make use of them only during nine months of the year. passing, as we have said, the other three months in the woods When they return, they take to their houses again ; unless, indeed, they have been burnt down in the meantime by their enemies, in which case they build themselves new ones of similar materials Such is the magnificence of Indian palaces"

Among the Indians to the westward of the Mississippi. particularly among the Mandans and kindred tribes, a somewhat different system of defence prevailed. The serpentine courses of the rivers, all of which have here high steep banks, leave many projecting points of land on elevated peninsulas, protected on nearly all sides by the streams. and capable, with little artificial aid, of being made effective for defensive purposes. Mr Catlin describes the principal village of the Mandans, while that remarkable tribe existed, as protected upon three sides by the river, and upon the fourth "by a strong picket, with an interior ditch, three or four feet in depth" The picket was composed of timbers a foot or more in diameter and eighteen feet high, set firmly in the ground, at a sufficient distance from each other to admit guns to be fired between them The warriors stationed themselves in the ditch during an attack, and were thus almost completely protected from their assailants These practices seem, however, to be of comparatively late introduction —(*N. A. Indians*, Vol I., p. 81 )

Brackenridge (*Views of Louisiana*, p. 242) mentions the ruins of an Indian town upon the Missouri River, fifty miles above the mouth of the Shienne. The spot was marked by "great piles of Buffalo bones and quantities of earthen-ware The village appeared to have been scattered around a kind of citadel or fortification, enclosing from four to five acres, in an oval form" The earth was thrown up about four feet. and a few of the palisades were remaining. The Shienne River is 1300 miles above the mouth of the Missouri Lewis and Clark also mention a number of remains of Indian fortifications of like character, but it is to be observed that they distinguish between them and the larger and more imposing ancient works which fell under their notice in the same region They describe an abandoned village of the Riccarees, called Lahoocat, which was situated in the centre of Goodhope Island. It contained seventeen lodges, surrounded by a circular wall and is known to have been occupied in 1797.—(*Exp.* p 72 ) They also mention the remains of a deserted village, erected by *Petit Arc* or Little Bow, an Omahaw chief, on the banks of a small creek of the same name, emptying into the Missouri. It was surrounded by a wall of earth about four feet high.—(*Exp*, p. 41 ) A circular work of earth, formerly enclosing a village of the Shiennes, was noticed by these explorers, a short distance above the mouth of the Shienne River —(*Exp*, p 80.) The ancient villages of the Mandans, nine of which were observed in the same vicinity, within a space of twenty miles, were indicated by the walls which surrounded them, the fallen heaps of earth which covered the huts, and by the scattered teeth and bones of men and animals —(*Exp*, p 84.)   Another defensive work, probably designed for temporary protection, was observed by these gentlemen in the vicinity of the mouth of the Yellowstone   "It was built upon the level bottom, in the form of a circle, fifty feet in diameter, and was composed of logs lapping over each other, about five feet high, and covered on the outside with bark set upright   The entrance was guarded by a work on each side of it, facing the river"   These entrenchments, they were informed, are frequently made by the Minaterees and other Indians at war with the Shoshonees, when pursued by their enemies on horseback.—(*Exp*, p. 622.)   Lieut. Fremont found similar constructions in the vicinity of the Arkansas   A much more feasible method of protection, under such circumstances, is mentioned by Pike   He states that the Sioux, when in danger from their enemies in the plains, soon cover themselves by digging holes with their knives, and throwing up small breastworks — (*Exp.*, p. 19.)   They are represented as being able to bury themselves from sight, in an incredibly short space of time.

The numerous traces upon the Missouri of old villages occupying similar positions, and having evidently been defended in a like manner with those above described, place it beyond doubt that this method of fortification was not of recent origin among those Indians   Mr Catlin mentions that there are several ruined villages of the Mandans, Minaterees and Riccarees, on the banks of the river, below the towns then occupied, which have been abandoned since intercourse became established with the whites.

Prince Maximilian notices a feature in the defences of the Mandan village of Mih-tutta-hang-kush, which does not seem to have been remarked by any other traveler.   This village is represented to have consisted of about sixty huts, surrounded by palisades, forming a defence, at the angles of which were "conical mounds, covered with a facing of wicker-work, and having embrasures, completely commanding the river and plain"   In another place, however, our author adds, that these bastions were erected for the Indians by the whites —(*Travels in the Interior of North America, by Maximilian, Prince of Weid*, pp , 173, 243.)

---

## DEFENCES OF THE ANCIENT MEXICANS AND PERUVIANS

It will be seen, from what has been presented, that, while the Indian tribes on the Atlantic coast and along the Gulf of Mexico, with few exceptions, defended themselves with simple stockades, the Indians to the west of the Mississippi frequently added an embankment of earth, though in other respects observing a very great uniformity with those nations first named   This difference may be accounted for, to a certain extent, by the nature of the soil, which, at the West, is generally readily excavated with the simplest tools.

Among the semi-civilized inhabitants of Mexico, Central America, and Peru, similar methods of defence were practised; but in the construction of their fortresses, they displayed a degree of superiority, corresponding to that which, in most other respects, they sustained over their savage contemporaries. Cortez found himself opposed, upon his first landing at Tobasco, by the town of that name, which, according to De Solis, was fortified after the usual method on the coast. The defences consisted of "a kind of wall made of the trunks of large trees, fixed in the ground after the manner of palisades, but so placed that there was room for the Indians to discharge their arrows between them. The work was round, without any traverses or other defences, and at the closing of the circle the extremity of one line covered the other, and formed a narrow, winding street, in which there were two or three little castles of wood, which filled up the passage, and in which were posted their sentinels. This," continues Solis. "was a sufficient fortress against the arms of the New World, when they were happily ignorant of the arts of war and of those methods to attack and defend, in which mankind has been instructed either by malice or necessity"—(*De Solis' Hist Mexico*, p 54 ) This town, corresponding entirely with those described by the followers of De Soto, in Florida seems to have been rudely fortified in comparison with others in the interior of the country, and nearer the seat of Aztec civilization.* Here the towns and cities were surrounded not only by palisades, but also by ditches and walls of earth and solid masonry. The skill with which the city of Mexico was protected is amply attested by the chroniclers of Cortez's expedition, and by that conqueror himself, who also inform us that walls were sometimes erected to guard the frontiers of provinces The great wall of Tlascalla furnishes. in its extent, a parallel to some of the more imposing defensive structures of the other hemisphere It was erected, according to Cortez, by the "ancient inhabitants" of that republic, as a protection against their enemies , and Clavigero asserts that other portions of the frontier were defended in a similar manner. De Solis describes it as "a great wall which ran across a valley from one mountain to another, entirely stopping up the way , a sumptuous and strong piece of workmanship, which showed the power and greatness of the builders. The outside was of hewn stone, united with mortar of extraordinary strength It was twenty feet thick and a fathom and a half high ; and on the top was a parapet after the manner of our fortifications The entrance

---

* The savage Indian tribes of South America possessed a like system of defence Those of Brazil fortified their towns with palisades, and the Indians of Buenos Ayres, Paraguay, and Chili, constructed additional ramparts and ditches Charlevoix describes those of the last named country as having forts, " surrounded by ditches and trenches, and protected by strong palisades, and pointed stakes of a very hard wood driven in the earth "—(*Southey s Hist Brazil*, Vol II., pp 162, 189 *Mendoza in Purchas* , Vol IV , pp, 1352, 1356, 1361 , *Charlevoix s Paraguay*, Vol 1 , p 156 , *Oralle s Chili, in Pinkerton*, Vol XIV , p 119 ) The natives of the Barbadoes Islands constructed defences of the same character They selected eminences for their forts, and protected them with trenches and palisades From these points they rolled down stones and logs upon their assailants —*Davis' Hist Barbadoes*, p 325

was narrow and winding, the wall in that part dividing and making two walls, which circularly crossed each other for the space of ten paces "* Clavigero states that it was six miles in length, eight feet in height, besides the parapet, and eighteen feet in thickness, composed of stone cemented with mortar. Works also existed in Mexico which approached more nearly to the character of the modern forts They were, for the most part, strong, natural positions, such as isolated eminences, or the summits of steep and rugged mountains.

One of these, enclosing the ruins of many imposing temples and edifices, is situated to the north of the city of Mexico, in the department of Zacatecas, which is supposed to have been formerly occupied by the Chichimecs and Otomies It is now known as the " Ruins of Quemada " The ruins are situated upon the summit of a high hill or *cerro*, and are inclosed upon the north, where the ground is sloping, by broad, double walls of massive stones cemented with mortar. Upon the south are rugged precipices, affording natural defences The walls have bastions at intervals, and are entered by four broad roads, or causeways, which extend in different directions over the adjacent plain

The hill of Xochicalco is three hundred feet in height, and a league in circumference, surrounded at the base by a deep and wide ditch. Whether designed as a temple or fortress, is not apparent It may have subserved both purposes, for there is ample evidence, in the records of the conquerors, that the sacred grounds of the Aztecs were their places of last resort, in the defence of which their valor was inflamed by religious zeal The summit of the hill of Xochicalco is attained by five spiral terraces, faced with cemented stones and supported by bulwarks, and is crowned by the ruins of edifices, which rank among the most imposing remains of the continent.

An ancient fortress, which no doubt well illustrates the character of the ancient Mexican defences, is figured and described by Du Paix A plan of it is presented in the subjoined engraving, Fig 30 " It occupies the summit of a steep, isolated rock, about a league west of Mitlan This rock is accessible only from the eastern side. The wall is of solid stone, twenty-one feet thick and eighteen high, and is about a league in extent. It forms, in its course, several salient and retiring angles, with curtains interposed On its assailable side, where is its principal entrance, it is defended by double walls, which mutually flank each other The first, or most advanced, forms an *enceinte*, or elliptical rampart, upon which, at short intervals, there are heaps of small round stones for slinging, and in the centre of the crescent there is an oblique gate, to avoid the enfilade or right line of arrows, darts, and stones The second wall, which is joined at its extremities to that of the fortress, is of greater elevation, and forms a sort of *tenaille* It differs from the other in having its sides or flanks more open It has likewise its rampart and heaps of stones. For greater security, batteries were disposed in the Aztec system of

---

* This feature is well illustrated in many of the defensive structures of the Mississippi valley, in which precisely similar expedients were adopted to secure the entrances See Vol I of these Contributions, Plates IV VI , VIII etc

defence, in front of the fortification, consisting of loose round stones, about three feet in diameter, placed high, and so balanced as to be easily precipitated below On the plain surface of the rock are various ruins of square buildings and edifices, of considerable size, which were probably the ancient barracks. In the point diametrically opposite the entrance, is a sally-port or postern, for furnishing the fort with men and provisions, or to facilitate a forced retreat."

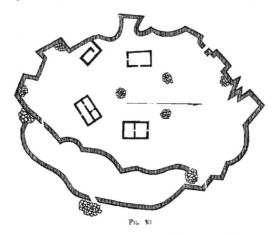

Fig. 30

Near the village of Molcaxac are the remains of an ancient fortress, much resembling that here described It occupies the summit of a mountain, and consists of four concentric walls of great strength and solidity.—(*De Solis*, Book II., p. 139.) Another fortress of similar character is mentioned by Clavigero as existing at Guatusco, twenty-five miles north of Cordova It consists of high walls of stone, and is only entered by high and narrow flights of steps

Although the above examples may serve to convey a very good idea of the nature of the defensive structures of the Mexicans, it is yet to be regretted that so brief and imperfect accounts of them have been transmitted to us by the early writers While we are constantly assured of their existence, their great extent and vast strength, we are left in the dark in respect to their details

More is known concerning the military works of Peru, and all accounts concur in representing them as clearly resembling those already described. According to Ulloa, a method of fortification existed, nearly allied to that practised by the ancient Celts It consisted in digging three or four ranges of moats quite around the tops of high and steep mountains, protecting them on the inside by walls of earth or stone. These were called *pucuras ;* and, in some of them, the outer circumvallation is represented as having been upward of three miles in extent. In respect to their number, he asserts that one scarcely meets with a mountain without them.—(*Ulloa*, Vol. I., p. 504, Vol. II., p 113.) Some were composed of rough stones, without arrangement, others of adobes The more irregular of these were attributed to the Indians before they were reduced by the Incas  La Vega describes the great fortress of Cuzco as constructed of three immense cyclopean walls, built rather of rocks than stones, surrounding a hill.  Acosta measured some of the stones, and found them thirty feet in length, eighteen in breadth, and six in thickness  The outer wall is said to have been twelve hundred feet in compass  Through the walls were gateways, communicating with the interior, where, according to La Vega, were three strong towers, two of which were square and one round , the latter appropriated to the use of the Incas, the former to the garrison. Under the towers were subterranean passages of great extent.—(*McCulloch*, p. 272 , *Bradford*, p. 169 , *Ulloa*, Vol. II., p. 457 )  It was supplied with water from a fountain in the centre  This is the fortress which so long resisted the attacks of the Spaniards.  Similar works exist near the village of Baños, in Huamalies, occupying the summits of two mountains, placed opposite to each other on either side of the river  The sides of the mountains are divided into galleries, ranged one above the other, in some places formed by artificial walls, and in others cut in the solid rock.—(*Mercurio, Peruano*, Vol V., p. 259 , *Stevenson*, Vol. II., p. 100 )  On the road from Potosi to Tacua, are the ruins of an ancient Peruvian city  Upon one side it is protected by a deep ravine, and on the other by a rampart, the stones composing which are dovetailed together in a very singular manner. Within the walls was a citadel, or place of last resort —(*Andrews' Travels in S  A.*, Vol. II., p. 161 )  Ulloa mentions the ruins of a fortified palace of the Incas, near Patasilca, one hundred and twenty miles from Lima  " The ruins are of very great extent : the walls are of tempered clay, and about six feet thick  The principal building stood upon an eminence, but the walls were continued to the foot of it, like regular circumvallations , the ascent wound round the hill, leaving many angles, which probably served as outworks to defend the place  It is called *Fortalesa*, and is supposed to have been a frontier point during the time of the Incas "—(*Ulloa*, Vol II , p. 27 , *Stevenson*, Vol. II , p  23 )

There are also evidences that, on the frontiers of certain portions of Peru, were constructed walls similar in design to that of Tlascalla.  Such a one is said to cross the valley of Guarmey —(*Ruschenberger*, p 361.)  Analogous works exist in Chili.—(*Frezier*, p. 262 , *Molina*, Vol II , pp  10, 68 )

The fortifications of Central America are very much of the same character with those already described  Juarros gives an account of one of these situated upon the river Socoleo. "The approach, as usual to such places, was by a single entrance, and that so narrow as scarcely to permit a horseman to pass it  From the entrance there ran on the right hand a parapet raised on the berme of the fosse, extending along nearly the whole of that side ; several vestiges of the counterscarp and curtain of the walls still remain, besides parts of other works, the use of which cannot now be easily discovered  In the court-yard there stood some large columns. upon which were placed quantities of pine wood, that being set on fire, gave light at night to the surrounding neighborhood  The citadel of this great fortification was in the form of a square graduated pyramid, rising twelve or fourteen yards from the base to the platform on the top, which was sufficient to admit of ten soldiers upon a side, etc  Every part of this fortress was constructed of hewn stones,

13

of great size; one of which being displaced, measured three yards in length by one in breadth.—(*Juarros' Hist Guat.*, p. 462)

The ruins of Uxmal, in Yucatan, described by Mr. Stephens, are represented to be enclosed by a wall of loose stones.—(*Stephens' Yucatan*, Vol I, pp. 165, 230.) It was not, however, completely traced by that gentleman  Enclosing the ruins of Tuloom he found a well-constructed wall of regular outline, as represented in Fig. 31.

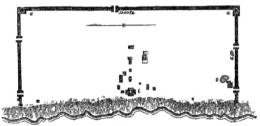

Fig 31

It forms three sides of a parallelogram, the fourth side, toward the sea, being bounded by a precipitous cliff  "It is of rude construction, and composed of rough, flat stones, laid upon each other without mortar or cement of any kind, and varies from eight to thirteen feet in thickness.  The south side has two gateways, each about five feet wide.  At the distance of six hundred and fifty feet, the wall turns at right angles and runs parallel to the sea  At the angle, elevated so as to give a commanding view, is a watch-tower, twelve feet square, which has two doorways  The interior is plain, and against the back wall is a small altar, at which the guard might offer up prayers for the preservation of the city  The west line, parallel with the sea, has a single gateway, at the angle is another watch-tower, like that before described, and the wall then runs straight to the sea. The whole circuit is 2,800 feet —(*Stephens' Yucatan*, Vol. II, p. 396.)

The remarkable structures within this work, seem to be of a religious origin, suggesting the probability that it was designed as a sacred enclosure  It is not impossible that, as in the case of some of the works of the Aztecs, it was the citadel of the surrounding population, within which, in times of danger, they sought the protection and assistance of their gods  The fortified hill in the vicinity of Granville, Ohio, has a small sacred enclosure within its walls.—("*Ancient Monuments of Mississippi Valley*," Plate IX)  May it not furnish a rude type of the more imposing work above described, and denote a similar practice?

## COMPARISON OF THE DEFENSIVE STRUCTURES OF THE AMERICAN ABORI-GINES, WITH THOSE OF THE PACIFIC ISLANDERS, CELTS, ETC.

THE resemblances which the defensive works of the mound builders, as well as of the later and existing Indian tribes, bear to those of many other rude nations, in various parts of the world, are no less striking than interesting. These resemblances have, however, had the effect of misleading superficial investigators, or those who have only paid incidental attention to these subjects. They have hastily inferred that, because certain monuments and aboriginal relics of the United States, such as entrenched hills, tumuli, and instruments and ornaments of stone and copper, sustain analogies, in some instances almost amounting to identities, with those occurring in the British Islands and on the Steppes of Russia, that relations must necessarily have existed between the builders, or that they had a common origin. These resemblances are, nevertheless, the inevitable results of similar conditions, and the ancient Celts and Scythians, the American Indians, and the natives of Australia, built their hill-forts, and fashioned their flint arrow-points and stone axes in like manner, because they thus accomplished common objects, in the simplest and most obvious mode. Human development must be, if not in precisely the same channels, in the same direction, and must pass through the same stages. We cannot be surprised, therefore, that the earlier, as in fact the later monuments of every people, exhibit resemblances more or less striking. What is thus true physically, or rather *monumentally*, is not less so in respect to intellectual and moral development. And it is not to be denied that the want of a sufficient allowance, for natural and inevitable coincidences, has led to many errors in tracing the origin and affinities of nations.

We not only find in the British islands, but also in the islands of the Pacific ocean, the almost exact counterparts of the defensive structures of our own country. "The places of defence of the Sandwich Islanders," says Ellis, " were rocky fortresses improved by art—narrow defiles or valleys, sheltered by projecting eminences—passes among the mountains, difficult of access, yet allowing their inmates a secure and extensive range and an unobstructed passage to some stream or spring. The celebrated *Pare* (fortress), in Atehuru. was of this kind, the mouth of the valley in which it was situated was built up with a stone wall, and those who fled thither for shelter were usually able to repel their assailants.

"Several of these places are very extensive. that at *Maeva* in Huahine, near Mouna Tabui, is probably the best in the islands. It is a square of about half a mile on each side, and encloses many acres of ground well stocked with bread fruit, containing several springs, and having within its precincts the principal temple of their tutelar deity. The walls are of solid stone-work, twelve feet in height. On the top of the walls, which were even and well paved, and in some places ten or twelve feet thick, the warriors kept watch and slept. Their houses were built within, and it was considered sufficiently large to contain the whole population There were four principal openings in the wall, at regular distances from each other, that at the west being called the king's road They were designed for ingress and egress, and during a siege, were built up with loose stones, when it was considered a *part haabuea*, an impregnable fortress."—(*Ellis' Polynesian Researches*, Vol I, pp. 313, 314.)

The New Zealanders were not deficient in defensive skill Cook describes one of their strongholds or *Heppahs* at length. His account, from the light which it affords as to the probable manner in which the embankments of the western works were surmounted, is subjoined entire

" Near this place is a high point or peninsula projecting into the river, and upon it are the remains of a fort, which they call Eppah or Heppah The best engineers could not have chosen a situation better adapted to enable a small number to defend themselves against a greater The steepness of the cliffs renders it wholly inaccessible from the water, which encloses it on three sides; and, to the land, it is fortified by a ditch, and a bank raised on the inside. From the top of the bank to the bottom of the ditch is twenty-two feet, the ditch on the outside is fourteen feet deep, and broad in proportion. The whole seemed to be executed with great judgment, and there had been a row of palisadoes, both on the top of the bank and along the brink of the ditch on the outside those on the outside had been driven very deep in the ground, and were inclined towards the ditch so as to project over it, but of these, the thickest only were left, and upon them were evident marks of fire, so that the place had probably been taken and destroyed by an enemy If occasion should make it necessary for a ship to winter or stay here, tents might be built in this place, which is sufficiently spacious, and might easily be made impregnable to the whole country "—(*Cook's Second Voyage* )

The following additional particulars respecting the construction and defence of the *Heppah*, by a later writer, and a long resident of New Zealand, may serve to explain some of the features of the aboriginal structures of our own country, as also the probable manner in which they were defended

" The fortifications of the natives are called *Pá* (*fort*), or *E' Pá* (*the fort*). The spots chosen for these defences equally evince sound judgment and habitual fear The position accounted as best adapted for the purpose, is the summit of a high hill, overlooking the surrounding country, or a mountainous pass, having at its foot a river or running stream Insular retreats, distant a few miles from the main, are also in especial repute. The first procedure is to *escarp* the hill, so as to render the ascent difficult and dangerous to a foe. Remains of such works are to be found on every remarkable elevation throughout the country The further defences consist of two, sometimes of three stout stockades of irregularly sized posts and poles, varying from eight to thirty feet high from the ground, into which they are thrust from three to seven feet The large posts are placed about a dozen feet apart, on which are often carved ludicrous representations of men and animals; the spaces between the poles being filled with stakes, placed close together, and bound firmly with horizontal pieces by a creeper called *toro-toro,* which is tough and serviceable for a long period.  These strongholds have often proved superior to any force the natives could bring against them   Few instances have occurred of a *Pá* being taken by a brisk siege, they have failed only when cowardice, treachery, or improvidence have aided the assailants.  The stockades that enclose the fort are within a few feet of each other, the outer gate or entrance being much less than the inner opening, which, in time of war, is entered by stepping-stones or small wooden posts like a turnstile.  The width is so contracted as scarcely to admit a large-sized man, and between the fences a fosse is often cut, about four feet in depth, sheltering the besieged while discharging their missiles at the enemy   A more confused scene can scarcely be conceived than a *Pá* during a siege   Some hundreds of low arched huts lie huddled together without regularity, streets, or paths, among these, some native palaces raise their roofs, and platforms (watás) built on trees for the preservation of food, and not for defensive purposes  Mounds are often erected during a night by an enemy, to overlook the interior of a fort, but they are of rare occurrence.  The huts near the *napa* or stockades are covered with earth and clay, to render them secure to the inmates

" Some forts have been selected with consummate skill, having the command of mountain gorges and narrow passes, which might keep in check an army, if defended by a handful of brave men   Various contrivances are invented to render an approach to a fortification difficult of access   Sometimes a wooden post with notches for the feet affords the only means of entering the fort.  The *Pá* formed by the celebrated E'Ongi, on a promontory jutting into Lake *Moperri,* was a work of much merit, and added greatly to the consequence of the self-taught engineer among his countrymen."—(*Pollock's New Zealand,* Vol. II., p. 26.)

It appears from these facts, that whatever estimate we may place upon the capabilities of the Pacific and South Sea Islanders, in other respects, they are, in the language of a close observer, " sufficiently advanced in civilization to construct fortifications, and adapt them to the nature of the country in which they are required."—(*Laing's Polynesian Nations,* p. 108.)

The defensive works of Great Britain present a great variety of forms, betraying different authors and different eras of construction   First of all, we have the works of the ancient Celts, of irregular outline, and occupying strong natural positions.  These are succeeded by the fortified camps and other defences of the Roman era, which are followed by the less regular but more laborious works of the Belgic or Saxon period

During the earliest or Celtic period, a large proportion of the barrows or tumuli scattered over the islands, were erected, then, also, were built those mysterious circles and long avenues which bear so striking a resemblance to the ancient structures of our own country

In the choice of their military positions, the ancient Britons were governed by the same obvious rules which regulated the mound builders, and the American Indians generally—advantage in all cases being taken of the natural features of

the country  Their defences were usually erected on headlands, a single wall
being carried along the brow of the promontory, while the level approaches were
protected by a succession of embankments and ditches, with occasional outworks
or advance posts.  In some instances, steep, isolated hills were selected, which
were defended by a series of concentric embankments, completely encircling the
summit, a method of construction, as we have already seen, most frequently
adopted by the Peruvians

The subjoined examples of ancient British fortresses, are reduced from plans
presented by Sir R. C. Hoare.

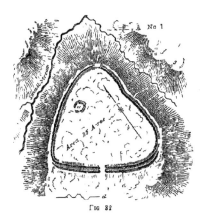

Fig 32

Fig. 32 is situated in the county of Wilts, in the parish of Colerne, near the road
leading to Bath, and is known to British antiquaries under the different titles of
" North Wood" and " Bury Wood Camp "  " Its shape resembles that of a heart,
its pointed part resting in an angle between two streams  Its area comprehends
twenty-five acres, and it appears to have had only one entrance towards the S W,
and that placed exactly in the centre of the ramparts, which on this side are double,
and rectilinear, the ground being level and must accessible on this side.  On the
N. W side, near the outward vallum, but within the area of the camp, is a small
earthen work (a), single ditched, with an entrance to the west"—(*Ancient Wiltshire*, Vol II., p 104

Fig 33 is situated in the same section of country with the work just described,
in the vicinity of Castle Combe. from which it is named  " It is placed," says
Hoare, " in a very strange and picturesque situation, on the point of a very steep
hill, at whose base flows a rapid brook  It is very difficult of access  The foundation of walls, a raised mound, and other circumstances induce me to attribute to
it a Saxon origin, and history reports its having been ravaged by the Danes.  Its
area is eight and a half acres; its form is rather oblong, but wider towards the
north, where the ground is most easy of access, and where the adit into the camp
has been placed  On entering the work at this point, and proceeding towards the

southern extremity, where the ground is most precipitate, we meet with three lines of ramparts, which intersect the area of the camp, through two of which there is an opening : the eastern point was fortified by a raised mound."—(*Ib*. Vol. II., p. 101.)

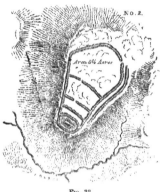

Fig. 33.

The singular *vitrified forts* of Scotland, are suggested in this connection.  They appear to have been composed of loose stones, which, by some process of vitrification, were made to present the outward features of solid rocks, and have long perplexed antiquarians.  Some have attributed the vitrification to lightning, others to accidental conflagration, while a few, more daring in their speculations, have considered them the craters of extinguished volcanoes !  It has also been supposed that vast defences of wood once surrounded and surmounted the ramparts, by the casual burning of which they were vitrified.  There is, however, every reason to believe, that this feature was the result of design, although it is not easy to explain how it was produced.  Dr. Anderson, in a communication to the Society of Antiquarians, in 1777, gives an account of a remarkable work of this description, called

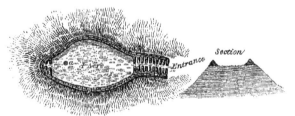

Fig. 34.

Knockferral, in Ross-Shire.  It is placed on a high ridge of an oblong shaped hill, very steep on three sides, the walls being raised on the edge of a precipice all round, except at the end admitting entrance into the area, the enclosed space of nearly an acre being level · features readily recognizable as also belonging to our American "Hill Forts" The approaches to this work, as those of all others of the same description, are strengthened by additional ramparts "Those at the entry," says our authority, "had extended, as I guessed, about one hundred yards, and seemed to have consisted of cross-walls, one behind the other, eight or ten in number; the ruins of which are still plainly perceptible. Through each of these walls there must have been a gate, so that the besiegers would have been under the necessity of forcing each of these gates successively, before they could carry the fort, on the opposite end of the hill. as the ground is considerably steeper, the outworks seem not to have extended above twenty yards. Not far from the farther end, was a well (a), now filled up. The wall all around from the inside appears to be only a mound of rubbish, consisting of loose stones: the vitrified wall is only to be seen from the outside Here the wall is covered with a crust of about two feet in thickness, consisting of stones immersed among vitrified matter; some of the stones being half fused themselves,—all of them having evidently suffered a considerable heat. The crust is of an equal thickness—of about two feet—from the top to the bottom, so as to lie upon, and be supported by. a backing of loose stones, forming in section an acute angle. Within the crust of the vitrified matter is another stratum of some thickness, parallel to the former, and consists of loose stones, which have been scorched by the fire, but present no marks of fusion."

It will be perceived that in position, mode of construction, etc., these defences are indistinguishable from those of America They might be regarded, so far as their apparent features are concerned, as the work of the same people; yet they were constructed by different races, separated from each other by ocean wastes, and having little in common, except the possession of those savage passions which have reddened every page of the world's history with blood. They serve only further to illustrate how naturally, and almost of necessity, men similarly circumstanced hit upon common methods of meeting their wants, and do not necessarily establish a common origin, nor a constant or casual intercourse

The Roman camps, vestiges of which are abundant throughout England and on the continent, also bear a close analogy to a large class of the more regular Western earth works, though probably differing widely from them in the purposes for which they were erected "The Romans, from the earliest period, paid particular attention to the security of their armies, by choosing the best situations for their camps that the circumstances would permit. They did not, however, trust to natural strength alone—making it an invariable rule, wherever they came, to enclose themselves within an entrenchment, consisting of a rampart and ditch strengthened with palisades The fortifications were of a stronger or weaker character, according to the nearness of an enemy, or the appearance of danger with which they were threatened at the time The form of the Roman camp was square, contrary to that adopted by the Greeks, who made theirs round, triangular, or of any other shape, as best suited the nature of the ground."—(*Roy's Military Antiquities of England*, p. 41.) The angles of the Roman camp were rounded, on a radius of about sixty feet, and there were gateways midway upon each side, sometimes, if the camps were of large size, there were several passages upon each side  These entrances were usually protected by exterior mounds, or by overlapping walls, and occasionally outworks were erected   The temporary camps, *castra æstiva*, or those not designed for constant occupation, had comparatively slight entrenchments, the ditch being about six feet deep, and the parapet behind it only about four feet high   The *castra stativa* were generally much smaller than the temporary camps, and were strongly protected.   They were designed to contain garrisons, either to guard a frontier or keep in awe newly conquered provinces. Two ranges of them were erected shortly after the time of Agricola, upon the frontiers of Caledonia, placed at short intervals apart between the Clyde and Forth, and the Tyne and Solway, nearly upon the line afterwards occupied by the walls of Hadrian, Antoninus Pius, and Severus.   The smaller sort of *castra stativa* were termed *castella*, answering in a great degree to the field-forts and redoubts made use of by modern armies

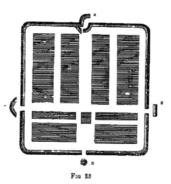

Fig. 35

The above cut, Fig. 35, is a plan of the camp of a single Roman legion, according to Polybius, and is introduced more to illustrate the different methods of protecting the gateways, than to serve any other purpose.   In some of the Western military works, as may be seen by reference to the first volume of these Contributions, gateways occur similar to that at A.   In the more regular structures of the West, however, the mound covering the gateway is invariably placed *interior* to the walls, which circumstance, joined to others less equivocal, goes to sustain the conclusion that such works were not constructed for defence   The Roman camps had frequently two, sometimes four or more, lines of embankment, with flanking defences, horn-works, etc   The stone and earth circles of England are all ascribed to the Celts , the rectangular works to the Romans   Throughout the islands, no works occur in which the two figures are combined, as in the Mississippi valley

14

WE have, in the quotation from Bartram, on page 68, evidence (not the most conclusive, it is true), that some of the mounds of the South were general cemeteries, and are not of a very high antiquity  Recent investigations have shown that burials in these were frequent, but this was seldom the primary purpose to which they were dedicated  Most of the mounds of the South were of sacred origin—the "high places" and temples of the aborigines.  Among the Natchez, the bones of the dead were placed in the temples of the tribe, and occasionally, if not always, finally buried there  These temples are represented to have been erected upon mounds or artificial elevations of earth, but it is not stated distinctly whether they were the work of this people, or simply appropriated by them  Within these temples, upon the death of the Suns or religious heads of the nation, were buried the victims which were put to death on the occasion —(*Charlevoix*, Vol II, p 264, *Du Pratz*, p. 356.)  These customs may account for the presence of numbers of human skeletons in some of these structures  The custom of burying in sacred places was of very general acceptance throughout the world  and the peculiar veneration which attached to tombs, often led to their consecration as temples.

In a letter dated Mt. Sylvan, Mississippi, August, 1847, Mr. R Morris presents the following facts respecting the mounds of that region  "A mound which I opened last summer, twelve miles southeast from this place, had in it not less than fifty full skeletons, all pretty near the surface.  They were packed without order, with layers of pounded clay between them  Those nearest the top were black and quite fresh, but lower down they were greatly decayed  No relics accompanied them. although in the graves where the later races buried their dead, are found many ornaments, utensils, and weapons.

"A few miles from Panola, there is a mound quite full of human bones.  Hundreds may be thrown out with a sharpened cane.  Another mound, about twelve miles north of the place just named. was opened a year or two since.  In the centre was found a structure like a cistern, nearly round, four feet across, and filled with soil  This being removed, an earthen vessel of singular form and material was taken out "

The burial-mounds of Florida, from what we can gather concerning them, have peculiarities in the arrangement of the skeletons. not elsewhere observed  These mounds are seldom of large size, and do not generally appear to be connected with other works  They range from four to eighteen feet in height, and are usually comprised of earth and sand, but are sometimes principally made up of decayed shells.  The skeletons, it is said, are found arranged in radiating circles, from top to bottom, with the feet outward and the heads a little elevated, and are generally accompanied by rude vessels of pottery   In one of the mounds, on the St John's River, a skeleton of large size was found, in a horizontal position, surrounded by others in a sitting posture.   It has been conjectured that these belong to a later era than the grand system of earth-works of the Mississippi valley.

Mounds designed as *general cemeteries*, if indeed there be any in the Western States, are certainly few in number and of modern date   One, containing many skeletons disposed in layers, formerly existed in Belmont county, Ohio   Whether it was secondarily appropriated by the Indians or built by them, it is not presumed to say, the remains found in it were indubitably of the recent tribes and of late deposit

The tumulus examined by Mr Jefferson on the low grounds of the Ravenna River, and described in his " Notes on Virginia," is attributed by him to the recent tribes of Indians, by whom it was probably built.   The stream on which it occurs is one of the lower branches of James River, which empties into the Atlantic. We have no satisfactory evidence that the race of the mounds passed over the Alleghanies, the existence, therefore, of a few tumuli to the east of these mountains, unless in connection with other and extensive works, such as seem to have marked every step of the progress of that race, is of little importance, and not at all conclusive upon this point, especially as it will hardly be denied that the existing races of Indians did and still do occasionally construct mounds of small size This mound was estimated by Mr. Jefferson to contain the skeletons of a thousand individuals, a portion of which, particularly toward the surface, were placed without order, while the remainder seemed to have been deposited with a certain degree of regularity   This is certainly a very large estimate of the contents of a barrow but forty feet base by seven feet in height   It will not be out of place to remark here, that by the unpractised observer, the bones of a hundred skeletons placed together would probably be mistaken for those of several hundred or a thousand.

We have, it is true, but very few accounts of the construction of mounds by the existing tribes of Indians   Lewis and Clarke noticed, in their travels west of the Mississippi River, a spot "where one of the great chiefs of the Mahas or Omahas had been interred   He was buried on a hill, and a mound twelve feet in diameter and six feet in height erected over him."*   Beck mentions a large mound on the Osage River, which had been erected within the last thirty or forty years, by the Osages, in honor of one of their dead chiefs †   Mention is made in the

---

* Exp, vol I, p 43   "Blackbird (Wash-ing-gah-sahba), chief of the Omahaws or Mahas, died in 1800, and was interred in a sitting posture on the back of his favorite horse, upon the summit of a high bluff of the Missouri, ' that he might see the white people ascend the river to trade with his nation '   A mound was raised over him, on which food was regularly placed for many years after, but this has been discontinued, and the flag staff which crowned it has been removed "—*James's Exp*, Vol I, p 204

† Gaz of Mo, p 308, James Exp  Vol II, p 34 —This is probably the same mound referred to by Mr Sibley, who derived his information from a chief of the Osages   " He stated that the mound was built, when he was a boy, over the body of a chief, called Jean Defoe by the French, who unexpectedly died while his warriors were absent on a hunting expedition   Upon their return, they heaped a mound over his remains, enlarging it at intervals for a long period, until it reached its present height "—*Featherstonhaugh's Trav*, p 70

documents accompanying the President's message for 1806, of a "mound of considerable size," erected by the Natchez Indians, near Nachitoches, when they were expelled from Louisiana, in 1728. They are also said to have fortified themselves near this place. Mr Catlin observed a conical mound, ten feet in height, at the celebrated pipe-stone quarries of the *Coteau des Prairies,* which had been erected over the body of a young chief of the Sioux tribe, who had been accidentally killed on the spot.—(*N A Indians*, Vol II, p 170) James also presents, upon what he deems good authority, an account of the discovery, by a hunting party, in 1816, on the banks of the La Mine River, in Missouri, of a newly made mound, which, when opened, disclosed the body of a white officer, clothed in regimentals, placed in a sitting posture on a mat, and surrounded by a rude enclosure of logs, twelve feet long, three wide, and four high. He had evidently met a violent death, and had been scalped.—(*Narrative,* Vol I, p 84) To what nation he belonged, and by whom the mound was erected, is unknown. The Mandans sometimes constructed little mounds of earth, not however for burial. They were connected, in some mysterious way, with their ceremonies for the dead. "Their dead," says Catlin, "are placed, closely enveloped in skins, upon scaffoldings, above the reach of wild animals. When the scaffolds decay and fall to the ground, the nearest relatives bury all the bones excepting the skull. The skulls are arranged in circles of a hundred or more, on the prairies, with their faces all looking to the centre. In the centre of each ring is erected a little mound, three feet high, on which are placed two buffalo skulls, a male and female; and in the centre is reared a medicine pole, supporting many curious articles of mystery and superstition, which they suppose to have the power of guarding and protecting this sacred arrangement. Here the relatives of the dead resort to hold converse with them, bringing a dish of food, which is set before the skull at night and taken away in the morning. Under each skull is constantly kept a bunch of fresh wild sage."—(*N A Indians*, Vol I, p 90)

The Indians, it is well known, often heaped a pile of stones over the graves of such of their tribe as met their death by accident, or in the manner of whose death there was something sufficiently peculiar to excite their superstition. Such was the case, in one instance, in Schoharie county, on the Cherry Valley trail. But the construction of mounds, whether for purposes of burial or as monuments, except perhaps among some of the Southern tribes, was far from common, and cannot be regarded as a custom of general acceptance. The few which they built were clearly, in most instances, the result of caprice or of circumstances; and we are not justified in ascribing to them more than a very trifling proportion of the numerous tumuli which dot the plains and valleys of the West, and which, in their numbers and uniformity of structure and contents, give conclusive evidence that they were constructed for specific purposes, in accordance with a well recognised design, and an established and prevailing custom.

The practice of depositing the property of the dead in the tomb with them (almost universal among the American Indians) is of the highest antiquity, and was widely diffused amongst all primitive nations. "In all early ages," remarks an erudite writer, "when the disengaged activity of man ever carries a keen and military edge with it, and his great employment is necessarily war and the chase, the weapons of both would naturally be deposited with the dead" We have a striking passage of Scripture, which shows the custom to have been as general as the spirit of ambition or the profession of arms "They shall not lie down with the mighty which are gone down to hell [the grave] with their weapons of war, and they have laid their swords under their heads" Josephus tells us, that in David's sepulchre was deposited such a quantity of treasure, that Hyrcanus, the Maccabean, took three thousand talents out of it, about 1300 years after David's death, to get rid of Antiochus, then besieging Jerusalem

Uniformity in the rites and ceremonies attending burial must not, however, be regarded as necessarily implying connections or relations between the nations exhibiting them, for most, if not all of those which may be esteemed of importance, had their origin in those primitive conceptions and notions which are inherent in man, and are in nowise derivative. In the universal recognition of a future existence, may be traced the origin of the immolations and sacrifices made at the tombs or on the pyres of the dead · the wife and the faithful servant sought to accompany their lord in his future life, and a numerous retinue was slain at the tomb of the Scythian King and the Peruvian Inca, that they might appear in a future state with a dignity and pomp proportionate to their earthly greatness. The Mexican slew the *techichi* at the grave of the dead, that his soul might have a companion in its journey along the dreary, terror-infested pathway, which, according to his superstitions, intervened between earth and the "blessed mansions of the sun" So, too, the faithful dog of the Indian hunter was placed beside him in the grave, that in the blissful "hunting-grounds of the West" he might "bear him company." The warlike Scandinavian had his horse sacrificed on his funeral pyre, and his weapons buried with him, so that, full armed and mounted, he might, with becoming state, approach the halls of Odin —(*Mallet*, Chap XII) In the almost universal belief that the soul of the dead, for a longer or shorter period, lingered around the ashes from which it was separated, we may discover the reason why food and offerings were deposited at the grave, why it was carefully preserved, and why, at stated intervals, the surviving relatives of the deceased decked it with flowers and performed games around it In some of these ceremonies it was believed the departed spirit silently participated, and with all it was supposed to be pleased and gratified.

MOUNDS are found in Oregon but little is known concerning them, except that they occur in the open prairies, are of small size (seldom more than six or seven feet in height), and are many thousands in number Some of them were opened by Com Wilkes, but found to contain nothing beyond a pavement of round stones. Their origin is involved in obscurity. Although professing to know nothing concerning them, the Indians nevertheless regard them with some degree of veneration. Their priests, or "medicine men," gather the wild herbs which grow upon them, for use in their incantations and superstitious rites It seems unlikely that they were built by a people so rude as those found in present occupation of the country.—(*Exploring Expedition*, Vol IV., p. 313.)

It is not known that any mounds occur in Upper or indeed in Lower California A few are found in New Mexico, and in the valley of the Gila, but we are ignorant of their character and contents. The aboriginal Mexicans often buried in the pyramidal structures constituting their temples; and it is presumed, although we have no direct evidence of the fact, that they sometimes erected tumuli over their dead The plain surrounding the great pyramids of Teotihuacan is covered with mounds, chiefly of stone, and disposed with a great deal of regularity; it is called *Micoatl*, or *Path of the Dead* * These pyramids are, however, ascribed to the Toltecs, who preceded the Aztecs in the possession of the valley of Anahuac; and it is reasonable to believe that the numerous tumuli which surround them, whatever then purposes, were built by the same hands

If the practice of erecting mounds over the dead prevailed at all among the Mexicans, it must have been to a very limited extent This is inferred from the silence of all the ancient authorities, who, although giving us very minute accounts of their burial customs, say nothing concerning such structures It was usual to burn the dead, and the rite was performed with many ceremonies. In cases where simple inhumation was practised, the body was placed in a sitting posture, in chambers of stone or brick, accompanied by their ornaments and the implements of their profession. Bernal Diaz mentions the explorations of Figuero, an officer among the conquerors who, in the territory of the Zapoticas, employed himself

---

* Mr Thompson, in his 'Recollections of Mexico' (pp 138 142), expresses the opinion that what have been very generally supposed to be sepulchral mounds around these pyramids, are not such in fact, but simply the ruins of the houses composing an ancient town His opinion, for reasons which the inquirer will find explained at large in his book, is entitled to consideration

"in discovering the burial places of the Caziques, and in opening their graves for the sake of the golden ornaments which the inhabitants of *olden times* were accustomed to bury with their chiefs   This employment he prosecuted with so much vigor and success, that he collected in this manner over 100,000 dollars worth of gold —(*Lockhart's Diaz*, Vol II., p. 322.)   It will be observed that Diaz speaks of these tombs as belonging to the people who inhabited the country in the olden time,—probably the Toltecs, amongst which branch of the American family the practice of mound-building seems to have been of universal prevalence.

Sepulchral mounds are abundant in many parts of Central America   In the vicinity of the ruins of Ichmul, in Yucatan, they are particularly numerous, covering the plain for miles in every direction   Some of these are forty feet in height   Several have been opened and found to contain chambers, enclosing skeletons, placed in a sitting position with small vessels of pottery at their feet — (*Norman's Yucatan*, p 146 )   In Honduras, says Herrara, were many tombs of the inhabitants , "some of which were large plain rooms, and others only like great heaps of earth.   In the territory of Zenu," continues this author, "abundance of graves were found in a field near a temple, so ancient that large trees were growing over them; and within them was an immense quantity of gold, besides what the Indians took, and what still is lost under ground   These graves were very magnificent, adorned with broad stones and vaults, in which the dead body was laid, and all their wealth, jewels, and arms, women and servants alive, with good stores of provisions and pitchers of their liquors, which denoted the knowledge they had of the immortality of the soul.   The dead were buried sitting, clothed and well armed."—(*Herrara*, Vol. IV , p 221 )

Mr Stephens excavated a sepulchral mound in the vicinity of San Francisco, in Yucatan   It was a square stone structure, with sides four feet high , and the top was rounded over with stones and earth   The interior was loose earth and stones, with some layers of large flat stones, the whole very rough.   After digging six hours, he came to a flat stone of large size, beneath which was a skeleton   The knees were bent against the stomach, the arms doubled from the elbow, and the hands supporting the neck or head.   With this skeleton was found a large vase, the mouth of which was covered with a flat stone.   It was empty, except some little, hard, black flakes at the bottom   Mr Stephens conjectures that it may have contained some liquid, or the heart of the skeleton —(*Trav. in Yucatan*, Vol I , p. 277.)

In South America, and particularly in Peru, the custom of erecting mounds over the dead was of general prevalence   The sepulchral tumuli of Peru were called *huacas* or *guacas*.   They exhibit many features in common with the burial mounds of the Mississippi valley, and establish that funeral customs, in many respects similar to those practised by the race of the mounds, prevailed among the ancient inhabitants of that country.   Their form is generally that of a simple cone , sometimes they are slightly elliptical, and occasionally rectangular   Their usual height is said to be not far from forty to fifty feet, though some are mentioned which are upwards of one hundred feet in altitude.   They are scattered in great profusion over the country , but, according to Ulloa, are "most abundant within the jurisdiction of the town of Cayambe, where the plains are covered with them, for the reason that formerly here was one of the principal temples of the ancient inhabitants, which it was supposed communicated a sacred character to the surrounding country, which was therefore chosen for the burial-place of the kings and caziques of Quito; and in imitation of them, all the chiefs of the villages were interred there The remarkable difference," continues this author, "in the magnitude of these monuments, seems to indicate that the guacas were always suitable to the character, dignity, or riches of the person interred, as indeed the vassals under some of the most potent caziques concurred in raising a mound over his body."—(*Ulloa*, Vol. I, p 480) It may be regarded as settled, that, as a general thing, none but the bodies of deceased chieftains and other persons of consequence were deposited in the *huacas*, and that those of the common people were buried in simple graves. Within the huacas, upon the original surface of the ground, are found chambers constructed of stone, brick, or timber, sometimes there are several of them, with connecting galleries, in which the dead were placed The bodies are usually found occupying a sitting posture With them were placed a great variety of articles, ornaments, and implements Vast quantities of pottery, of every variety of form and ornament, articles of gold and silver, comprising ear-rings, pendants, bracelets, and little images of men and animals, axes of hardened copper and of stone, differing but slightly in shape from those in use at the present day; spear-heads and mirrors of obsidian (*gallinazo* stone), cloth of cotton, of the wool of the lama, and of other materials, implements of palm-wood, marine shells, and a thousand articles of similar character Vast numbers of these tombs have been opened for the sake of the treasures they contain *

In Chili, sepulchral mounds of earth and stone are of frequent occurrence. In them are found, besides the bones of the dead, earthenware, axes, and vessels of stone, admirably worked, and occasionally edged tools of hardened copper Molina describes, with considerable minuteness, the funeral ceremonies of the Chilian Indians, which, from the light they may throw upon the customs of the mound-builders, are worthy of notice "As soon as one of their nation dies, his friends and relations seat themselves on the ground round the body, and weep for a long time, they afterwards expose it, donned in its best clothes, upon a high bier, where it remains during the night, which they pass near it, weeping, or in eating or drinking with those who come to console them. This is called the black entertainment black being with them, as with us, the sign of mourning. The following day, or within two or three days, they carry the corpse to the burial-

---

* The amount of treasure found in some of the huacas is very great Stevenson states that in the year 1576, a huaca was opened in which was found gold amounting to 46,810 golden ounces, according to Humboldt, 5 000 000 francs We are not surprised at the great value of some of these deposits, in view of the almost incredible quantities of gold and silver possessed by the ancient Peruvians According to Proctor (*Peru in* 1823-24), the excavation of the ancient tombs for their contents is still carried on, though it seems that considerable quantities of the precious metals are seldom found Mr Proctor mentions that in some instances the spindles of the ancient inhabitants, with the cotton thread still perfect on them, have been found in the huacas

place of the family, which is usually situated on a hill or in a wood   The corpse is preceded by two men at full speed on horseback, and is followed by the relations, with loud cries and lamentations, while a woman strews ashes on the track, to prevent the soul from returning   On arriving at the place of burial, the corpse is laid on the surface of the ground, surrounded, if a man, with his arms, if a woman, with female implements, and with a great quantity of provisions, and with vessels filled with *chica* and with wine, which, according to their opinion, are necessary to subsist them during their passage to another world   They sometimes even kill a horse and inter it in the same ground   After these ceremonies, they take leave, with many tears, of the deceased, wishing him a prosperous journey, and cover the body with earth and stones in a pyramidal form, upon which they pour a great quantity of *chica* "—(*Molina's Chili*, Vol II, p 82 )

The Esquimaux cover their dead with rude heaps of stone, above which they pile the sledges and canoes of the deceased   The bodies are usually closely wrapped in skins, and placed in a sitting posture.—(*Capt Lyon's Narrative*, p 68 ) Kotzebue mentions a structure of stones which he designates as a "round tower, four fathoms in height," at Kotzebue Sound   It was probably a sepulchral monument of the savages —(*Voyage*, Vol I., p. 210 )

---

## SEPULCHRAL MOUNDS AND MONUMENTS OF THE ANCIENT WORLD

"THE most enduring monuments of the primeval ages of society," observes a learned archæologist, "were those erected in memory of the dead ; and it seems that the further we go back into the history of mankind, the deeper we find man's veneration for his departed brethren   The simplest, and also the most durable, method of preserving the memory of the departed, was by raising a barrow, or mound of stones, over his remains , and accordingly, we find instances of this mode of interment in almost all countries of the globe "   The extent to which it prevailed in America, we have already indicated , and the coincidences in form and structure between the sepulchral monuments of this continent and those of the Old World, have been the subject of incidental remark.   These coincidences are, however, sufficiently remarkable to merit further attention ; and it is believed a brief review of the character of the primitive sepulchral monuments of the other continent will serve greatly to illustrate and explain those of our own country, at the same time that it establishes the general prevalence of the custom of mound-burial in past ages

The earliest of human records distinctly refer to the practice of erecting mounds of earth or stone over the dead, but we find in the pyramids of Egypt—

which may be regarded as perfected tumuli—the evidence of its prevalence at a period long anteceding the dawn of written history. In the deep night of antiquity, step by step, had the rude heap of stones which filial regard first gathered over the dead, developed itself, until in its massive proportions and solid strength it emulated the mountains, and bade defiance to time. Homer speaks frequently of the sepulchral tumuli of the heroic age of early Greece, and gives many curious details relating to the ceremonies of the interment. The description of the burial of Patroclus is familiar to most readers; it, however, conveys so accurate and lively an idea of the practices common to ancient burials, that we cannot do better, in illustration of our subject, than to quote it here. It should be premised that the Homeric heroes were burnt before interment.

> " They still abiding heaped the pile
> A hundred feet of breadth from side to side
> They gave to it, and on the summit placed,
> With sorrowing hearts, the body of the dead
> Many a fat sheep, with many an ox full-horned,
> They flayed before the pile, busy their task
> Administering , and Peleus' son, the fat
> Taking from every victim, overspread
> Complete the body with it of his friend
> Patroclus, and the flayed beasts heaped around
> Then, placing flagons on the pile, replete
> With oil and honey, he inclined their mouths
> Towards the bier, and slew and added next,
> Deep groaning and in haste four martial steeds
> Nine dogs the hero at his table fed ,
> Of which beheading two, their carcasses
> He added also   Last, twelve gallant sons
> Of noble Trojans slaying (for his heart
> Teemed with great vengeance), he applied the force
> Of hungry flames that should devour the whole "
>
> *Iliad*, Book XXIII , Cowper's *Version*

The sacrifices done, and the body consumed, the bones are next collected and the tumulus heaped above

> " The Greeks obey '  Where yet the embers glow,
> Wide o'er the pile the sable wine they throw,
> And deep subsides the ashy heap below
> Next the white bones his sad companions place,
> With tears collected, in the golden vase
> The sacred relics to the tent they bore ,
> The urn a veil of linen covered o'er
> That done, they bid the sepulchre aspire,
> And cast the deep foundations round the pyre ,
> High in the midst they heap the swelling bed
> Of rising earth, memorial of the dead "—*Iliad*, Book XXIII

The Trojans are made to bury the body of Hector in the same manner   during nine days they collect the wood and raise the pile ; and when fire has completed its part of the work, they also quench the fires with dark wine, and collect the bones of the hero in a golden urn, which they cover with a rich cloth, and place in a "hollow trench ," above this they pile large stones, and over all heap the tumulus.

The body of the dead was not always burned among the Greeks , on the contrary, burial both by inhumation and incremation was practised from the earliest times, though one practice may have been more common than another at a particular period   In Magna Græcia, unburnt skeletons have been found, and in tombs close by vases containing the ashes of the dead.—(*Tischben and Bottiger.*)   Both skeletons and ashes have been found in Greece itself —(*Stackelberg, die Graber der Hellenen* )   There are no certain accounts as to whether the body was burned at the place of sepulture, or at a spot designated for that purpose   At any rate, the remains were collected and deposited in a *cinerary* made of clay or bronze. The coffins of the unburned were sometimes of wood, but generally the work of the potter, though in some cases of masonry or stone   The tombs were usually in a spot designated for the purpose.   Sometimes they were placed in the person's own house   After it was forbidden to bury in the city, it became common to select a certain quarter for burials.   The favorite place of sepulture was in the fields or by some frequented highway   The tombs were the inviolate property of the family, so that no other person might bury therein.   A variety of articles were placed with the dead—vases, mirrors, ornaments, etc   In cases of burning, they were placed on the pyre   Feasts and offerings to the dead were customary   At stated times the tombs were decked, and sometimes bloody sacrifices were made   In the order of funeral ceremonies, it should be mentioned that the first thing done was to insert a small coin (an *obolus*) in the mouth of the dead, as a ναῦλον for the ferryman of Hades   A similar custom existed among the ancient Mexicans, who inserted a gem of some kind in the lips of the deceased, which was to serve as a heart in the next world

The funeral customs of the Romans were nearly identical with those practised by the Greeks   Their tombs were often simple tumuli, and so denominated. Burial by inhumation and by fire were common practices   In the tombs were placed coins, urns, flasks for holding tears or perfumes, sepulchral lamps, etc Games were celebrated in honor of the dead, and sacrifices and libations made on their tombs

Among both Greeks and Romans, the expenditures at funerals became so great, and the ambition to erect large and costly monuments so general, that it was found necessary to prescribe their dimensions, and check extravagance by law.

A pillar or upright stone, in ancient times a sacred emblem, was usually placed upon the tumulus of the dead.   Paris wounded Diomedes from behind the pillar on the barrow of Ilus.   These pillars were called *stelæ*   Alexander, when he crossed the Hellespont, performed solemn games at the barrows of the Grecian heroes who fell before the walls of Troy, and anointed with perfumes the *stelæ* on their tops.   They were erected on the taphos of the Athenians who fell at

Marathon, and on that of the Lacedæmonians who died at Thermopylæ, and bore the names of the slain  The stelæ were continued when the barrows were no longer erected; and the idea of their sanctity is still retained in the monumental stones which plead for safety, by professing to be *sacred* to the memory of the person above whose grave they are erected

Sometimes the arms or implements of the dead were suspended around the *stelæ* or crowned the barrow of the dead  A spear was fixed on the tomb of the Trojan Hector, and Misenus, the trumpeter of Hector, and pilot of the Trojan fleet of Æneas, had reared upon his tomb the symbols of his deeds

> " On it Æneas piously heaped
> A mighty mound sepulchral  The oar, the trumpet,
> Arms of the man, the airy summit crowned,
> From him Misenus named  It still retains
> That name, and holds it through the lapse of time "[*]
>                                                    *Æneid*, IV , 232

Even in the later periods of Grecian history, mounds are occasionally raised over the illustrious dead.  Plutarch says that Alexander, on the death of Demaratus, " made a most magnificent funeral for him, his whole army raising him a monument of earth eighty cubits high and of vast circumference '  Semiramis endeavored to eternize the memory of Ninus her husband, by raising a high mound for his tomb  The Scythians, whose tumuli are scattered in great abundance over the plains of Russia, southern Siberia, and Tartary, labored, says Herodotus, " to raise as high a monument of earth for their dead as possible "  This author has left us a remarkable description of their mode of interment, which is amply confirmed by the exploration of their tombs  " The body of the king, having been transported through the various provinces of the kingdom, was brought at last to the Gerri, who live in the remotest parts of Scythia, where the sepulchres are  Here the corpse was placed upon a couch, encompassed on all sides by spears fixed in the ground . upon the whole were placed pieces of wood, covered with branches of willow.  They strangled one of the deceased's concubines. his groom, cook, and most confidential servant, whose bodies they placed around the dead ; they slew horses also, and deposited with him the first fruits of all things, and the choicest of his effects, and finally some golden goblets, for they possessed neither silver nor brass  This done, they heaped the earth above with great care, and

---

[*] The practice here indicated was one of general prevalence, not only in ancient but in more modern times, and alike amongst savage and polished nations  The Indians around the Upper Mississippi, to this day, place a pole above the graves of their dead, from which his arms and ornaments are suspended , so, too, do the Indians of Oregon , who, however distrusting the veneration of their fellows, break holes in the kettles, and bend the barrels of the guns which they place on the tombs  The arms and crest of the titled dead are still graven on their monuments, and the unstrung lyre and broken sword indicate the graves of the poet and the warrior  The stelæ are still to be seen on the barrows of the ancient Scythians and Scandinavians, though none are found crowning the sepulchral mounds of America

endeavored to make as high a mound as possible "—(*Melpomene*, LXXI.)  The richness of the Scythian barrows is extraordinary, and according to Strahlenberg, the local governors of Siberia used formerly to authorize caravans or expeditions " to visit and ransack the tombs," reserving to themselves a tenth of the treasures recovered —(*Siberia*, p 366)  In the second volume of the British Archæologia. is an account of the opening of one of the large tumuli in southern Siberia.  After removing the superincumbent earth and stones, three vaults, constructed of unhewn stones and of rude workmanship, were discovered  The central one was largest, and contained the remains of the individual over whom the tumulus had been erected  It also contained his sword, spear, bow, quiver, arrows, etc  In the vault at his feet, were the skeleton and trappings of a horse, in the vault at his head, a female skeleton, supposed to be that of his wife  The male skeleton reclined against the head of the vault, on a sheet of pure gold extending from head to foot, and another of like dimensions was spread over it  It had been wrapped in a rich mantle, studded with rubies and emeralds  The female skeleton was enveloped in like manner  a golden chain of many links, set with rubies, went round her neck, and there were bracelets of gold upon her arms.  The four sheets of gold weighed forty pounds.

In some instances, the bodies were burned before interment  All of the Scythian barrows contain numerous relics of art, ornaments of gold and silver and precious stones, weapons and implements of war, domestic utensils, mirrors, images and idols, vases of metal and pottery, grains of the millet kind, etc, etc —(*Strahlenberg*, pp 264, 268; *Rennel's Herodotus*, p 110)

These ancient tombs, which are called *Bogri* by the Russians, are often plain mounds  Some were set round with rough stones in a circle or square  others with hewn stones.  In the squares the corner-stone was usually higher and broader than the others, and sometimes bore inscriptions.  Occasionally, the barrow was surmounted with a stone, or *stela*

In Rajast'han, the practice of burying the distinguished dead under tumuli still exists  Previous to interment, the body is burned, as is also the wife of the deceased, who in all cases accompanies her lord  Monumental pillars are also erected, rudely carved with emblematic figures.  They are placed in lines irregular groups, and in circles, and are numerous in the vicinity of every large town  These tombs are places of sacrifice, and to them the Rajpoot repairs at stated intervals, to make offerings to the manes of his ancestors.—(*Tod's Rajast'han*, Vol I. pp 72, 75)

A singular variety of tumular structures, maintaining a certain resemblance to those of other portions of the globe, but having many essentially peculiar features. is found in Sweden  They are, for the chief part, circular. sometimes, however, there is a square enclosure of upright stones, with a conical barrow in the centre, which has its base surrounded with upright stones, midway between this and the summit, the circumference is marked by a second ring of upright stones, close to the summit a third belt encircles it, and the crest of the barrow is crowned by a *cromlech*, or group of stones.  Another variety has a circle of upright stones around the base of a *carnedd*, or stone mound  A third variety has a circular belt of upright stones around a conical barrow, which is surmounted by a single upright stone. In connection with these, is a remarkable variety of stone enclosures. Some consist of a simple circle of upright stones, two of which, placed opposite each other, are larger and taller than the rest. Others are circular, with a small avenue of approach of four stones on each side, others are large circles, with every sixth stone of larger size than the others, and the two north and south, of still greater dimensions; others are triangular, with a large stone in the centre, and another at each corner; others triangular, with each side curving inward, but without the large stones in the centre and corners, others are square. The structures last named are frequently surrounded by *valla*, and enclosures are seen contiguous to and even forming part of tumuli.—(*Sjoborg Samlingar for Nordens Fornalskare, &c*, 2 Vols 4to, *Stockholm*, 1822, *Zur Alterthumskunde des Nordens, Von J J A Worsaœ, Leipzig*, 1847)

Mr Worsaæ divides these barrows, according to the character of their contents, into three classes ·

FIRST.—*Barrows of the Stone Age*.—These contain unburned corpses, enclosed in rude stone chambers: the implements and utensils found in them are of stone or flint.

SECOND —*Barrows of the Bronze Age* —Containing burned human remains, deposited in vases or little stone chests  also, arms and utensils of bronze or copper

THIRD.—*Barrows of the Iron Age* —Burned human remains : arms and utensils of iron, etc  These barrows are often of regular forms, triangular, square, oval, ship-form, etc , generally surrounded by upright stones, as above.

This classification differs somewhat from that usually adopted, in which the "age of fire" and the "age of hills" distinguish the earlier and later periods of Scandinavian monumental history. Odin is said to have introduced the practice of burning, and also that of the wife sacrificing herself with her deceased lord *— (*Mallet's Northern Antiq*, Chap XII ) Among all the rude nations of the north and west of Europe, for an indefinite period before the dawn of civilization, burial customs, strictly analogous to those already described, existed. The dead were buried with or without burning, and with them were deposited numerous relics of art, which, in the greater or less skill which they exhibit, mark the eras of burial, and the gradual advance of the builders. The Germans, says Tacitus, " added to the funeral pile the arms of the deceased and his horse," and both Cæsar and Pomponious agree in saying that the inhabitants of Belgium and Gaul buried or burned with the dead whatever was valued by them in their lifetime.

---

* A recent Stockholm paper has the following paragraph relating to the excavation of certain Runic barrows, in Sweden

"The crown Prince has lately directed several of the Runic Barrows or 'giant's graves,' in the neighborhood of old Upsula, to be opened at his cost  Odin's Hill was the first opened, when clear proofs were found that the hill was not formed by nature but by human hands, although the urn, with the bones of the individual inhumed therein, and which, in all probability, is in the centre of the hill, had not been found  A hearth, formed of extraordinary large bricks, was first discovered in the interior, and at a distance of about twenty three yards, a strong wall, of large pieces of granite, resting on a solid floor made of clay, the wall formed the corner of a large grotto of from four to six feet in height  Within it there were ashes and other traces of fire  Unfortunately, the advanced period of the year has, for the present, interrupted the works, but they will be resumed in the summer "

The burial-mounds of the ancient Britons, both of the Celtic and Saxon periods, evince similar practices on the part of their builders   For obvious reasons, the mounds of the United States have oftenest been compared to these; and, upon the narrow basis of certain coincidences in structure, a common origin has been ascribed to both   This circumstance, in connection with others, justifies a more detailed notice of the British barrows than would otherwise be required.   They have been systematically investigated by many learned and indefatigable antiquarians, the result of whose inquiries, so far as they relate to the modes of interment practised by the ancient inhabitants, are compendiously presented by Sir R. C Hoare, in his splendid work, entitled " Ancient Wiltshire "

"Four distinct modes of interment were practised by the ancient Britons —

1. The body placed generally in a cist, with its legs bent up towards the head, and frequently accompanied by daggers of brass, drinking cups, &c

2. The body extended at full length, accompanied by articles of brass and iron, such as spear-heads, lances, swords, and the umbos of shields.

3. Interment by incremation   when the body of the deceased was consumed by fire, and the bones and ashes deposited either on the floor of the barrow, or in a cist cut in the chalk   This is called a simple interment.

4. Urn burial, with incremation, when the body was burned, and the bones and ashes deposited within a sepulchral urn, which is generally, though not in all cases, reversed.   By the web of cloth still remaining in some instances, it appears that the ashes were wrapped up in a linen cloth and fastened by a small brass pin, several of which, intermixed with the ashes, have been found

" Of these modes of burial, the first was probably most primitive   articles of iron bespeak a later period; and it is further probable, that the two modes of burying the body by fire were adopted at one and the same period   We have instances where the body has been enclosed in a wooden chest, riveted with brass, or within the more simple covering of an unbarked timber tree "

A very remarkable resemblance in form exists between the various kinds of British barrows and the mounds of this country; in this respect, indeed, there is scarcely a perceptible difference between them   The curious will find in Hoare's Ancient Wiltshire, 1812, Stukeley's Stonehenge and Itinerarium , Rowland's Antiquities of Anglesey, 1723 , Camden's Britannia , Grose's Antiquities; in the British Archæologia, thirty volumes, quarto; Higgins's Celtic Druids, 1827 , Borlase's Ancient Cornwall; and in numerous other works upon the subject, abundant illustrations of the correctness of this observation   Sir R C Hoare has attempted to make the variety of form exhibited by these barrows the basis of a classification, distinguishing the eras of their construction, and even the caste and condition of the dead which they cover   It is probable that some varieties of form may have predominated at a particular period, and that the dimensions of the barrow may have, in some degree, corresponded with the rank of the dead.   Further than this, however, the theory is not well sustained.   Sir Richard enumerates not less than eleven kinds of tumuli, distinguished from each other by their form, viz .—

1st. *The Long Barrow*, which resembles half an egg, cut lengthwise, one end a little broader than the other, generally ditched around the base, sometimes enclosed in a circle, and occasionally set round with upright stones  Supposed to be the oldest form of the Celtic barrows  *Contents*  usually a number of skeletons at the broad end, lying in a confused manner, and generally covered with a pile of stones or flints  In other parts, stags' horns, fragments of rude pottery, and burnt bones

2d. *The Bowl Barrow*, the form of which is indicated by the name, with or without a ditch, and having a slight depression in the top.  Supposed to be a family mausoleum

3d  *The Bell Barrow*, a modification of the *Bowl Barrow*, supposed to have been formed by placing a new top thereon, for additional interment

4th. *The Druid Barrows*, enclosed by a vallum and ditch, the latter always interior to the former, the number of mounds within the enclosure varying from one to fifteen or twenty  *Contents*: skeletons, small cups, beads of amber, glass, and jet, small lance-heads, and, very rarely, sepulchral urns, all of elegant workmanship.  Sir Richard supposes, from the predominance of ornaments, that they were devoted to females.  Supposed to be family cemeteries.

5th  *The Pond Barrow*, consisting of a simple circular vallum or ditch  Fosbroke doubts whether these should be denominated barrows, and suggests that they may have been Druidical tribunals  They are identical in form with many of the small circles of the West.  No remains found in them.

6th. *The Twin Barrow*, comprised of two barrows joining each other, and enclosed in a circle.  Supposed by Sir Richard to be the monuments of individuals closely allied to each other by blood or friendship.

The remaining classes are but slight and hardly appreciable modifications of those already described.

The rude natives of New Zealand erect tumuli over their dead, who are sometimes burned previous to interment.  Their arms and ornaments are deposited with them.  Custom rigorously enjoins that these monuments to the departed shall be carefully watched over.  A woman at Clarence River, who neglected to weed and trim her husband's tumulus, was put to death in consequence of her neglect —(*Angas' Australia and New Zealand*, Vol II , p  280 , *Gray's Australia*, Vol I , p. 227.)  Similar monuments, most usually constructed of stone, and sometimes of great size and regularity, were often erected over the dead, by the natives of the larger Polynesian Islands, where they still remain, enduring records of the primitive customs of the islanders —(*Ellis's Polynesian Researches*, Vol III , pp  242, 325; *Beechey's Nar*  pp  20, 37; *La Pérouse Voy*, Vol. III., p. 194 )

Without noticing further the burial customs of nations, ancient and modern, in the various quarters of the globe, enough has been presented to show the general prevalence of mound-sepulture, and the nearly uniform practices which attended it  As remarked at the outset, it is the simplest method of perpetuating the memory of the dead  Its general adoption by different and widely separated people, must not, therefore, be taken to indicate any extraordinary dependence,

## PROBABLE FUNERAL RITES OF THE MOUND-BUILDERS

FROM various features discovered in the sepulchral mounds of the West, it has been suggested that sacrifices or ceremonies of some kind, in which fire performed a part, were solemnized above the dead. The general occurrence of a layer of charcoal at some point near the surface of the mound, bearing evidence of having been heaped over while burning, and sometimes having mingled with it human bones, the bones of animals, and relics of art, affords ample basis for the conjecture We have seen that in the burials of Chili, sacrifices and libations were made at the tumuli of the dead; in Peru, the burial rites were very similar, and in cases where the deceased was of the Inca race, or a person of consequence, his wives and domestics were put to death, that they might accompany and serve him in another world On the death of the Inca Huyana Capac, it is said that over one thousand victims were slain at his tomb. Similar practices prevailed among many of the South American savage tribes, also in Central America and in Mexico In the latter country, the arms, implements, and ornaments of the deceased were burned or buried with him; and, as we have already said, an animal resembling a dog, called by the Mexicans *techichi,* was killed, to accompany his soul in its journey to the world of spirits If the body was burned, the ashes were collected in an earthen pot, in this was deposited a gem, which it was supposed would serve in the next world for a heart; and the urn was buried in a deep ditch * Eighty days thereafter, oblations of meats and drinks were made over the grave On the decease of persons of consequence, their slaves and servants were put to death, sometimes in great numbers. Analogous customs prevailed among the Natchez, when, on the death of the Suns, many human victims were sacrificed Among the savage North American tribes, no custom was more general than that of making oblations at the tombs of the dead . dogs were sometimes sacrificed at the burial; and horses are now occasionally slain by the Western tribes, upon the graves of their owners

---

* "They (the Mexicans) made it the office of the priests to inter the dead and perform the funeral obsequies They buried them in their own gardens, and in the courts of their own houses Some were carried to the places of sacrifice in the mountains, others were burnt, and the ashes afterwards buried in the temples, and with all were buried whatever they had of apparel stones, and jewels They did put the ashes of the dead in pots, and with them their valuables, how rich soever they might be If it were a king or lord who was dead, they offered slaves to be put to death, and gave apparel to such as came to the interment  *  *  * They did set food and drink on the graves of the dead, imagining that their souls did feed thereon "—(*Acosta in Purchas,* Vol III, p 1029 )

16

Libations in some cases were made at the tomb, and repeated at intervals for years. According to Charlevoix, at the "Feasts of the Dead," or general burial of the Hurons and Iroquois, dances, games, and combats constituted part of the ceremonies of the occasion

Vanegas (*Hist California*, I. p 104) says, The California Indians bury or burn their dead indifferently, as chances to be most convenient Vancouver (*Voy.* III, pp 182, 242) mentions two instances, in which the natives of the Northwest coast burned their dead, but we are not left to infer that the custom was general A singular funeral custom is mentioned as prevailing among the *Takah*, or Carriers, one of the Oregon tribes, and a branch of the great Algonquin family They always burn their dead upon a pyre, in case the deceased has a wife, she is obliged to lie by the side of the corpse until the fire is lighted and the heat becomes intense If, in the estimation of the spectators, she abandons the pyre too early, she is thrust back, and thus often falls a sacrifice. The Medicine-men of this tribe pretend to receive the spirit of the dead in their hands, after the corpse is burned, and to be able to transfer it to any one they choose, who then bears the name of the dead, in addition to his own —(*Narrative of U S. Exploring Expedition*, Vol IV, p 453)

Father Creux, a Jesuit Missionary in Canada, in 1639, notices a fact which affords a curious antithesis to the customs of the Mexicans, above presented by Clavigero namely, that the Hurons cut off the flesh from the bones of those who were drowned or frozen, and burned it; the skeleton alone was buried. Charlevoix (Vol. II., p 189) confirms this statement He adds, that the bodies of those slain in battle were burned, probably for the more easy transportation of their ashes to the burial-grounds of their fathers.

La Hontan (Vol. II, p 53) states that "The savages upon the Long River [Mississippi ?] burn their dead, reserving the bodies until there are a sufficient number to burn together, which is performed out of the village, in a place set apart for the purpose" This statement does not find support in other authorities

"They appease the souls of the dead with offerings of meats and drinks. Every woman whose child dies at a distance from home, makes a journey, once a year, if possible, to its place of burial, to pour a libation on its grave."—(*Loskiel*, p. 76.)

With these facts and the suggestions of analogy before us, we are certainly justified in the inference that the burials in the mounds were attended with sacrifices, perhaps of human victims, with oblations, and, it is probable, with games and ceremonies corresponding with those which prevailed, at one period, in the Old World

It was remarked, in a preceding chapter, that the highest points of the hills and the jutting bluffs of the table-lands bordering the valleys of the Western rivers, are often crowned with mounds Although generally supposed to have been designed for "look-outs,' or places of observation, investigation has shown that a portion of them, at least, were sepulchral in their original purposes. Clavigero observes of the Mexicans, that they had no particular places assigned for the burial of their dead, but entombed them in the fields and on the *mountains*. It is possible that an ambition like that which governed the selection of the place of sepulture of the Omahaw chief, Blackbird, also influenced the ancient people in the disposal of their dead   He was buried sitting on his favorite horse, on the summit of a high hill overlooking the Mississippi, " that he might see the strangers coming to trade with his people "*   So, too, the chiefs of the mound-builders may have desired, at their death, to be placed where, with the eyes of a spirit, they might watch over their people thronging the fertile valleys beneath their tombs   Thus an early Greek poet speaks of the tomb of Themistocles overlooking the Piræus :

> " Then shall thy mound  conspicuous on the shore,
> Salute the mariners who pass the sea,
> Keep watch on all who enter or depart,
> And  be the umpire in the naval strife "
>
> *Plato comicus, ap  Plut  vit  Themist*

A somewhat similar sentiment occurs in the Iliad, where Hector, speaking of one he is to slay in single combat, says .

> " The long-haired Greeks
> To him, upon the shores of Hellespont,
> A mound shall heap, that those in after-times
> Who sail along the darksome sea shall say,
> ' This is the monument of one long since
> Borne to his grave  by mighty Hector slain ' "

The ancient Anglo-Saxon was not without a similar ambition.   The dying Beo-wulf enjoins :

> " Command the famous in war
> to make a mound,
> bright after the funeral fire,
> upon the nose of the promontory
> Which shall for a memorial
> to my people
> rise high aloft
>
> on Hronesness ,
> that the sea-sailors
> may afterwards call it
> Beowulf's barrow
> when the Brentings
> over the darkness of the floods
> shall sail afar "—*Beowulf*, v  5599

The size of the aboriginal mounds of the  West was no doubt regulated in a degree by the dignity of the individuals over whose remains they were erected, or by the regard in which they were held by their people.   In the number or value of their enclosed relics, the various mounds, great and small, exhibit little difference   We have, however, seen, according to Ulloa, that the character of the deposites

---

* Kemble, in a note to Beowulf, quotes an Icelandic Saga describing the ceremonies attending the burial of a hero, as the death feast, the raising of the mound, the casting of treasures therein, the slaughter of his horse, and the placing of the hero in his chariot

as well as the size of the mound was, in Peru, a sure indication of the state and power of the dead. Such was the case among the ancients. Beowulf requests that his people may raise a barrow over him proportionate in size to the respect entertained for his memory

"Old of life, he spake a whole multitude of words, and commanded me to greet you, he bade that ye should make, according to the deeds of your friend, on the place of the funeral pile, the lofty barrow, large and famous, even as he was of men the most worthy warrior"—(*Beowulf*, I, 6183)

In the subsequent burial of Beowulf, the burning of the body, the sacrifices, the games, the songs and orations in praise of the dead and in commemoration of his deeds, we have a vivid picture of the funeral customs of the olden time,—customs not peculiar to the old Continent, but prevailing among the nations of the New World, and probably attending the burials of the ancient people whose monuments we are investigating   Beowulf's people carry into effect his desire, and the poem ends with this description of his interment —

"For him then prepared the people of the Geats a funeral pile upon the earth, strong, hung round with helmets, with war-boards (shields), and with bright byrnies, as he had requested   The heroes, weeping, then laid down in the midst the famous chieftain, their dear lord   Then began on the hill the mightiest of funeral fires the warriors to awake ·  the wood-smoke rose aloft dark from the fire; noisily it went, mingled with weeping   The mixture of the wind lay on till it the bone-house [body] had broken, hot in his breast   Sad in mind, sorry in mood, they mourned the death of their lord   *   *   *   Made then the people of the Westerns a mound over the sea; it was high and broad, by the sailors over the waves to be seen afar   And they built up, during ten days, the beacon of the war-renowned, the [king] of swords   They surrounded it with a wall, in the most honorable manner that wise men could desire   They put into the mound rings and bright gems, all such ornaments as the fierce-minded men had before taken from the hoard   they suffered the earth to hold the treasures of warriors, gold on the sand; there it yet remaineth, as useless to men as it was of old   Then round the mound rode of beasts of war, of nobles, a troop, twelve in all , they would speak about the king, they would call him to mind, relate the song of words, speak themselves ;  they praised his valor, and his deeds of bravery they judged with honor, as it is fitting that a man his friendly lord should extol, should love him in his soul, when he must depart from his body to become valueless.  Thus mourned the people of the Geats, his domestic comrades, their dear lord ;  they said that he was of the kings of the world the mildest of men and the most gentle. the most gracious to his people, and the most jealous of glory "—(*Beowulf*, v. 6268 )

## THE MOUNDS NOT GENERAL BURIAL-PLACES, GREAT INDIAN CEMETERIES OF THE WEST

ALLUSION has been made, in the body of this work, to the large cemeteries which have been discovered at various places in the Mississippi valley, and the suggestion ventured that they owe their origin to practices similar to those which prevailed among the Indians of New York and Canada, of collecting, at stated intervals, the bones of the dead, and depositing them in pits or trenches. There are many interesting facts connected with these cemeteries, which merit attention, and justify a recurrence to the subject.

Nothing is more common in the accounts given of Western mounds, than the loose and very vague remark, that certain ones or all of them "contain vast quantities of human bones" To this circumstance seems attributable, in a great degree, the prevailing and very erroneous impression, that the mounds are simple tombs, or rather grand cemeteries, containing the remains of an entire race. The Grave Creek mound is spoken of by Atwater, Doddridge, and other writers, as a grand mausoleum "undoubtedly containing many thousand human skeletons" An investigation has shown it to contain but a very few skeletons; and examinations of several other tumuli, characterized in similar extravagant terms, have been attended with like results. *The mounds of the West can be regarded only to a very limited extent as the burial-places of the people who built them* But little more than one-half of their number are clearly sepulchral in their character; and these, except in extraordinary cases, contain but a single skeleton each *

---

* The authority of Mr Samuel R Brown, author of the "Western Gazetteer, or Emigrant's Directory," published in 1817, has been quoted by various writers on American antiquities, and has been supposed to sustain the conclusion that the mounds were vast receptacles of the dead, slain in battle. It will be seen, however, from Mr Brown's account of his explorations, that the mounds which he examined contained *deposites of different dates*, one of which was clearly of the modern Indians, though the fact does not appear to have suggested itself to the mind of the explorer, or to have occurred to the writers who have followed him. The material portions of Mr Brown's account are subjoined.

"We examined from fifteen to twenty of these mounds. In some, whose height was from fifteen to twenty feet, we could not find more than four or five skeletons. In one, not the least appearance of a human bone was to be found. Others were so full of bones as to warrant the belief that they originally contained at least one hundred bodies; children of different ages and the full grown seemed to have been piled together promiscuously * * * In the progress of our researches, we obtained ample testimony that these masses of earth were the work of a savage people. We discovered a piece of glass resembling the bottom of a tumbler, but concave; several stone axes etc * * * There was no appearance of *iron*; one of the skulls was found pierced by an arrow, which was still sticking in it, driven about half way

We must seek elsewhere for the general depositories of the dead of the mound-builders   It has been suggested that the caves of the limestone regions of Kentucky and Tennessee were used as sepulchres.   Some of these are represented to have contained thousands of bodies, preserved by the natural properties of these caves, clothed in strange fabrics, composed of a coarse species of cloth interwoven with feathers, in fanciful and tasteful patterns, resembling the feather-cloth of Mexico, of which such glowing descriptions were given by the conquerors.*   Extensive, however, as these cave depositories may have been, they fail, in view of

---

through before its force was spent   It was about six inches long   The subjects of this mound were doubtless killed in battle and hastily buried   In digging to the bottom of them, we *invariably* came to a stratum of ashes, from six inches to two feet thick, which rests on the original earth   These ashes contain coals, fragments of brands, and pieces of *calcined bones*   From the quantity of ashes and bones, and the appearance of the earth underneath, it was evident that large fires must have been kept burning for several days previous to commencing the mound, and that a considerable number of victims must have been sacrificed by burning on the spot "—(*Brown's Gazetteer of the West*, p 58 )

"That some of the mounds served for tombs, we have the conclusive evidence that they abound in human bones   It has often been asserted, that some of the mounds are full of bones that are perforated, as though the living subjects were slain in battle , and  that the skeletons are heaped together in promiscuous confusion, as if buried after a conflict, without order or arrangement   The bones which we have seen were such, and so arranged, as might be expected in the common process of solemn and deliberate inhumation '  —(*Flint* )

"The vulgar opinion has been circulated by various writers, that under these mounds were buried the bodies of those who were slain in battle   They probably pertained to the particular tribe of a country, and were restricted to the principals among them, for it is not to be supposed that the inhabitants were indiscriminately buried under tumuli   Their burial-places must be sought elsewhere "—(*Sir Richard C Hoare, on the Barrows of Great Britain* )

* The nitrous caves of Kentucky were found to contain a considerable number of desiccated human bodies , they were termed *mummies*, and, for a time, created much speculation   They were generally enveloped in skins, in a species of bark, or in feather cloth, and placed in a squatting posture   It is said that hundreds of these were taken from a cave near Lexington, and burned by the early settlers   The bodies appear to have owed their preservation entirely to natural causes   It has been inferred, from the resemblance between the envelopes of these bodies and the feather-cloths of Mexico, that the people who thus deposited their dead were very ancient, and probably an offshoot from Mexico   We have, however, abundant evidence to show that fabrics of this kind were manufactured by the Southern Indian tribes   The chronicler of Soto's expedition reports having found "a great many mantles made of white, red, green, and blue feathers, very convenient for the winter "  Du Pratz also describes this feather fabric as of common use   and Adair observes  "They likewise make turkey-feather blankets, twisting the inner end of the feathers very fast in a double, strong thread of the inner bark of the mulberry," etc —(*Am Inds* , p 423 )

In May, 1835, a cavern cemetery was discovered on the banks of the Ohio River, opposite Steubenville   It was thirty or forty feet in circumference, and filled with human bones   "They were of all ages, and had been thrown in indiscriminately after the removal of the flesh   They seemed to have been deposited at different periods of time, those on the top alone being in a good state of preservation ' —(*Morton's Crania Americana*, p 235 )   Dr Morton regards these remains as of no great age, and as undoubtedly belonging to individuals of the barbarous tribes

A similar cave was discovered, some years ago, at Golconda, on the Ohio River, Illinois   It contained many skeletons —(*Crania Am* , p 284 )   Henry, in his travels, mentions a cave in the island of Mackinaw in Lake Huron, the floor of which was covered with human bones   He expresses the opinion that it was formerly filled with them   The Indians knew nothing concerning the deposite , our author, nevertheless, ventures the conjecture, that the cave was an ancient receptacle of the bones of prisoners sacrificed at the Indian war-feasts   'I have always observed," he continues, ' that the Indians pay particular attention to

the abundant evidences of a vast ancient population, to answer the question, What became of the dead of the ancient people? In Tennessee, as well as in Kentucky and Missouri, extensive cemeteries have been discovered. For a description of some of those of Tennessee, the public are indebted to Prof. TROOST, of Nashville —(*Trans. Am. Ethnol. Soc.*, Vol. 1, p. 358.) One is mentioned by him in the immediate vicinity of that town, which is about a mile in length, and of indefinite breadth. No less than six others equally extensive are found within a radius of ten miles. The graves are lined with flat stones, and occur in ranges. Within these, skeletons much decayed are found, also various relics, some of which are recognised as identical with those found in the mounds of Ohio, suggesting a common origin. This identity is further indicated, though not established, by the presence of mounds and other structures in the vicinity of these cemeteries. Beads, composed of perforated shells, of the genus *Marginella*, were discovered by Dr. Troost in the graves. These have been found in both the sepulchral and sacrificial mounds north of the Ohio; as have also beads and other ornaments, made probably from the columella of the *strombus gigas*, similar to those found by this explorer in the graves above mentioned. How far these coincidences may be traced, can only be determined when the same mind which has investigated one class of remains shall be able to investigate the other.

Near Sparta, in Tennessee, are several extensive cemeteries, in which the bones of the dead were deposited, enclosed in short coffins or boxes, made of flat stones. These coffins measure about two feet in length and nine inches in depth. A small, rude, earthen vessel, accompanied by some small shells, is usually found near the head of each skeleton.—(*Featherstonhaugh's Trav.*, p. 48.) Similar burial-places are found in Missouri, particularly in the vicinity of the Marimec River. The

the bones of sacrifices, preserving them unbroken, and depositing them in some place exclusively appropriated to the purpose."—(*Travels*, p. 111.)

In the State of Durango, Mexico, some cave depositories have been discovered, which have given rise to very exaggerated accounts. Some of them have represented that as many as a million of bodies were found in a single cavern. All the information which we have, that can be regarded as authentic, is contained in Dr. Wishzenus's Memoir of the Expedition under Doniphan, published by order of Congress, p. 69. After crossing the Rio Nasas, we arrived at San Lorenzo. "On the right hand, or south of us, was a chain of limestone hills running parallel to the road. At the foot of a hill belonging to the chain, Señor de Gaba pointed out a place to me where, some years ago, a remarkable discovery had been made. In the year 1838, a Mexican, Don Juan Flores, perceived the hidden entrance to a cave. He entered, and found nearly one thousand well preserved Indian corpses, squatted together on the ground, with their hands folded below their knees. They were dressed in fine blankets, made of the fibres of lechuguilla, with sandals made of a species of hana and were ornamented with colored scarfs, with beads of seeds of fruits polished bones, etc. This is a very insufficient account of this mysterious burying place. The Mexicans supposed it belonged to the Lipans, an old Indian tribe which from time immemorial has roved and still roams over the Bolson de Mahimi. I had heard at Chihuahua of this discovery, and was fortunate enough to secure a skull which had been taken from the cave."

Among the South American nations, cave burial seems to have been common. Humboldt describes a cave-sepulchre of the Atures, which he discovered on the sources of the Orinoco. It contained nearly six hundred skeletons, regularly arranged in baskets and earthen vases. Some of the skeletons had been bleached, others painted, and all, it is worthy of remark, had been deposited after the removal of the flesh,

" coffins" are neatly constructed of long flat stones, planted vertically, and adapted to each other edge to edge, so as to form a continuous wall.  At either end of the grave the stones project a little above the surface.  These stone sarcophagi are usually from three to four, but sometimes as many as six feet in length.  The bones in these appear to have been deposited after having been separated from the flesh, in accordance with a practice well known to have been common amongst many Indian tribes.—(*Beck's Gaz. of Missouri*, p 274, *James's Exped*, Vol I, p. 55 ) Other extensive cemeteries are found in various parts of the country.  One near Alexandria, in Arkansas, is said to be a mile square *

A very extensive cemetery has been discovered in Bracken county, Kentucky, occupying nearly the whole of the "*bottom*" or plain, on the south bank of the Ohio, between Bracken and Turtle creeks  The village of Augusta has been built upon it in latter times  The following account of this cemetery was communicated to the author by Gen. John Payne, of Augusta.  It will be observed that iron was discovered in some of the graves; which demonstrates that a portion of the burials took place since communication was established between the whites and Indians, and very likely within the 18th century

" The beautiful bottom upon which it stands, extends from one creek to the other, about a mile and a half, and averaging about 800 yards wide  The town is laid off at the upper end of the bottom.  The hill back of it is high, but not precipitous , and upon arriving at the summit, it almost immediately falls towards the south with a gentle but deep descent, and immediately there rises another hill  I am thus particular, that you may have a knowledge of the ground where now rest the skeletons of hundreds, perhaps thousands, of an ancient race, as well as of the surrounding localities  The soil of the bottom-land is alluvial

" The village rests upon one vast cemetery : indeed, the whole bottom appears to have been a great burying-ground ; for a post-hole can hardly be dug in any part of it without turning up human bones, particularly within three or four hundred yards of the river bank.  The ground appears to have been thrown up into ridges, one end resting on the river bank, and the other extending out some two, others three hundred yards, with depressions between of about one hundred feet, the ridges rising to an elevation of about three feet, and are about fifty or sixty yards wide  These ridges are full of human skeletons *regularly buried*  My house, at the lower end of the village, stands upon one of these ridges . and in excavating a

---

* Accounts of a number of these ancient cemeteries are given by Gen Lewis Collins, in his recently published History of Kentucky, from which the following notices are condensed  Six miles N E of Bowling Green, Warren county, there is a cave which has a perpendicular descent of about thirty or forty feet.  At the bottom are vast quantities of human bones —(p 541 )  On the north bank of Green River, in the vicinity of Bowling Green, are a great many ancient graves , some of which are formed of stones set edgewise  A similar cemetery occurs near the mouth of Peter's creek, on Big Barren River, the bones are enclosed in stone coffins, which are about three feet long  and from one to one and a half wide  On the same river, three miles above Glasgow, and on Skegg's creek, five miles S W of the same place, are caves containing human bones , those in the last named cavern seem to be exclusively the bones of small children —(p 177 )  Similar caverns are found in Union and Meade counties, all of which are said to contain human bones in abundance

foundation for the basement story, seventy by sixty feet, and four feet deep, we exhumed one hundred and ten skeletons, numbered by the skulls, but there were several more, the skulls of which were so much decayed and intermingled with others that I did not take them into the calculation. I have no doubt that there were at least one hundred and forty bodies buried within the bounds above mentioned ; and then on every side the skeletons had been severed, a part taken away while the remains were left sticking in the wall  My garden, extending one hundred and fifty feet back from my house, is manured with human bones, and is very productive  I cannot turn up a spadefull of earth without disturbing the remains of the ancient dead.

"Those exhumed by me, I have said, appeared to have been regularly buried, they were about two feet below the surface generally, but some not more than a foot or eighteen inches, invariably with their heads toward the river—the river at this point running south 70° west ; some had rough unhammered stones extending on both sides the full length, with a head and foot stone, and a stone covering the head, others, again, would have only a stone on each side of the head, a head and foot stone, and a stone covering the head, others, only a head and foot stone, and others, and much the greatest number, had 'nothing to mark the ground where they were laid.'  Most of the bones were entire, but when exposed to the atmosphere, many soon crumbled into dust, though others remained quite firm  Several of the skulls, in a good state of preservation, I had in my house for months, until they were broken up  The teeth appeared sound: I do not recollect an instance of defective teeth, there were many absent teeth, but this evidently arose from their dropping out after burial.  There were some skeletons of children : the bones of those mouldered into dust almost immediately

"Many articles of Indian ornament, use, and warfare were excavated, such as arrow-heads of flint and bone, glass beads, and that peculiar kind of ancient Indian pottery, formed of clay and pulverized or pounded muscle-shells, which had evidently received the action of heat to harden it  Some of the specimens of the latter were very perfect, with well formed ears, like our pottery ware, some well formed, handsome stone pipes, glass beads, both black and blue, ornaments of bone, etc.  The other ridges, where they have been opened, have exhibited like results. they are full of human bones, apparently regularly buried, but the skeletons have not been always found to lie at right angles with the river, but sometimes parallel, and at other times diagonally  Upon this bottom, and covering these remains in 1792, when the bottom was first settled, stood some of the largest trees of the forest.  We have sycamores now standing on the bank, between these remains and the river, five feet in diameter at the stump

' There is another fact which perhaps I should mention  Maj Davis, who owned a farm on the Augusta bottom, about half a mile below the village, passing opposite his lands where a part of the bank had fallen into the river, discovered a bone sticking out of the bank, and upon drawing it out, it proved to be the bone of the right arm, and upon the wrist there were *three hammered iron rings.*  They were evidently of manufactured iron, round and formed to fit the wrist  the ends brought together but not welded or closed, the iron was destroyed,—it had been so

17

completely oxydized as to break very easily, the workmanship was rough, and the print of the hammer was upon them

"A full cart-load of bones, taken from the basement story of my house I had wheeled off into my garden over them I erected a mound, and crowned it with a summer-house, and there they shall rest for the future

"About forty years ago, Dr Overton, then of Lexington, was upon a visit to Augusta. I had heard of a large pile of stones upon the spur of a hill overlooking the Ohio, about three miles above. We went to visit it, worked hard nearly all day, and, at the depth of about five feet in the centre of the pile, found about a half bushel of charcoal and ashes; this was all that we could discover

"I know of no fortifications, nor of any mounds or tumuli, in the county of Bracken At Claysville. near the bank of Licking River, there is a very large mound; but I have not been informed that either curiosity or scientific research has induced the citizens to open it."

Cemeteries, analogous to those in Tennessee and Kentucky, as already observed, exist in Ohio. One, in the extreme northeastern part of the State, at Conneaut, on Lake Erie, covers about four acres. "It is in the form of an oblong square, and appears to have been laid out in lots running north and south, and exhibits all the order and propriety of arrangement deemed necessary to constitute Christian burial The graves are distinguished by slight depressions, disposed in straight rows, and were originally estimated to number from two to three thousand. Some were examined in 1800. and found to contain human bones, blackened by time, which, on exposure, crumbled to dust. On the first examination of the ground by the early settlers, they found it covered with a primitive forest. A number of mounds occur in the vicinity. The pioneers observed that the lands around this place exhibited signs of having once been thrown up in squares and terraces, and laid out in gardens."—(*How's Gaz. of Ohio*, p 40 )

A cemetery also occurs in Coshocton county, in the same state, which is described by Dr Hildreth of Marietta, in Silliman's Journal of Science and Art. It is situated a short distance below the town of Coshocton, on an elevated, gravelly alluvion; in 1830, it covered about ten acres The graves were arranged regularly in rows, with avenues between them, and the heads of the skeletons were placed to the west Traces of wood were observed around some of the skeletons, from which circumstance it is supposed the bodies were deposited in coffins The interments had evidently been what may be denominated *bone burials,* and were not made until after the decomposition of the flesh The graves, consequently, measure but little more than three feet in length, the bones being dismembered and packed upon each other, or flexed together, thus giving rise to the popular error of an aboriginal *pigmy race.* No relics are described as accompanying the human remains * Near this cemetery is a large mound

---

* It is said that in one of the graves were found pieces of oaken boards, together with some wrought iron nails If such were the fact the burial must have been made subsequent to the commencement of European intercourse It is possible that this was a burial of later date than the others

How far these cemeteries may be regarded as the depositories of the mound-builders, we are unprepared to say. Dr. Troost is disposed to regard the "pigmy graves" as of comparatively late origin, and distinguishes between them and the cemeteries of the more ancient race. He observes. Some consider these places as battle-grounds, and the graves, those of the slain, but that is not the case. The Indians do not bury fallen foes: they leave them to be devoured by wild animals, their own slain they carry to their towns, or hang up in mats, on trees. They have their burying festivals, when they collect the bones thus preserved, and bury them. In my opinion, the numerous small graves which are attributed to a race of pigmies, had this origin. I have opened numbers of them, and found them filled with mouldering bones, which, judging from the fragments, belonged to common sized men. The bones in these graves lay without order. This is not the case with the old extinct race, whose graves are much larger, the skeletons being generally stretched out. Nevertheless, I have found these also more or less doubled up."* It is extremely probable that the large cemeteries of Ohio, and those of Kentucky and Tennessee, had a common origin. The absence of stone coffins in the former may perhaps be ascribed to the greater difficulty of procuring stones for the purpose of constructing them. Quite a number of stone graves have, nevertheless, been found in Ohio, entirely corresponding in structure with those above described; all of which answer perfectly to the *cistvaen* or *kistvaen* of the British antiquaries.

It is the opinion of Dr. Morton, founded upon an examination of the human remains found in some of the "pigmy graves" of Tennessee, that "the so-called pigmies of the Western country were merely children, who, for reasons not readily explained, but which actuate some religious communities of our own time, were buried apart from the adult people of their tribe."—(*An Inquiry into the Distinctive Characteristics of the American Race*, p. 44.)

---

* Trans. Am. Ethnog. Soc., Vol I, p 358. Dr. Troost describes these graves as "rude fabrics, composed of rough flat stones (mostly a kind of slaty lime and sandstone, abundant in Tennessee). These were laid on the ground, in an excavation made for the purpose. upon them were put, edgewise, two similar stones of about the same length as the former, and two small ones were put at the extremities, so as to form an oblong box of the size of a man. When a coffin was to be constructed next to it, one of the side stones served for both, and consequently they lay in straight rows, in one layer only. I never found one above the other."

The vulgar notion of a pigmy race, founded upon the small size of some of the ancient stone graves, was for a time associated with another equally absurd. Some skulls of old persons were taken from those cemeteries, the teeth had been lost and the *alveolæ* obliterated, exposing the sharp edge of the jaw bone, whence it was inferred that the ancient pigmies were destitute of teeth, and had jaws like those of a turtle!

It has elsewhere been observed, " that the structure, not less than the form and position, of a large number of the aboriginal enclosures of the Mississippi valley, render it certain that they were designed for other than defensive purposes."— (*Ancient Monuments of the Mississippi Valley*, p 47 ) They are distinguished for their regularity most are circular, others are square or rectangular, and a few are elliptical or octagonal Sometimes these figures are combined in the same group While the defensive works for the most part occupy high hills and other commanding positions, and in their form correspond to the natural features of the ground upon which they are built, the sacred enclosures almost invariably occur upon the level river terraces, where the surface is least undulating The ditch, in the few instances where that feature is discovered, is, with rare exceptions, interior to the embankment, and, in procuring the material comprising the latter, great care seems to have been exercised by the builders to preserve the surface of the surrounding plain smooth and, as far as practicable, unbroken. The further fact that many of these regular works are commanded from neighboring eminences, not to mention the absence of supplies of water, seems conclusively to establish, that whatever may have been their secondary purposes, they were not primarily connected with any military system

It has also been observed that these enclosures contain mounds, evidently of sacred origin Some of them correspond in form with the ancient pyramidal temples of Mexico and Central America, and others cover altars upon which were offered the sacrifices prescribed by the aboriginal ritual

Upon the basis of these facts, it is assumed that the enclosures of the West, not manifestly defensive in their purposes, were in some way connected with the superstitions of their builders ; an assumption supported by the well known fact that the most imposing monuments of human labor and skill, in early times, were those which were erected under the influence of religious zeal

Proceeding upon this assumption, we next inquire what relations these works sustain to the sacred structures of the various aboriginal nations of this continent, and to those erected by the primitive nations of the Old World, and to what extent they may be regarded as indicating the religious beliefs and conceptions of their builders ?

## TEMPLES OF THE NORTH AMERICAN INDIANS

The temples of most of the North American Indian tribes were of the rudest character, and distinguished only by their greater size from the ordinary huts of

the natives.  The ground which they occupied was considered sacred, and an area
around them was sometimes enclosed and consecrated to religious rites.  Like the
religious structures of the Druids, they were usually places of deliberation and
council , within them the priests performed the ceremonies of their religion, and
within them the chiefs and warriors gathered to consult on public affairs, to make
war and conclude peace.  Within them also was maintained the sacred fire of
those nations which adhered to the requirements of sun-worship.  The Narragan-
sett Indians of New England, and the nations of Virginia, both kept up perpetual
fires in their temples, as did also the Natchez and the other tribes which assimilated
to the semi-civilized natives of Central America.—(*Purchas's Pilgrims*, IV., p 1868 ,
*McCulloch's Researches*, p 3 , *Loskiel*, p 39 , *Catlin's N A Indians*, Vol. I., pp
88, 158 )  Amongst the Natchez, these temples were sometimes decorated with
rude carvings and paintings, which probably were not without their significance

Berkley describes with some minuteness a *Quioccosan* or sacred building of
the Virginia Indians  It was constructed in precisely the same manner with their
cabins generally, but was somewhat larger  It was thirty feet long by eighteen
broad , and around and at some distance from it, were " set up posts, with faces
carved on them and painted "  The entrance was barricaded with logs , thus there
was neither window nor passage for the light, except the door.  In the centre of
the building was a fire-place, and near one end was suspended a partition of mats,
behind which, on shelves, were found three other mats, carefully rolled up  " In
one of them," says our author, " we found some bones, which we judged to be
the bones of men , in another we found some Indian tomahawks, finely graven and
painted , and in the third, some materials which, when put together, formed a rude
figure of a man, which was their *okee, kiwassee, Quioccos*, or idol "—(*Hist Virginia*,
p 166 )

Smith, in his description of Virginia, says, that " in every territory of a We-
rowance is a temple and a priest—two or three, or more "  He mentions also,
" upon the top of certain red sandy hills, great houses filled with images of their
kings and devils, and tombs of their predecessors.  Which houses are neere sixty
foot in length, built arborwise  This place they account so holy, that none but
priests or kings dare come into it, nor the savages dare not go up in boats by
it, but that they solemnly cast some pieces of copper, white beads, or pocones in
the river  In this place are commonly resident seven priests "—(*Smith in Purchas*,
Vol IV , p. 1701 )

Marchand mentions a temple among the natives of Coxe's Channel (N W
Coast), which had some relation to the primitive open temples of the Old World
" It is surrounded by strong posts, seven or eight feet high, in which are preserved
all the tall trees that are then growing ; but all the shrubs are carefully torn up,
and the ground is everywhere put in order and well beaten.  In the midst of this
enclosure, where a cave is sometimes made, is seen a square and uncovered edifice,
constructed with handsome planks, the workmanship of which is admirable , and
a stranger cannot behold without admiration that they are twenty-five feet in
length, by four in breadth, and two and a half inches in thickness "—(*Marchand's
Voy*, Vol I., p. 409 )  Vanegas states that there was a temple, in his day, at the

Island of St. Catherines, on the coast of California, which had a spacious level court, where the Indians performed their sacrifices  The place of the altar was a large circular space, with an enclosure of feathers of divers colors; and within the circle was an image strangely painted, representing some devil, according to the manner of the Indians of Mexico, holding in his hand the figures of the sun and the moon.—(*Vanegas's California*, Vol I, p. 105.)

Prince Maximilian has described to us the "Medicine lodge ' of the Minataree Indians, of which the subjoined engraving (Fig 36) is a plan  It is situated in the centre of the village, and consists of an elliptical space, one hundred and

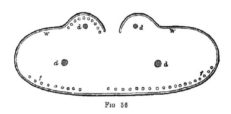

Fig 36

twenty feet in length, enclosed by a fence ten or twelve feet high, composed of reeds and poles somewhat inclining inwards  It has an entrance to the left; *d, d, d, d,* are four fires; and in the semi-elliptical recesses, the medicine men and elders of the tribe have their seats —(*Travels in America*, p 419.)  The place occupied by the spectators, is indicated by *f, f*  The Mandans had similar "medicine lodges,' except that they were circular in form  They had also a sacred area in the centre of their village  and within it was placed a shrine of high mystery. around which their religious dances were performed.

It would be profitless to inquire further into the character of the sacred edifices, "medicine lodges," or "council houses' of the hunter tribes.  It will be seen at once, that they reflect little if any light upon the structures under notice.

No sooner, however, do we pass to the southward, and arrive among the Creeks, Natchez, and affiliated Floridian tribes, than we discover traces of structures which, if they do not entirely correspond with the regular earth-works of the West, nevertheless seem to be somewhat analogous to them  These natives, it will be remembered, had made some slight advances in civilization  were agricultural in their habits, lived in considerable towns, had a systematized religion, and sustained many other resemblances to the semi-civilized nations of the continent.

Adair, in his account of these Indians, frequently mentions "*the Holy Square*" surrounding their temples, and within which their religious rites were performed  He does not, however, descend to particularize; and we are left to conjecture what were its dimensions, and how its boundaries were designated.  It must have been of considerable size, for he several times speaks of it as receiving an entire village or tribe, at the time of the great annual festivals  He is so absorbed, however, in his favorite theory, that he cannot describe any feature except by the name borne by its fancied counterpart among the Jews  So we are not surprised in finding, within "the Sacred Square," and standing near its western side, a *Sanctum Sanctorum*, or most holy place, enclosed by a mud-wall about breast high It was here that the consecrated vessels of earthen ware, conch-shells, etc., were deposited This sacred place, according to our authority, could not be approached by any but the *magi* or priests Indeed, so great a holiness attached to the sacred squares themselves, that it was believed if the great annual sacrifice were made elsewhere, it would not only be unavailable for the purposes required, but bring down the anger of the god to propitiate whose favor it was instituted, viz. the genial god, the god of almost universal adoration amongst rude people, the fountain of heat and light, the divine fire, *The Sun !* Within this square, at least at the time of the great festival, the women were not allowed to enter, nor those persons who had neglected to comply with certain prescribed purifying ceremonies, or who had been guilty of certain specified crimes

The deficiencies in Adair's account are supplied to a considerable extent by Bartram, in a MS. work on the Creek Indians, now in possession of Dr S. G. Morton, of Philadelphia. He not only describes the "public squares' alluded to by Adair, in which the religious ceremonies of the Indians were performed, and their deliberative councils held, but also communicates the interesting and important fact that they sometimes appropriated to their purposes the ancient enclosures and other monuments found in the country, and concerning the origin of which they professed no knowledge His account, apart from its bearings on the questions before us, has a general interest which justifies its insertion entire

"CHUNK YARDS.—The 'Chunk Yards' of the Muscogulges or Creeks, are rectangular areas, generally occupying the centre of the town The Public Square and Rotunda, or Great Winter Council House, stand at the two opposite corners of them They are generally very extensive, especially in the large, old towns. some of them are from six to nine hundred feet in length, and of proportionate breadth. The area is exactly level, and sunk two, sometimes three feet below the banks or terraces surrounding them, which are occasionally two in number, one behind and above the other, and composed of the earth taken from the area at the time of its formation These banks or terraces serve the purpose of seats for spectators In the centre of this yard or area there is a low circular mound or eminence, in the middle of which stands erect the 'Chunk Pole,' which is a high obelisk or four-square pillar declining upwards to an obtuse point.* This is of wood, the heart or inward resinous part of a sound pine tree, and is very durable ; it is generally from thirty to forty feet in height, and to the top is fastened some object which serves as a mark to shoot at, with arrows or the rifle, at certain appointed times. Near each corner of one end of the yard stands erect a less pole or pillar, about twelve feet high. called a 'slave post,' for the reason that to them are bound the captives condemned to be burnt These posts are usually

---

* This pole, it may here be observed, corresponds in position with certain erect stones found by Mr Stephens and other travellers, occupying the centre of the areas enclosed by the temples of Central America and Yucatan, and which, as will be seen in due time were undoubtedly *phallic* emblems

decorated with the scalps of slain enemies, suspended by strings from the top. They are often crowned with the white dry skull of an enemy.

"It thus appears that this area is designed for a public place of exhibition, for shows, games, etc. Formerly, there is little doubt, most barbarous and tragical scenes were enacted within them, such as the torturing and burning of captives, who were here forced to run the gaunlet, bruised and beaten with sticks and burning chunks of wood. The Indians do not now practise these cruelties; but there are some old traders who have witnessed them in former times. I inquired of these traders for what reason these areas were called ' *Chunk Yards ;*' they were in general ignorant, yet, for the most part, concurred in a lame story that it originated in the circumstance of its having been a place of torture, and that the name was but an interpretation of the Indian term designating them.*

"I observed none of these yards in use in any of the Cherokee towns; and where I have mentioned them, in the Cherokee country, it must be understood that I saw only the remains or vestiges of them among the ruins of ancient towns, In the existing Cherokee towns which I visited, although there were ancient mounds and signs of the yard adjoining, yet the yard was either built upon or turned into a garden plat, or otherwise appropriated. Indeed, I am convinced that the Chunk Yards now or lately in use among the Creeks are of very ancient date, and not the work of the present Indians; although they are now kept in repair by them, being swept very clean every day, and the poles kept up and decorated in the manner I have described.

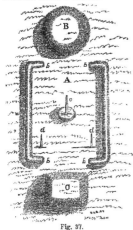

"The following plan, Fig. 37, will illustrate the form and character of these yards.

"A. The great area, surrounded by terraces or banks.

"B. A circular eminence, at one end of the yard, commonly nine or ten feet higher than the ground round about. Upon this mound stands the great *Rotunda, Hot House,* or *Winter Council House* of the present Creeks. It was probably designed and used by the ancients who constructed it, for the same purpose.

"C. A square terrace or eminence, about the same height with the circular one just described, occupying a position at the other end of the yard. Upon this stands the *Public Square.*

"The banks enclosing the yard are indicated by the letters *b, b, b, b; c* indicates the ' *Chunk Pole,*'

Fig. 37.

and *d, d,* the ' *Slave Posts.*'

---

* According to Adair, Du Pratz, and other writers, the Cherokees and probably the Creeks were much addicted to a singular game, played with a rod or pole and a circular stone, which was called *chungke*. Mr. Catlin describes this game as still existing under the name of " *Tchung-kee*," among the Minitarees

"Sometimes the square, instead of being open at the ends, as shown in the plan, is closed upon all sides by the banks  In the lately built or new Creek towns, they do not raise a mound for the foundation of their rotundas or public squares.  The yard, however, is retained, and the public buildings occupy nearly the same position in respect to it  They also retain the central obelisk and the slave posts.

### ARRANGEMENT OF THE PUBLIC BUILDINGS

"The following engraving, Fig 38, exhibits the most common plan or arrangement of the Chunk Yard, Public Square, and Rotunda, in the *modern* Creek towns

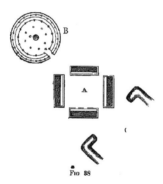

Fig 38

"A  The Public Square
"B  The Rotunda·  *a*, the entrance opening towards the square; the three circular lines show the rows of seats or rude sofas, the punctures show the posts or columns which support the building, *c*, the great central pillar, surrounded by the spiral fire which gives light to the edifice,*
"C. Part of the Chunk Yard.
"Within this Rotunda, they seem to keep the Eternal Fire, where it is guarded

and other tribes on the Missouri  It also prevailed among some of the Ohio Indians  It has been suggested that the areas called *chunk* or *chunky yards* by Bartram, derived their names from the circumstance that they were, amongst other objects, devoted to games, among which, that of the *chungke* was prominent  This suggestion derives some support from Adair, who says, " They have, near their State House, a square piece of ground, well cleared, and fine sand is strewn over it when requisite to promote a swifter motion to what they throw along it '—(*American Indians*, p 402)  It is therefore not improbable that these square areas were denominated *chungke* yards

* It is to be regretted that our author has not given the dimensions of the "Rotunda"  It would be interesting to know how it would compare, in that respect, with the small circles so common throughout the West,

18

by the priests   Within it the new fire is kindled on the occasion of the Feast of
the First Fruits   No woman is allowed to step within the Rotunda, and it is death
for any to enter   None but a priest can bring the sacred fire forth   The *spiral
fire* in the centre of the building is very curious   it seems to light up into a flame,
of itself, at the appointed time , but how this is done I know not.

THE PUBLIC SQUARE

"The Public Square of the Creeks consists of four buildings of equal size,
placed one upon each side of a quadrangular court.   The principal or Council
House, is divided transversely into three equal apartments, separated from each
other by a low clay wall   This building is also divided longitudinally into two
nearly equal parts , the foremost or front is an open piazza, where are seats for
the council   The middle apartment is for the king (*mico*), the great war chief,
second head man, and other venerable and worthy chiefs and warriors   The two
others are for the warriors and citizens generally.   The back apartment of this
house is quite close and dark, and without entrances, except three very low arched
holes or doors for admitting the priests   Here are deposited all the most valuable
public things, as the eagle's tail or national standard, the sacred calumet, the drums,
and all the apparatus of the priests.   None but the priests having the care of these
articles are admitted , and it is said to be certain death for any other person to
enter *

"Fronting this is another building, called the 'Banqueting House ,' and the edifices upon either hand are halls to accommodate the people on public occasions, as
feasts, festivals, etc   The three buildings last mentioned are very much alike, and
differ from the Council House only in not having the close back apartment

"The clay-plastered walls of the Creek houses, particularly of the houses comprising the Public Square, are often covered with paintings   These are, I think,
hieroglyphics or mystical writings, of the same use and purpose with those mentioned by historians to be found upon the obelisks, pyramids, and other monuments
of the ancient Egyptians   They are much after the same style and taste; and
though I never saw an instance of perspective or *chiaro-oscuro,* yet the outlines
were bold, natural, and turned to convey some meaning, passion, or admonition,
and they may be said to speak to those who can read them.   The walls are plas-

---

* This is probably the apartment designated by Adair as the *sanctum sanctorum.*   Du Pratz (p 351)
states that the temples of the Natchez were divided into two apartments, in the larger of which the eternal
fire was kept   "The inner apartment," he observes, ' was very dark, receiving no light except what
came in at the door   I could meet nothing here but two boards, on which were placed some things like
small toys, which I had not light to peruse "   These sacred inner rooms cannot fail to remind us of the
dark chambers of Palenque and Copan, within which Mr Stephens discovered the mystical tablets described
in his volumes on Central America   Nor is it difficult to trace a correspondence between the pictured walls
of these buildings, as described in the text, and the sculptured fronts and elaborately painted walls of the
Central American temples

tered very smooth with red clay, then the figures or symbols are drawn with white clay, paste, or chalk: if the walls are plastered with white clay, the figures are sketched in red, brown, or blueish paste.

"Almost all kinds of animals, sometimes plants, flowers, trees, etc, are depicted, also figures of men in various attitudes, some very ludicrous and even obscene In some instances, the *membrum generationis virile* is represented, but I saw no instance of indelicacy in a female figure. Men are often pictured with the head and other members of different kinds of animals, as the wolf, buck, hare, horse, buffalo, snake, duck, turkey, tiger, cat, crocodile, etc, etc All these animals, on the other hand, are depicted having the human head and other members, as also the head and members of other animals, so as to appear monstrous

### CREEK TOWNS AND DWELLINGS

"The general position of the Chunk Yard and Public Buildings of the Creeks, in respect to the dwellings of the Indians themselves, is shown in the following engraved plan:

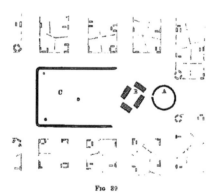

Fig 39

"A is the Rotunda, B, the Public Square, C, the grand area, or Chunk Yard The habitations of the citizens are placed with considerable regularity in streets or ranges, as indicated in the plan."*

The inference might not unreasonably be drawn, from Bartram's language, that the rectangular areas, surrounded by embankments, as also the square and circular

---

* "The dwellings of the Upper Creeks consist of little squares, or rather of four oblong houses enclosing a square area, exactly on the plan of the Public Square Every family, however, has not four of these houses some have but three, others not more than two, and some but one, according to the circumstances of the individual or the number of his family Those who possess four buildings have a particular use for

mounds above mentioned, were constructed by the Creeks. He, however, states explicitly, in his Travels. that the country in which these remains occur was occupied subsequently to the arrival of Europeans by the Cherokees, who were afterwards dispossessed by the Creeks; and that " it was probably, many ages preceding the Cherokee invasion, inhabited by a single nation or confederacy, governed by common laws, possessing like customs, and speaking the same language, but so ancient, that neither the Creeks nor the Cherokees, nor the nations they conquered, could render any account by whom or for what purposes these monuments were erected." He also inclines to the belief, that the uses to which these structures were appropriated, by the existing Indian tribes, were not widely different from those for which they were originally built. Upon this point he adds. " The mounds and large areas adjoining them seem to have been raised in part for ornament and recreation, and likewise to serve some other public purpose, since they are always so situated as to command the most extensive prospect over the country adjacent. The square terraces may have served as the foundations of fortresses, and perhaps the great pyramidal mounds answered the purpose of look-outs, or were high places for sacrifice "—(*Travels*, p. 518.)

From this account we gather the important fact, that in the centre of the Creek (as also of the Cherokee) towns was a " public square," surrounded by edifices devoted to public purposes, and that accompanying this square, and placed in a fixed position in respect to it, was an edifice, circular in form, which was more

---

each one serves for a cook room or winter lodging-house another as a summer lodging house and hall for visitors, and another for a granary or store-house, etc.

" The accompanying cut (Fig 40) illustrates the plan of the dwelling or villa of a Creek chief known

Fig. 40.

among the traders by the name of Bosten A is the area enclosed by four buildings the one upon the left, *e*, was his lodging house, and was large and commodious, the building opposite was a large, square, open pavilion, covered by a cedar roof, which was supported by two rows of posts or pillars Between each range of pillars was a platform, raised about two feet and ascended by two steps, this was covered with checkered mats of curious workmanship, woven of splints of canes variously colored In the centre of the pavilion was a square platform, raised somewhat higher than the others, and also covered with mats In this delightful, airy place, visitors were received and entertained The remaining two buildings were used, the one as a cook-house, the other as a store house

" The Lower Creeks, or Seminoles, are not so regular in their buildings, public or private The private houses of the Cherokees consist of one oblong log building, divided transversely into several apartments,

Fig. 41

with a portico in front a round house, D, stands a little distance off, and is used as a winter lodging house " especially dedicated to religious purposes, and within which was kept up the eternal fire. In some cases these structures, it seems, were elevated upon mounds.

Mr Payne, in his MSS, thus describes the great Council House of the Cherokees, which corresponds with the "Rotunda' mentioned by Bartram After remarking that it was near this that the dwellings of the *Uku* and head men of the tribe were erected, and that it was always situated in a town capable of accommodating a great number of people, he proceeds

"Every part bore a mystical reference to the sanctity with which they regarded the number *seven* Seven posts were set deep in the ground, equi-distant from each other, so as to form seven equal sides, though generally the roof, when it touched the ground, as it sometimes did was entirely circular. Upon the seven posts seven very long beams were so placed, as to rest one end on the ground, or periphery *raised two or three feet with earth*, while the other end stretched high in air, and all soon met at a point directly over the centre of the floor Other pieces of timber were fastened transversely to these, answering for ribs at first they were thatched with grass, and over it a layer of clay, surmounted with another layer of grass, so as to make it water-proof The external appearance of the entire building very much resembled an immense charcoal-pit There was an opening in the roof for the escape of the smoke The fire was in the centre Anciently, they say, this was the sacred fire handed down from above

"The Council House door was always on the eastern side directly toward the rising sun Before it was a portico. The seven posts which supported the house were so set, that one stood directly opposite the entrance, on the west side of the structure It was painted white, and had pins and shelves attached to it, on which were hung or laid all the holy things connected with their worship * * The space which was regarded as most sacred, was that immediately back of the seat of the *Uku*, near the white post already mentioned Among the sacred things kept here were the sacred arks, and smaller arks of clay for conveying the holy fire * * * Adjacent to the Council House, there was a large public square, the sides formed by four one-story structures The entrances at each corner were wide and open These structures were open in front like piazzas, and each one was partitioned off into several divisions, etc "

The embankment designating the outlines of the structure here described, may be regarded as throwing direct light upon the origin of the small circles so abundant in the valley of the Ohio

In the account of La Salle's last expedition to the mouth of the Mississippi, published by the Chevalier Tonti, we have a brief notice of the *Taencas* or Tenzas, from which the following interesting passages, relating to the questions before us, are extracted.

"As the first village of the *Taenca* stands on the other side of a lake which is eight leagues in circumference, and half a league over, we were forced to take a canoe to cross it As soon as we landed, I was surprised to see the grandeur of the village, and the order of the cottages; they are placed in divers rows, and in a straight line, round about a large space, being all made of earth and covered over with mats of cane We presently took notice of two, fairer than the rest, one of which was the prince's palace, and the other the temple. Each of them was forty feet square, and the walls ten feet high and two feet thick, the roof in the form of a cupola, and covered with a mat of divers colors. * * * As to their religion, the prince told me that they worship the sun; that they had their temples, their altars, and their priests. That in their temple there was a fire which burned perpetually, as the proper emblem of the sun. That at the decrease of the moon, they carried a great dish of their greatest dainties to the door of the temple, as an oblatory sacrifice; which the priests offered to their God, and then carried it home and feasted themselves therewith. * * * The next day I had the curiosity to see their temple, and the old gentleman led me thither The structure of it was exactly the same with that of the prince's house. *As to the outside, it is encompassed with a great high wall, the space betwixt that and the temple forming a kind of court where people may walk* On the top of the wall were several pikes to be seen, upon which were stuck the heads of their own most notorious criminals, or of their enemies On the top of the frontispiece, there is a great knob raised, all covered round with hair, and above that a heap of scalps, in the form of a trophy * * The inside of the temple is only a *Nave*, painted on all sides, at top with all sorts of figures, in the midst of it is a hearth raised in the form of an altar, upon which there is burning continually three great billets of wood, standing up on end, and two priests, dressed in white vestments, are ever looking after it to make up the fire and supply it It is round this the people come to say their prayers with strange kind of hummings The prayers are three times a day at sunrise, at noon, and at sunset. They made me take notice of a sort of closet cut out of the wall, the inside of which was very fine I could only see the roof of it, on the top of which there hung a couple of spread eagles, which looked towards the sun * I wanted to go in, but they told me it was the tabernacle of their God, and that it was permitted to none but their high priest to go in. And I was told it was the repository of their wealth and treasures, as jewels, gold and silver, precious stones, and some goods that came out from Europe, which they had from their neighbors.—(*La Salle, Trans. N Y. Hist. Soc*, Vol. II, pp. 269, 272.)

THE TEMPLES OF MEXICO, CENTRAL AMERICA, AND PERU

The pyramidal temples of the Aztecs, which perhaps better deserve the name of altars, or the scriptural name of " high places," were always surrounded by large enclosures, most usually of a square form. The great temple of Mexico, which is described by all the early authors as nearly identical in form and structure with all the principal temples of Anahuac, consisted first of an immense square area, " surrounded by a wall of stone and lime, eight feet thick, with battlements, ornamented with many stone figures in the form of serpents " The extent of this enclosure, which occupied the centre of the ancient city, may be inferred from the

---

* Adair speaks of " cherubimical figures in the Synhedria" of the Muscogulges or Creeks —(p 30 )

assertion of Cortez, that it might contain a town of five hundred houses. It was paved with polished stones, so smooth, says Bernal Diaz, that "the horses of the Spaniards could not move over them without slipping." The four walls of this enclosure corresponded with the cardinal points, and gateways opened midway upon each side, from which, according to Gomera, led off broad and elevated avenues or roads—(*Purchas*, Vol III, p. 1133) In the centre of this grand area rose the great temple, an immense pyramidal structure of five stages, faced with stone, three hundred feet square at the base, and one hundred and twenty feet in height, truncated, with a level summit, upon which were situated two towers, the shrines of the divinities to which it was consecrated. It was here the sacrifices were performed and the eternal fire maintained. One of these shrines was dedicated to Tezcatlipoca, the other to Huitzlipochtli, which divinities sustained the same relation to each other, in the Mexican mythology, as Brahma and Siva in that of the Hindus. Both are the same god, under different aspects, and with the God of the Rain, Tlaloc, constitute a Triad, almost identical with that which runs through all the mythologies of the East.

Besides this great pyramid, according to Clavigero, there are forty other similar structures, of smaller size, consecrated to separate divinities, one was called *Tezcacalli*, "House of the Shining Mirrors," which was covered with brilliant materials, and sacred to *Tezcatlipoca*, the God of Light, the Soul of the World, the Vivifier, the Spiritual Sun, another to *Tlaloc*, the God of Water, the Fertilizer; another to *Quetzalcoatl*, said to have been the God of the Air, whose shrine was distinguished by being circular, "even," says Gomera, "as the winds go round about the heavens. for that consideration made they his temple round"

Besides these, there were the dwellings of the priests (amounting, according to Zarate, to 5,000) and of the attendants in the temples, and seminaries for the instruction of youth; and, if we are to credit some accounts, houses of reception for strangers who came to visit the temple and see the grandeur of the court, ponds and fountains, groves and gardens, in which flowers and "sweet smelling herbs" were cultivated for use in certain sacred rites, and for the decoration of the altars. "And all this," says Solis, "without retracting so much from that vast square but that eight or ten thousand persons had sufficient room to dance in, upon their solemn festivals" The area of this temple was consecrated ground; and it is related of Montezuma, that he only ventured to introduce Cortez within its sacred limits after having consulted with and received the permission of the priests, and then only on the condition, in the words of Solis, that the conquerors "should behave themselves with respect." The Spaniards having exhibited, in the estimation of Montezuma, a want of due reverence and ceremony, he hastily withdrew them from the temple, while he himself remained to ask the pardon of his Gods for having permitted the impious intrusion

There is a general concurrence in the accounts of this great temple given by the early authorities, among whom are Cortez, Diaz, and others, who witnessed what they described. They all unite in presenting it as a type of the multitude of similar structures which existed in Anahuac. Their glowing descriptions, making due allowance for the circumstances under which they wrote, are sustained by the imposing ruins of Cholula, Papantla, Mitla, Xoxachalco, Misantla, Quemada, and the thousand other monuments which are yet unrecorded by the antiquary, and which invest every sierra and valley of Mexico with an interest hardly less absorbing than that which lingers around the banks of the Nile.

From the number of these religious structures, we gather some idea of the predominance of Mexican superstitions.  Sohs speaks of eight temples in the city of Mexico, of nearly equal grandeur with that above described, and estimates those of smaller size to amount to two thousand in number, "dedicated to as many idols of different names, forms, and attributes"  Torquemada estimates the number of temples in the Mexican empire at *forty thousand*, and Clavigero places the number far higher   "The architecture," he adds, " of the great temples was for the most part the same with that of the great temple of Mexico, but there were many likewise of a different structure, composed of a single body in the form of a pyramid, with a staircase, etc "  Gomera says, " they were almost all of the same form; so that what we shall say of the principal temple, will suffice to explain all the others."  Cortez, in a letter to Charles V, dated October 30, 1520, states that he counted four hundred of these pyramidal temples at Cholula

From all sources we gather that the principal temples, or rather sacred places of Mexico, consisted of large square areas, surrounded by walls, with passages midway at their sides, from which sometimes led off avenues or roads, and that within these enclosures were pyramidal structures of various sizes, dedicated to different divinities, as also the residences of the priests, with groves, walks, etc.

Proceeding to Central America, we still find, so far as we are informed concerning the remains of these countries, the sacred enclosure and the pyramidal temple.   The enclosure surrounding the sacred edifices of Tuloom, already described in another connection (page 98), was most probably the consecrated ground of the ancient inhabitants   Its rectangular form and the position of its gateways go far to connect it with the corresponding structures of Mexico and the United States   Grijalva, the first discoverer of Yucatan, alluding perhaps to these very structures of Tuloom, "saw several places of worship and temples, wide at the bottom and hollow at the top, stately stone buildings, at the foot of which was an enclosure of lime and stone."   Del Rio assures us that the principal structures, the temples, of Palenque, were placed in " the centre of a rectangular area, three hundred yards in breadth, and four hundred and fifty in length "  Assuming the word " yard " to be a translation of the Spanish *vara*, which is thirty-three inches in length, we have the dimensions of this area, 825 by 1240 feet.  Herrara relates, concerning the building of the town of Mayapan, by the ancient inhabitants of Yucatan

" 'They pitched upon a spot, eight leagues from the place where Merida now stands, and fifteen from the sea, where they made an enclosure of about half a quarter of a league [on each side?], being a wall of dry stone with only two gates They built temples, calling the greatest of them *Cuculcan*, and near to the enclosure the houses of the prime men   *   *   It was afterwards ordered that, since the *enclosure was only for the temples*, the houses of the people should be built round about ' —(*Herrara*, Vol. IV., p 162.)

The accounts which we possess of the ancient religious structures of Peru, although glowing with admiration of their splendor and riches, are yet extremely vague as respects their plan of construction. Enough, however, is easily gathered to assure us that they consisted of large consecrated courts or areas, like those of Mexico, in which the temples proper were situated, together with fountains, gardens, and the residences of the priests.

The great Temple of the Sun at Cuzco, in the description of which the early Spaniards have expended every superlative of their language, consisted of a principal building and several chapels and inferior edifices, covering a large extent of ground, in the heart of the city, and completely encompassed by a circular wall, which, with the edifices, was constructed of stone. Aqueducts opened within this sacred enclosure; and within it were gardens, and walks among shrubs and flowers of gold and silver, made in imitation of the productions of nature. It was attended by four thousand priests. "The ground" says La Vega, "for two hundred paces around the temple was considered holy, and no one was allowed to pass within this boundary but with naked feet." Nor even under these restrictions were any permitted to enter, except of the blood of the Incas, in whom were centred the priestly and civil functions of the government.

Besides the great Temple of the Sun, there was a large number of inferior temples in Cuzco, estimated by Herrara at three hundred. Numerous other temples are scattered over the empire, all of which seem to have corresponded very nearly in structure with that already described. The most celebrated temple in Peru, next to that of Cuzco, was situated on an island in Lake Titicaca, where it was believed Manco Capac first made his appearance on earth. The whole surface of the island was considered sacred. The Temple of Pachacamac is described as being enclosed by walls, and to have "more resembled a fortress than a temple." According to Roman, "the temples of Peru were built upon high grounds or the tops of hills, and were surrounded by four circular embankments of earth, one within the other. The temple stood in the centre of the enclosed area, and was quadrangular in form."

A structure, corresponding very nearly with this description, is noticed by Humboldt, who denominates it, in accordance with local traditions, *Ingapilca*, "House of the Incas," and supposes it to have been a sort of fortified lodging-place of the Incas, in their journeys from one part of the empire to the other. It is situated at Cannar, and occupies the summit of a hill. The "citadel" is a very regular oval, the greatest axis of which is 125 feet, and consists of a wall, built of large blocks of stone, rising to the height of sixteen feet. Within this oval is a square edifice, containing but two rooms, which resembles the ordinary stone dwellings of the present day. Surrounding these is a much larger circular enclosure, which, from the description and plate, we infer is not far from five hundred feet in diameter. This series of works possesses few military features, and it seems most likely that it was a temple of the sun. This opinion is confirmed by the fact that, at the base of the hill of Cannar was formerly a famous shrine of the Sun, consisting of the universal symbol of that luminary formed by nature upon the face of a great rock. Humboldt himself admits an apparent dependence between this shrine and

19

the structures above described —(*Humboldt's Res.*, Vol, pp. 242, 248, fol plates, No. 17 ) Ulloa describes an ancient Peruvian temple situated on a hill near the town of Cayambe, perfectly circular in form, and open at the top It was built of unburnt bricks, cemented together with clay.—(*Ulloa*, Vol I., p 486.)

TEMPLES OF POLYNESIAN ISLANDERS HINDUS, ETC

Enclosures ruder in construction, yet nevertheless analogous in form and identical in purpose with those here described, were found among the Polynesian Islanders The area of their temples was frequently a square or parallelogram, protected by stone walls, within which were pyramidal structures, sometimes of great size. One of these, within the great enclosure of *Atehuru*, was two hundred and seventy feet long, by ninety-four feet broad, and fifty feet high, flat on the summit, which was reached by a flight of steps, much after the manner of the Mexican Teocalli. Within the sacred area, and at the base of these pyramidal structures, the idols were placed and their altars erected Here also were the dwellings of the priests and of the keepers of the idols. The trees and other objects within the walls were sacred —(*Ellis's Polynesian Researches*, Vol. I, p 340 ) In some instances, instead of an unbroken wall, the sacred area was indicated by a series of pyramidal heaps of stones, placed at intervals, so as to constitute the leading points of a square, within which was placed the temple proper. The ruins of a temple of this kind, called *Kaih*, still exist in the island of Hawaii.—(*U S. Exploring Exped.*, Vol IV, p 100.)

When we extend our inquiries to the eastern shores of the old continent, we find in India the almost exact counterparts of the religious structures of Central America analogies furnishing the strongest support of the hypothesis which places the origin of American semi-civilization in southern Asia. A close and critical comparison of these monuments, in connection with the systems of religion to which they were respectively dedicated, and the principles which governed their erection, may lead to most interesting and important results.

In another connection, some of the more obvious analogies will be pointed out; with no view, however, of establishing dependencies, but for the purpose of illustration and elucidation. It is sufficient for our present objects to remark, that the temples of India and of the islands of the Indian seas, both of modern and ancient date, are constructed and enclosed in like manner with those already described The consecrated area is sometimes of vast extent, equalling if not exceeding in this respect the largest of those which existed in Mexico These enclosures are square, and usually have their entrances corresponding to the cardinal points. " The general style of these buildings," says Bishop Heber, "is a large square court, sometimes merely surrounded by a low brick wall, with balustrades, indented at the top, with two or sometimes four towers at the angles In the centre of the principal front is, for the most part, an entrance, often very handsome. In the middle of the quadrangle, or in the middle of one of its sides opposite the main entrance, is a pyramid, which is the temple of the principal deity. The structure is sometimes octagonal, but mostly square."—(*Heber's Travels*, Vol I., Chap 3) "Sometimes a number of temples are built within this sacred area One at Chanchra, in Jesson, has twenty-one temples, and one thousand acres of ground" —(*Ward*, Vol. III, p 230) The Pagoda of Seringham is one of the most magnificent in India. It stands on an island in the river *Careri*, in the dominions of the Rajah of Tanjore Seven square enclosures, formed by walls twenty-five feet high, four feet thick, and three hundred and fifty feet distant from each other, enclose a court in the centre, in which are sacred pyramidal structures, the abodes of the gods of the Hindu pantheon, and among them the sanctuary of the Supreme Vishnu These various deities are believed really to animate their respective pyramids or shrines Four large gates, one in the middle of each side, each surmounted by a tower, are the entrances to the several courts. The outer wall is four miles in circumference. The number of the enclosures has a symbolical signification, and refers to the several regions into which the Universe, the abode of the gods, was supposed to be divided, according to the theory of the age in which the structure was built —(*Dudley's Naology*, p 104, *Colman's Mythology of the Hindus*, p 157, *Maurice's Indian Antiquities*, Vol III, pp 13, 50) The great temple of Jaggenath, at Orissa, the general resort of all Hindu sects, is regarded as possessing such exceeding sanctity. that the earth for twenty miles round is considered holy The most sacred spot is an enclosed area about six hundred and fifty feet square, which contains the temples of the idol and his sister, surrounded by fifty lesser temples, all of pyramidal form —(*Colman's Myth. of the Hindus*, p 52)

In the Island of Java are the remains of many ancient temples, of similar character and construction A large number of these, designated as the ruins of Prambanai, exist in the district of Pajang. One of the most perfect of the groups occurring here is termed by the natives "the Thousand Temples" The group occupies a rectangular area six hundred feet long and five hundred and fifty feet broad, and consists of four rows of small pyramidal structures. enclosing a court, in which is placed a large pyramidal edifice. The whole is surrounded by a wall, having entrances midway on each side Some of these groups are disposed in squares of greater or less dimensions, but all have a common character —(*Crawford's Indian Archipelago*, Vol II, p 196; *Asiatic Researches, Calcutta*, Vol XIII.) There are also single temples of like form, occasionally of great size, and generally surrounded by a series of enclosures

The religious edifices and pyramidal shrines of the Japanese are described by Kæmpfer as "sweetly seated" in the midst of large square enclosures, approached by spacious avenues, and embracing within their walls springs, groves, and pleasant walks "The empire," observes our authority, "is full of these temples, and their priests are without number Only in and about Miaco, they count nearly 4,000 temples and 37,000 priests "—(*Kæmpfer's Japan*, Vol. II., p 416)

These examples might be greatly multiplied, so as to extend the chain of analogies quite around the globe. Passing, however, over the intermediate space, we come at once to the British Islands.

The British Islands, and the portion of the continent adjacent to them, abound
in ancient monuments, closely allied to those under consideration    They have
been very accurately investigated and described by Camden, Borlase, Douglas,
Hoare, Cunnington, Higgins, Deane, and numerous others, and the world is familiar
with their character.    The researches of these investigators have directed upon
them all the lights of erudition    Availing ourselves at once of the results of their
labors, we apply them to the elucidation of the mysterious monuments of our own
country

The analogies which exist between one class of ancient British remains and a
corresponding class of American structures, have already been briefly pointed out
There is, however, another large division, more numerous and more interesting
than these, of widely different form and manifestly different design    These consist, for the most part, of circular structures, of greater or less dimensions, composed of earth or of upright stones placed at short distances apart.    These circles
are sometimes of great size, embracing many acres of ground, but most are of
moderate dimensions, corresponding in this as generally in other respects with
those of this country    They are regarded by all well informed British antiquaries
as religious in their origin, and connected with the ancient Druidical system.    This
conclusion is not entirely speculative, but rests in a great degree upon traditional
and historical facts.    Borlase observes, "The grandeur of design, the distance of
the materials, the tediousness with which all such massive works are erected, all
show that they were the fruits of peace and religion"    "That they were erected,"
says Hoare, "for the double purpose of civil and religious assemblies, may be
admitted without controversy    They were public edifices, constructed according
to the rude fashion of the times, and at a period when the Deity was worshipped
in the most simple and primitive manner, under the open canopy of heaven."—
(*Ancient Wiltshire*, Vol. II., p. 122.)    Cæsar, writing of the Druids, is understood
to allude to their sacred structures in the following terms.    "*Druides, certo anni
tempore, considunt in* LOCO CONSECRATO    *Huc omnes undique qui controversias habent
conveniunt, eorumque judiciis decretisque parent*"—(*Cæsar, de Bello Gallico*, Lib. VI.)
"Once a year the Druids assemble at a *consecrated place*.    Hither such as have
suits depending flock from all parts, and submit implicitly to their decrees"    It
need not be added, that the Druids were priests and judges, the expounders of
religion and the administrators of justice, they were entrusted with the education
of youth, and taught the motions of the stars, the magnitude of the earth, the
nature of things, and the dignity and power of the gods.    They officiated at sacrifices and divinations, they decided controversies, punished the guilty, and rewarded
the virtuous.    Their power was superior to that of the nobles, over whom they
wielded the terrors of excommunication from a participation in the imperative rites
of their religion    They centred in themselves the occult learning of the day,

which seems to have been closely allied to that of Phœnicia, if not, indeed, mainly derived from the East.

" The sacred places of the Druids were enclosed sometimes with a fence of palisades, and sometimes with a mound of earth, or with stones, to keep off the profane, and prevent all irreverent intrusion upon their mysteries.* Tacitus relates that the early Germans considered their groves and woods as sacred : these spots were consecrated to pious uses, and the holy recess took the name of the divinity who filled the place, and whose sanctuary was never permitted to be seen but with reverence and awe.   Agreeable to this was the early practice of the Britains, who, according to the same authority, used similar customs with the Germans."—(*Germania*, C. ix. and C. xl.)   In the form of their temples, the Druids, for the most part, adopted the circle; and the generally received opinion is, that all *circular monuments* were originally intended for devotional purposes.

There are some earth-works in the British Islands, which were clearly not defensive, but yet are rectangular.   To these, authors have hesitated in ascribing a date.   One of the most singular of these, which corresponds very nearly with that discovered near Tarlton, Pickaway county, Ohio (*Ancient Monuments of the Mississippi Valley*, Plate XXXVI., No. 1), occurs upon Banwell Hill, county of Wilts, England.   The accompanying engraving (Fig. 42) is reduced from the plan given

Fig. 42.

by Sir R. C. Hoare, who notices it briefly as follows : " Before quitting this interesting eminence, I must not omit to take notice of a very singular little earth-work, situated towards the village of Banwell.   Its form proclaims it to be Roman ; but I cannot conceive to what use it was destined.   The embankment enclosing the cross is two hundred and thirty yards in extent, and encloses nearly three-quarters of an acre."—(*Ancient Wiltshire*, Vol. II.; *Roman Era*, p. 43.)   There is certainly a most striking coincidence ; yet it is one which it would be unsafe to regard as any other than accidental.

It may not be wholly inappropriate to mention that some of the most ancient temples of India are built in the form of a cross ; such is the shape of the great

---

* Salopia Antiqua, p. 10.  Hermoldus, in his Chronicon de Rebus Salivæ, says that the Sclavonians prevented all access to their groves and fountains, which they considered would become desecrated by the entrance of Christians.   They had their sacred oaks, which they surrounded by a fence of wicker-work. The *tabooed* palms and other trees of the Marquesas and South Sea Islanders are protected from profane contact in a like manner.

temple at Benares, and that at Mathura At the intersection of the four arms rises a lofty dome Such also is the shape of the subterranean temple of New Grange, in Ireland —(*Tavernier* Vol III, pp 30, 47; *Faber's Pag. Idol.*, Vol. III., p. 287, *Higgins's Celtic Druids*, p. 40.)

The circular form is certainly best adapted for the reception of the devotees desiring to see and hear, or to participate in parts of the sacrificial rites practised within them But it is claimed, and upon an array of evidence which will admit of no dispute, that the form of the primitive temple was, with great uniformity, that of the symbol of the religion to which it was consecrated, or of the god to whose worship it was dedicated

The circle is the uniform symbol of the sun, alike among the most savage as the most enlightened nations, and the fact that most of the ancient religious structures of the British islands are of that form, would seem to imply that the god of Celtic adoration was symbolized as the Sun, and that the ancient Celtic religion was a modification of what is usually termed sun or fire worship This implication is sustained by abundant evidence, into which it is impossible. as it would be out of place, to enter here. We have every reason for believing that the objects of the Druidical worship were identical with those of the followers of Baal, (the Sun).* Like them, the Druids were addicted to the study of the heavens, and in the same way they offered up sacrifices to Baal. Bel, Belus, Belinus, Moloch, Apollo, or the Sun The connection of Druidism with the name of Baal, is well known in the lines of Ausonius—himself a Druid—who writes.

> " Tu Baiocassis stirpe Druidum satus,
> Si fama non fallit fidem,
> Belini sacratum ducis e templo genus "

Cæsar says the Gauls worshipped Apollo the Gauls were followers of the Druidic rites according to the same authority.

·

## SYMBOLISM OF TEMPLES

The rationale of symbolism, as connected with temples, next claims our attention Not only was the doctrine of occasional presence of universal acceptance amongst the followers of every early religious system, but they believed that the gods made temples and sacred structures their places of constant abode. Their presence, in some instances, was supposed actually to animate their shrines, and

---

* Salopia Antiqua, p 7 The evidence upon this point, as remarked in the text, is alike abundant and conclusive The Phœnicians, who undoubtedly penetrated into the British islands at a very early day, introduced many of their own habits and superstitions They were the carriers of customs and opinions, as of wares, and dispensed the seeds both of African and Asiatic idolatry in Europe This conclusion is sustained not only by the striking resemblance between many of the religious rites of the ancient Celts and those of Assyria and Egypt, but by etymological evidences of a most positive character —(*Thackeray's Ancient Britain*, Vol I, pp 10, 14 also *Introduction to Ancient Wiltshire*, and *Higgins's Celtic Druids*, ubi supra )

to consecrate the earth around them. The Jews were assured that Jehovah dwelt between the emblematic cherubim. In the hope of rendering his homage in the actual presence of his God, the Mohammedan pilgrim makes his weary journey to Mecca, and the Hindu devotee seeks, from the remotest provinces, the shrine of Jaggenath. The same idea of a living presence is manifested in the superstition of the savage, who regards every remarkable tree, rock, cave, spring, or stream, as the evidence or actual impersonation of a divinity, and renders his homage in accordance with his belief.

The presence of the gods was formerly supposed to be favorable, and powerfully conducive, if not indispensably necessary, to the prosperity of cities and nations; and as such was ever desired and ever a cause of joy and exultation. The poet Horace addresses the goddess Venus in terms significant of the benefits resulting from her presence.

> ' O Goddess in blest Cyprus dwelling,
> And Memphis wanting of Sithonian snow '"

So, too, Homer alludes to the celestial mountain of Greece.

> " Olympus famed, the safe abode of gods,
> By winds is never vexed, nor drenched with rain
> Snow falls not, but the cloudless arch serene
> Widely expands with brightness ever clear "

Influenced by opinions such as these, we can readily understand how the temple might take the symbolical form of the god to whose worship it was dedicated, thereby being made more acceptable as his abode, at the same time that its form proclaimed his presence. Sallust, in his treatise on the Gods and the World, illustrates this ancient doctrine in the following words: "As the providence of the gods is everywhere extended, a certain habitude or fitness is all that is necessary in order to receive their beneficent communications. But all habitude is produced through imitation and similitude; and hence temples imitate the heavens, but altars the earth; statues resemble life, and on this account are similar to animals, etc."*

The earth, remarks an ingenious writer, being regarded as God by a large portion of the heathen world, any structure bearing that form might justly be considered as a symbol of the Deity, indicative of his power and his presence. The

---

* The Pantheon at Rome was dedicated to all the gods, who instead of rude shrines consecrated to each, as in the great temple of Mexico, had their statues placed within the vast rotunda. The great concave dome, we are expressly told by Pliny, was designed to represent the vault of Heaven, 'quod forma ejus convexa fastigiatam cœli similitudinem ostenderet.' Yet it seems to have been eminently a temple of the solar Apollo, whose colossal image was placed immediately in front of the entrance, the first and most imposing object which met the eye of the spectator.— (See Faber, Pagan Idolatry, Vol III, p 284, Maurice, Ind Antq Vol III, p 185) Mr Dudley, who claims that the circle and the square were the symbols of the reciprocal powers of nature, assumes that the circular Pantheon, with its quadrangular portico was intended to signify the union of the two principles or powers —(Naology, p 390)

import of the symbol caused the conviction and assurance that all sacred structures ought, of necessity, to be constructed in its form —(*Dudley on Symbolism*, p 43.)

This conviction seems to have prevailed among the Hebrews : the " Ark of the Covenant," in which were deposited the tables of the law, was essentially symbolical in its form  The form of the Tabernacle in the wilderness, and of the great temple on Mount Zion, we may infer, was regarded as a matter of importance, from the specific directions given for their construction.  And the primitive Christians, we are assured, were in a like manner influenced in the form of their sacred edifices *

Vesta, in the later mythologies, was the igneous element personified; her globular temple on the banks of the Tiber represented, we are told, the Orb of the Earth, cherished and made prolific by the central fire —(*Maurice, Ind Antq*, Vol. III., p 130 )  The reason for the obicular or oval form of her temple was recognised in Ovid's day   He writes

> ' What now is roofed with brass, was then of straw,
> And the slight osier formed the wattled wall
> This spot, that now the fane of Vesta bears,
> The palace was of Numa, king unshorn
> 'Tis said the form is now, as erst of old ,
> And the true reason may be well approved
> Vesta and Earth are one   A ceaseless fire
> Burns in them both, and both alike pervades
> The earth  a globe supported on no prop,
> Hangs, heavy weight  in all-subjected air "
>
> Ovid, Fast, Lib  VI , 261

Plutarch alludes, in similar terms, to the symbolical significance of the form of this temple   " Numa built a temple of orbicular form, for the preservation of the sacred fire; intending by the *fashion* of the edifice to shadow out, not so much the earth, or Vesta considered in that character, as the *whole universe ;* in the centre of which the Pythagoreans placed fire, and which they called Vesta and Unity."†

---

* " In respect to the form and fashion of their churches it was for the most part oblong, to keep (say some, vide *Consist Apost* L ii , C 57) the better correspondence with the fashion of a ship , the common notion or metaphor by which the church was wont to be represented "—( *Cave's Prim  Christianity*, p 65 )

† *Plutarch, de Iside et Osiride*  M Ramée has well expressed this idea in his " *Histoire Generale de l'Architecture*," from which we translate the following passage

" Among all the people of antiquity, intimately connected with the idea of God, was that of the Earth as his habitation, and Heaven as his eternal home   The universe, and especially the visible heavens, was for this reason considered as a true Temple of the Divinity, built by Himself, and was held as the primitive Temple, to be taken as a model, as the type of all temples to be raised by the hand of man   It was, therefore, considered unworthy of God and contrary to the idea held of Him, to erect sanctuaries to the Supreme Being on the same plan as the houses which man built for himself as a shelter and protection against the changes of the seasons   A habitation for God, it was thought, should resemble the Universe , and for that reason it would bear a divine character, and the Divinity would therein be, as it were, at home   Hence the construction of temples was regarded, in all antiquity, as a religious or hieratic art, the inventors and masters of which, at first, were the gods themselves "

The notions already alluded to as influencing the *forms* of temples, controlled also the choice of their position, the nature of their materials, and, when they were advanced from their primitive rudeness, the character of their ornaments The crescent crowns the minaret of the Mohammedan, the symbolic trident of Siva, the dome consecrated to his worship, and the cross, in like manner, designates the church of the Christian   The significance of the trident is not less obvious to the Hindu, than that of the crescent to the Turk, or the symbol of his religion to the Christian, yet to the stranger to each, they would possess no higher value than might attach to them in their character of ornaments

Were it necessary to our purpose, the illustrations of the various points here indicated might be greatly extended   Enough has, however, been said to place in a plausible light the fact (which probably no one would be disposed to deny), that the form of the primitive temple was, to an eminent degree, symbolical.  In the words of Deane, " The figure of the temple, in almost every religion with which we are acquainted, is the hierogram of its God   The hierogram of the sun was always a circle   the temples of the sun were *circular.*  The Arkites adored the personified ark of Noah   their temples were built in the form of a *ship*   The Ophites adored a serpent deity   their temples assumed the form of a *serpent*   And to come home to our own times and feelings, the Christian retains a remnant of the same idea when he builds his temples in the form of a *cross,* the cross being at once the symbol of his creed, and the hierogram of his God "—(" *Observations on Dracontia, by Rev J B Deane, British Archæologia,* Vol XXV, p 191 )

It is the fact that the religious conceptions, the philosophy and physical speculations of the ancients, exerted a controlling influence upon the construction of their sacred edifices, that invests those monuments with interest, not only as works of art, but as illustrations of man's primitive beliefs,—his notions of cosmogony, and his philosophy of the earth and heavens   " On every review." observes an eminent author, " and from every region, accumulated proofs arise, how much more extensively than is generally supposed the designs of the ancients in architecture were affected by their speculations in astronomy, and by their mythological reveries."— (*Maurice, Ind Antiq*, Vol III, p 199 )

Having already taken this brief survey of the character of the various primitive religious structures of various parts of the world, and having indicated the principles upon which those with the origin of which we are acquainted, sustaining the closest analogy to those of our own country, were constructed, we return with new aids to the investigation of the latter

As has already been several times observed, the aboriginal temples. or rather sacred enclosures. of the Mississippi valley are nearly all of regular figures, usually circular or elliptical, sometimes square or rectangular, exhibiting in this respect, as also in their manner of combination, a uniformity which could only result from a fixed and well recognised design   Nothing can be more obvious than that they were built in accordance with a general plan, founded upon certain definite principles: and it is impossible to resist the conviction that their various forms and combinations possessed some degree of significance, and sustained some relation to the worship to which they were dedicated   We arrive at these conclu-

20

sions from a simple contemplation of the monuments themselves, unaided by the suggestions of analogy, or the evidence furnished by the concurrent practice of all early nations *

When, however, we find these conclusions sustained by analogies of the most striking character, and discover that the mythological and philosophical notions of primitive nations exhibited themselves in a symbolical system which extended even to the form, position, and ornaments of their temples, then our conclusions become invested with a double value, and we proceed with some degree of confidence to inquire how far we are justified in supposing that the ancient structures of the Mississippi valley indicate the character of the worship to which they were dedicated. We have, it is true, neither the light of tradition nor of history to guide our inquiries; the very name of the mysterious people by whom these works were erected is lost to both, and a night darker than that which was prophesied should shroud the devoted "cities of the plain" rests upon them. Under these disadvantages, every attempt to clear up the darkness may fail; if, however, but partially successful, if but a single ray of light be directed upon the subject of our inquiries, the attempt will not be in vain, nor stand in need of an apology.

By far the larger proportion of the sacred structures of our country are circular in form, so also were the temples of the ancient Celts, for the received reason that they were dedicated to the worship of the Sun, whose most obvious and almost universal symbol is the circle. Assuming, upon the basis of this and other analogies, that their circular form is allusive to the former existence, among the people by whom they were built, of a similar system or form of worship, what further support do we find for the assumption, in the known religious notions of the various American tribes and nations? If, in answer to this question, it should be found that *Sun Worship*, if not of universal prevalence, greatly predominated throughout the continent, the assumption already so well sustained by analogy rises into the dignity of a well supported hypothesis.

It has already been remarked, in another connection, that the worship of the Sun was not less general in America than it was at one period among the primitive nations of the Old World. It existed among the savage hunter-tribes and among the semi-civilized nations of the South, where it assumed its most complicated and imposing form, and approximated closely to that which it sustained at an early period among the Asiatic nations,—the Egyptians, Assyrians, Hindoos, Scythians, and their offshoots in Europe. It is well known that it predominated in Peru, and was intimately connected with the civil institutions of that empire. The race of the Incas claimed their descent from the sun, to that luminary they erected their most gorgeous temples; and the eternal fire, everywhere emblematic of its influences, was watchfully maintained by the virgins consecrated to its service. The royal Inca himself officiated as priest of the sun, on every return of its annual festival. The Peruvians also paid adoration to the moon, as the "wife of the sun,"—a clear recognition of the doctrine of the reciprocal principles. In

---

* "Nothing says M Leibnitz "happens without a *reason* why it happens so rather than otherwise."

Mexico also, as in Central America, we still discover, beneath a complication of strange observances and bloody rites, the simplicity of Toltican Zabianism. Upon the high altars of Aztec superstition, reeking with the blood of countless human victims, we still find the eternal fire, no longer, however, under the benign guardianship of consecrated virgins, but consigned to the vigilance of a stern and rigorous priesthood. And, as the Inca trusted at his death to be received to the bosom of his father, the Sun, so too did the fiercer Aztec look forward with confidence to eternal existence and beatitude in the " House of the Sun "*

The Natchez and their affiliated tribes were worshippers of the sun, to which they erected temples and performed sacrifices. And from what can be gathered concerning their temples, it is rendered probable that they erected structures analogous to those under notice. They also maintained a perpetual fire, and their chiefs claimed the sun as their father. The chiefs bore the distinguishing title of *Suns*, and united in themselves the priestly and civil functions.—(*Charlevoix, Canada*, Vol II, p 273, *Du Pratz, Hist Louisiana*, Vol II, pp. 178, 212, *Herriot, Hist. Canada*, p 508.) The natives of the Barbadoes and the West India islands generally, worshipped the same celestial body in conjunction with the moon.—(*Edward's Hist W Ind*, Vol I, p 80, *Davis's Barbadoes*, pp 216, 236, *Herrara*, Vol I, p 162.) The Hurons derived the descent of their chiefs from the sun, and claimed that the sacred pipe proceeded from that luminary.—(*Charlevoix, Canada*, Vol I, p 322, *Lafiteau*. Vol I, p 121.) The Pawnees, Mandans, and Minatarees had a similar tradition and a kindred worship.—(*Nutall's Arkansas*, p. 276.) The Delawares and the Iroquois offered sacrifices to the sun and moon, and, in common with the southern Indians, had a festival in honor of the elementary fire, which they considered the first parent of the Indian nations. It is probable that their council-fire was an original symbol of their religion.—(*Loskiel*, pp 41, 43; *Colden's Hist Five Nations*, Vol I, pp 115, 175, *Schoolcraft's Narrative*, p 20; *Bradford's Res*, p 352.) The Virginian tribes were also sun worshippers, and sustained the perpetual fire in some of their temples. The same is true, as we have already had occasion to show, in a remarkable manner, of the Floridian tribes, who, if we are to credit the accounts of the early voyagers, sacrificed human victims to the sun.—(*Ribauld, MS, Le Moyne*, in *De Bry, Herrara, Florida, Lafiteau, Moeurs des Sauvages*, Vol I, p 158, *Rochefort, Hist. Antilles*, Chap 8.)

The Esquimaux, the natives of the Northwest Coast, and the California Indians, all shared in this worship.—(*Hall's Voy* (1631), pp 38, 61, *Vanegas's California*. Vol I, p 164.) It prevailed to an equal extent among the savage tribes of South America. In connection with the worship of the moon, it existed among the Muyscas of Colombia, among the Araucanians, the Puelches, and the Botucados of Brazil.—(*Herrara*, Vol V, p. 90; *Molina*, Vol II, p 71, *Dobrizhoffer*, Vol II, p 89, *Mod Trav in Brazil*, Vol. II., p 183.) The caziques of the Gua-

---

* *Clavigero*, Vol II, p 3 " They held for an assured faith that there were nine places appointed for souls and the chiefest place of glory was to be near the sun "—(*Gomera*, in *Purchas*, Vol III p 1137.)

ranies, like those of the Natchez, were called *Suns*, and claimed a like lofty lineage. The evidence upon this point might be greatly extended, but enough has been adduced to establish the general predominance of Sun Worship in America.*

It will be seen, from this hasty survey, that the hypothesis which ascribes to the square, circular, and other regular structures of the Mississippi valley a religious origin, and to their forms a symbolical significance, is sustained not only by the most obvious circumstances of structure and position, but also by striking analogies, derived from the form and known character of corresponding structures in other parts of the world It is further sustained by the nature of the worship, which, from its wide diffusion and great prominence amongst the American nations, we are justified in supposing was elementary and pervaded the American continent from the earliest period

It may be objected that a portion of these structures are square or octangular, and cannot, therefore, whatever may be said of those bearing a circular form (and which are by far the most numerous), be regarded as symbolizing the sun, or indicating the prevalence of sun worship among the builders   Any attempts to answer this question would doubtless involve a very extended inquiry into the form and connections which this worship assumed, both in the Old and New Worlds, and would perhaps, after all, bear too much the character of a mere speculation to be satisfactory, or in any degree conclusive.  For this reason no attempt of the kind will be made.   The observations which follow are thrown out suggestively, as furnishing the possible if not the probable principles upon which some of these structures were built, and the reasons which may have influenced the singular combinations which we observe between them

It can be shown that the doctrine of the reciprocal principles of nature, which entered so largely into the early idolatry of the Eastern World, prevailed also in America   The sun and the moon, or oftener, the sun and the earth, emblematized these principles   According to Mr Dudley and other writers on symbolism, these powers among the primitive idolaters were figuratively represented · the male principle by the *circle*, the female principle by the *square*.†  The same authorities lay it down as a rule, subject to few exceptions, that whenever the circular form is adopted in sacred structures, the worship of the male principle is indicated ; but when the quadrangular, then the female principle   " At one time," says Mr. Dudley, " the ancient world was divided in the worship of the two powers , but time

---

* " Sun worship existed extensively in North as well as South America   There is reason to believe that the ancestors of all the principal existing tribes of America worshipped the *Eternal Fire*   Both from their records and traditions, as well as their existing monuments, this conclusion is irresistible   *  *  * Among the North American tribes, the graphic *Ke ke-win*, which depicts the sun, stands on their pictorial rolls as the symbol of the Great Spirit , and no important rite or ceremony is undertaken without an offering of tobacco to him   The weed is lit from fire generated anew on each occasion "—(*Schoolcraft, Address before N Y Hist Soc*, 1846, p  29 )   " They believe in the sacred character of fire, and regard it as the mysterious element of the universe typifying divinity "—*Ib* , p  35

† " The Chinese have consecrated two temples, one to the Heavens, the other to the Earth   the first is round, the second square, according to the theory of their learned men, who, with the Pythagoreans, regard the earth as a *cube*, and the heavens a *sphere* "—(*De Pau, Res China and Egypt*, Vol II , p  42 )

and various circumstances contributed to effect a compromise, which resulted in the combination of the two figures, or the adoption of the octagonal form instead" Mr. Dudley instances several examples of these combinations among the early Grecian and Celtic remains, and observes, "if the sacred structures of early antiquity were examined with reference to this doctrine, many and ample proofs of its truth would be discovered"—(*Naology*, pp 345, 358, *ubi supra.*)

If we were to adopt the hypothesis advanced by Mr Dudley, the fact that the American nations almost universally entertained the idea that the earth was square, would become invested with importance

But, as already observed, these latter suggestions are simply thrown forward as plausible, and not as indicating a settled opinion   The refinement of symbolism which they imply, will, however, appear less improbable, when we come to learn to what extent the semi-civilized nations of America, in their religious beliefs and conceptions, display an identity with the primitive nations of the Old World

The hypothesis of a symbolical design in the forms and combinations of these structures may seem somewhat new and startling to most minds   There are, however, many other facts and considerations having a direct bearing upon it, which will appear in a succeeding work   Meantime, and before passing to collateral inquiries, it will not be out of place to repeat, that the great size of many of the structures to which we have assigned a sacred origin, precludes the idea that they were temples in the ordinary acceptation of the term   It is probable that, like the great circles of England, the squares of India, Peru, and Mexico, they were the sacred enclosures within which were erected the shrines of the gods of the ancient worship, and the altars of the ancient religion.   They may have embraced consecrated groves, and, as they did in Mexico, the residences of the ancient priesthood   Like the sacred structures of the country last named, some of them may have been secondarily designed for protection in times of danger

---

## STONE-HEAPS—STONES OF MEMORIAL—STONE CIRCLES

It has been noticed, on a preceding page, that occasional large heaps of stone, owing their origin to the aborigines, are to be found in the State of New York. Particular reference was made to one in Schoharie county, which is described more in detail in Howe's Gazetteer of New York, as follows

"Between Schoharie Creek and Caughnawaga was an Indian trail, and near it, in the north bounds of Schoharie county, has been seen, from time immemorial, a large pile of stones, which has given the name of 'Stone Heap Patent' to the tract on which it occurs, as may be seen from ancient deeds   Indian tradition says that a Mohawk murdered his brother on this spot, and that this heap was erected to commemorate the event   Every individual who passed that way added a stone to the pile, in propitiation of the spirit of the victim."—(*Howe's Gaz of New York*, p 278.)

Dwight, in his travels, mentions a heap of stones of this description, which was raised over the body of a warrior killed by accident, on the old Indian trail between Hartford and Farmington, the seat of the Tunxis Indians, in Connecticut.  Rude heaps of stone of similar character are of frequent occurrence throughout the West   A very remarkable one occurs upon the dividing ridge between Indian and Crooked Creeks, about ten miles south-west of Chilicothe, Ohio.  It is immediately by the side of the old Indian trail which led from the Shawanoe towns, in the vicinity of Chilicothe, to the mouth of the Scioto River, and is described in detail in the first volume of these Contributions, p 184

Another heap of stones, of like character, but somewhat less in size, is situated upon the top of a high, narrow hill overlooking the small valley of Salt Creek, near Tarlton, Pickaway county, Ohio   It is remarkable as having large numbers of crumbling human bones intermingled, apparently without order, with the stones A very extensive prospect is had from this point.  Upon the slope of a lower hill, near by, appears to have been formerly an Indian village   Many rude relics are uncovered on the spot by the plough

Smaller and very irregular heaps are frequent among the hills.  These do not generally embrace more than a couple of cart-loads of stone, and almost invariably cover a skeleton   Occasionally the amount of stones is much greater.  Rude implements are sometimes found with the skeletons   A number of such graves have been observed near Sinking Springs, Highland county, Ohio , also in Adams county in the same State, and in Greenup county, Kentucky, at a point nearly opposite the town of Portsmouth, on the Ohio

A stone-heap, somewhat resembling those first described, though considerably less in size, is situated on the Wateree River, in South Carolina, near the mouth of Beaver Creek, a few miles above the town of Camden.  It is thus described in a MS letter from Dr Wm Blanding, late of Camden, addressed to Dr S G Morton, of Philadelphia :

" The land here rises for the distance of one mile, and forms a long hill from north to south.  On the north point stands what is called the ' Indian Grave.'  It is composed of many tons of small round stones, from one to four and five pounds weight   The pile is thirty feet long from east to west, twelve feet broad, and five feet high , so situated as to command an extensive view of the adjacent country as far as ' Rocky Mount,' a distance of twenty miles above, and of the river for more than three miles, even at its lowest stages "

A large stone-heap was observed, a number of years since, on a prairie, in one of the central counties of Tennessee   " Upon removing the stones, near the centre of the pile was found a stone box, six feet long and three broad, formed by joining with care the edges of flat stones   Within it was found the decayed skeleton of a man   No weapons or other relics accompanied the skeleton "

The smaller stone-heaps of the West seem to have been connected with some system of burial, and were perhaps designed to protect the bodies of those who casually met their death among the hills, or in some encounter with an enemy, from the attacks of wild animals, as well as to point out their places of sepulture * It is still customary among some of the Indian tribes to carefully envelope the bodies of their dead, and place them in trees or on scaffoldings, for the same purpose †

Occasionally, after interment in the earth, stakes are driven around the graves for the sake of protection  Whether the large heap first described was raised over the body of some distinguished savage, or as a simple mark or monument upon the Shawanoe trail, it is difficult to determine  The absence of human remains would seem to favor the latter conclusion  However this may be, there is certainly nothing very singular in the existence of these monuments  A spot remarkable in any respect, seldom failed to arouse the superstitions of the Indians, or attract their reverence, and to become in time a great "medicine" or mystery  According to Acosta, the Peruvians had a practice of casting a stone as an offering upon any remarkable spot, at the crossings of paths, and on the tops of hills or mountains  "It is therefore," observes our authority, "that we find by

---

* " To perpetuate the memory of any remarkable warriors killed in the woods, I must here observe that every Indian traveller as he passes that way, throws a stone on the place, according as he likes or dislikes the occasion or manner of death of the deceased  In the woods we often see innumerable heaps of small stones in these places, where, according to tradition, some of their distinguished people were either killed or buried, till the bones could be gathered ; then they add Pelion on Ossa, still increasing each heap, as a lasting monument and honor to them, and an incentive to great actions "—*Adair's History of the American Indians*, p 184

"At or soon after burial, the relations of the deceased sometimes cover the grave with stones , and, for years after, occasionally resort to it, and mourn over or recount the merits and virtues of the silent tenant "—*Hunter's Narrative*, p 309

"They have other sorts of tombs , as when an Indian is slain, in that very place they make a heap of stones (or sticks, when stones are not to be found), to this memorial, every Indian that passes by adds a stone, to augment the heap, in respect to the deceased hero "—*Lawson's Carolina* (1709) p 22

Losc describes an Indian burial-place near Piqua, Ohio, where the dead were placed upon the bare limestone rocks and covered over with slabs of stone  No order was displayed in the arrangement of the graves  A cemetery of like character, in which each grave is marked by a heap of stones, is said to exist in Westmoreland county, Pennsylvania

The Bheels of the mountain district of India still raise *cairns*, or rude piles of stones, over the bodies of their chiefs, the tops of which, at particular periods, are covered with oil, red lead, and vermilion —*Coleman's Hindu Mythology* p 271

† "Among the Blackfeet, the dead are not buried in the ground, if it can be avoided  The body is sewn up in a buffalo robe, dressed in his best clothes, his face painted red, but without his weapons, and laid in some retired place  in ravines, rocks, forests, or on high, steep banks  It is often covered with wood and stones, so that the wolves may not reach it  Frequently the corpse remains above ground in a kind of shed  At the funeral of rich Indians, several horses are often killed on the spot , we were told of instances in which ten and twelve, and even one hundred and fifty, were killed "—*Maximilian's Travels in North America*, p 259

the highways great heaps of stones offered, and such other things "* So, too, an early writer on the Housatonic Indians observes " There is a large heap of stones, I suppose ten cart-loads, in the way to *Wanhktukook*, which the Indians have thrown together as they passed by the place for it used to be their custom, every time one passed by, to throw a stone upon it; but what was the end thereof they cannot tell, only that their fathers used to do it, and they do it because it was the custom of their fathers. Some suppose it was designed as an expression of their gratitude to the Supreme Being, that he preserved them to see the place again " —(*Hopkins's Memoirs of Housatonic Indians*, p. 11 ) The " Elk-horn pyramid," on the Upper Missouri, is regarded with deep reverence, and no hunter passes it without adding another horn to its proportions. This accumulation has been going on for a long period, and the pile is now reported to be not far from fifteen feet high, and of corresponding lateral proportions It is composed entirely of elk-horns, many of which are to be found upon the adjacent prairies An instance of this practice of accumulating stones and other materials, is mentioned by Mr Schoolcraft, in which the offerings consisted of sticks and twigs It is highly probable that most of the great heaps of stone scattered over the country owe their origin to this practice It is further possible that some of them may have originated in a practice mentioned by Beverly, who states that the Indians sometimes signalized the conclusion of a peace, or some other memorable action, by burying a tomahawk, and raising over it a heap of stones.—(*Hist Virginia*, p 164 ) If such was the fact, "burying the hatchet" was not a mere rhetorical figure among the Indian orators

Customs, similar in all respects to those described as existing among the Indians, prevailed among the ancient Celts, and have hardly become extinct among the Highlanders of Scotland. A *cairn*, or heap of stones, was a common monument of the dead, and hence arose the saying, " *I'll add a stane to yer cairn,*" in acknowledgment of a service, or in token of regard Two motives, however, appear to have existed for throwing a stone, in passing, to a cairn. In the one case, says Logan, it arose from respect to the deceased, whose memory it was wished to prolong by increasing the size of his funeral mount. The soul of the departed was believed to be pleased with this mark of attention The other motive for throwing stones to augment a cairn was, to mark with execration the burial-place of a criminal, a practice which, according to Dr. Smith, was instituted by the Druids. "It is curious," continues the above author, "that the same practice should result from views so different; yet the fact is so, and the author has often, in the days of his youth, passed the grave of a suicide, on which, according to custom, he never failed to fling a stone" "A *carn* or *cairn*," says O'Connor

---

* *Acosta* in *Purchas*, Vol III , p 1028 The ancients erected heaps of stones in the crossways, and every traveller augmented it by adding a stone These were termed *Thermulæ* The pilgrims of the Middle Ages did the same, when they came within view of the end of their journeys , the piles which they erected were called *Montjoyes* In the passes of the Alps, rude heaps of stones are visible, marking the spot of some deed of violence, or of some catastrophe

(*Chronicles of Eri, Introduction*, Vol. I., p 297), " is a heap of stones, upon which an inferior order of priesthood, called Carneach, used to officiate, they are also found on the summits of hills, whereon Breo—that is, fire—blazed for beacons as signals, but they were also the only heaps raised over those who came to a sudden or violent death, and in Ireland, the custom is practised to this day, of throwing a small stone on passing the place where one has been accidentally killed, which was considered so great an evil, that a more bitter malediction could not be uttered than, ' *Bi an Carn do leact,*' May the Cairn be thy bed "

We may infer from the following passage, ascribed to Virgil, on a noted robber named *Balista*, that stones were sometimes heaped over the graves of criminals, amongst the Romans, in token of obloquy .

> " Monte sub hoc lapidum tegitur Balista sepultus
> Nocte, die, tutum carpe viator iter "

At the death of Absalom, we are informed, in execration of his memory, his body was cast into a pit, and a heap of stones raised over him  " And they took Absalom, and cast him into a great pit in the wood, and laid a very great heap of stones upon him, and all Israel fled, every one to his tent "—(2 *Samuel*, xviii 17.) A similar expression of popular hatred was visited upon the avaricious Achan " And all Israel stoned him with stones, and they raised over him a great heap of stones "—(*Joshua* vii. 25, 26.)

Nothing can be more certain than that the erection of stones, like the elevation of tumuli over the dead as sepulchral monuments, was the first and simplest means of commemorating events  And it is not unlikely that worship was often paid to such as were of ancient date, not so much on the score of symbolical significance, as in consequence of long association with interesting or important circumstances. Monuments of this kind were perpetuated at so late a date, upon the old continent, as to become charged with inscriptions declaring to us the objects for which they were erected. Olaus Magnus observes of Scandinavia, " There are also high stones  by the aspect and signature thereof the ancient possessions of provinces, governments, forts, communities of men, are to continue to every man in peace, without laws, suits, or arbitration, giving an example that among these nations there is more right to be found in these stones, that are boundaries, than elsewhere in the large volumes of laws, where men think themselves more learned and civil "

The first instance, recorded in the Bible, of the erection of such stones is that of Jacob, who raised a stone at Bethel, to commemorate the vision which he saw, and attest the engagement which he formed in consequence.  In fixing their respective boundaries, Laban said to Jacob, " Behold this heap, and behold this pillar, which I have cast up betwixt thee and me  This heap be witness, and this pillar be witness, that I will not pass over this heap to thee, and thou shalt not pass over this heap and this pillar to me for harm ' —(*Gen* xxxi  51, 52 )  In reading this account, it is impossible to resist the conviction that the parties were

21

not originating a new practice, but acting in conformity with usages well known and established   The stone set up by Joshua under the oak at Shechem, was assuredly an evidence and memorial of the covenant into which he had entered with God.   The incidental references to stones of this kind, in the Bible, show that they were numerous   Thus, there is "the stone of Bohan the son of Reuben" (*Josh* xviii ), and the great stone known as " the stone of Abel," upon which the ark was placed in returning from the Philistines.—(1 *Sam.* vi )   The Hebrews also set up stones as monuments of victories , such was the *Ebenezer,* " the stone of help," set up by Samuel —(*Sam* vii )   Greek historians inform us that a similar custom existed among that people, derived from their ancestors   Every memorable field of battle throughout Greece has its tumulus or *polyandrion*

Among the aborigines of America, stones were sometimes erected for precisely similar purposes.   We have an instance, mentioned by Col. Emory, in which an erect stone was raised by some of the Indians of Northern Mexico, in commemoration of a treaty or compact.   He says   " At this point (on the plains bordering the Moro River, New Mexico), we were attracted to the left by an object which we supposed to be an Indian , but on coming up to it, we found it to be a sandstone block standing on end, surmounted by another shorter block.   A mountain man, versed in these signs, said it was in commemoration of a talk and friendly smoke between some two or three tribes of Indians "—(*Military Reconnoissance from the U S to California* )

The superstitions of the Indians exhibit themselves in a thousand forms, and extend to almost every remarkable object in nature   A stone which, from the action of natural causes, has assumed the general form of a man or an animal, is especially an object of regard; and the fancied resemblance is often heightened by artificial means, as by daubs of paint, indicating the eyes, mouth, and other features.   Mr Schoolcraft has presented the public with sketches of a number of

Fig 43

these rude idols, all of which were found to the north-west of the Great Lakes No. 1 in the cut was brought to the Indian Office at Mackinaw, in 1839 , number 2 was found on Thunder Bay Island, in Lake Huron, in 1820, where it had been set up under a tree   The island is small and barren, and in its solitary, desolate aspect furnished a place eminently appropriate, according to the Indian superstition, for the residence of a Manitou or spirit.  No 3 was found by Mr School-craft, about one thousand miles above the Falls of St. Anthony, on the Mississippi. It had been set up in a shadowy nook, and was almost entirely concealed by shrub-bery —(*Indian in his Wigwam*, p  292.)  Fig  44, No  1, was found in East

Fig  44

Hartford, Connecticut, and deposited in the Museum of Yale College in 1788.  It is thirty-one inches high and seventeen wide; the material is white granite  It is said the Indians placed their dead before it previous to burial, and afterwards returned and danced around it.—(*Trans, Am. Acad Arts and Sciences*, Vol III, p  192)  Number 2 was found at the base of a mound in South Carolina, and is now in the possession of Dr S  G. Morton, of Philadelphia  It is small, not more than six inches in height, and has evidently undergone some artificial modi-fication.

Single erect stones, or a group of them, of large size, in isolated situations, were also venerated.  They are sometimes covered with rude figures, and sacri-fices made at their base.  James, Lewis and Clarke, Prince Maximilian, and other travellers mention some of these, which in size and general disposition closely resemble the Celtic *cromlech* —(*Lewis and Clarke*, pp  79, 83, *Prince Maximilian's Travels*, pp. 381, 417, *James's Narrative*, Vol. I, p. 252)  Catlin observed a singular group of five large boulders, at the *Coteau des Prairies*, which were regarded with the utmost veneration by the Indians  None venture to approach nearer than three or four rods; and offerings are made in humble attitude, by throwing tobacco towards them from a distance.—(*N. A Indians*, Vol. II., p. 202)

In the State of New York also, at various points, are remarkable stones, with which the Indians connected their traditions, and which they were accustomed to hold in high regard.  Such was the celebrated "Oneida Stone," from which the Oneidas figuratively represent themselves to have sprung  It stands in the town of Stockbridge, Madison county, on a very commanding eminence, from which the entire valley, as far as Oneida Lake, can be seen, under favorable cir-cumstances  It was the altar of the tribe, and a beacon-fire lighted near it was the signal for the warriors to assemble in cases of emergency  It is a large boulder of sienite, and is figured by Mr Schoolcraft, in his "Notes on the Iro-quois," p. 77.  In the county of Westchester, town of Yonkers, on the bank of the Hudson, in an obscure nook, is also a singular stone, which once received the reverence of the Indians  Another, bearing some resemblance to the human head, is found in the town of New Rochelle, in the same county.—(*Hist. County of West-chester*, By ROBT. BOLTON, JR., Vol. I., p. 374: Vol. II., p. 403.)  In the township last named is also a very remarkable rock, supported by five others, as shown in the following wood-cut, Fig. 45:

FIG. 45.

From its entire correspondence with the Celtic *cromlech*, this has attracted some considerable attention.  Its position is, however, entirely the result of accident. The rock itself is granite, and the supporting stones limestone.  The members of the New York Geological Survey decided that it owes its position to the washing away of the earth from among the stones upon which the boulder accidentally rested when transported to this spot.—(*Ib.*, Vol. I., p. 374 )

It is well known that among the nations of the East, a plain, unwrought stone placed in the ground, was an emblem of the generative or procreative powers of nature.  In India such such stones are very abundant, and are denominated Lin-gams; and in Central America the same symbol was extensively adopted.  It is not improbable that the erection of an obelisk of wood in the centre of the con-secrated areas of the Creeks, as described by Bartram, on page 135, had its origin in the primitive practice of erecting these symbolical stones; which in India, as also in Central America, almost invariably occupy the centres of the sacred enclosures.  Stones arranged in a circle, around a central larger one, or amidst several disposed in a peculiar manner, was a very primitive form of the solar temple.  The remains of these temples, notwithstanding their rudeness, constitute some of the most imposing and interesting monuments of the Old World.  If we may credit Beverly, the Indians of Virginia not only erected sacred stones, but had sacred enclosures, corresponding very nearly with the ancient stone circles. He says: "The Indians have posts fixed around their *Quioccasan* (temple of the idol), which have men's faces carved upon them, and are painted.  They are like-wise set up around some of their other celebrated places, and make a circle for them to dance about in on certain solemn occasions.  They very often set up pyramidal stones and pillars, which they color with *puccoon* and other sorts of paint, and which they adorn with *peak, roanok*, etc.  To these they pay all outward signs of worship and devotion, not as to God, but as they are hieroglyphics of the permanency and immutability of the Deity; because these, of all sublunary bodies, are the least subject to decay or change  they also, for the same reason, keep baskets of stones in their cabins "—(*Hist Virginia.* p 184 )

Besides the rough, upright, and wrought stones. constituting enclosures, or occupying the areas of sacred structures, in Central America and Yucatan, accounts of which are given by Mr Stephens, we have intelligence of the recent discovery of monuments in New Granada (South America), which exhibit a still closer relationship to the primitive stone circles and other analogous structures of the other continent  The subjoined account is given in a letter from Signor Velez, dated Bogota, December, 1846 :

" In traversing, at different times, the province of Tunja, with the sole purpose of examining the country, I acquired some vague information respecting the presumed existence, in the province of Leiva, of some ruins belonging to a temple or a palace of the times of the ancient Indians.  As the account varied each time that I attempted to inform myself by inquiries as to the existence of remains of buildings anterior to the conquest, and as no one affirmed that he had seen them himself, I began to doubt the truth of the report.  Nevertheless, as the subject was one that interested me exceedingly, I undertook a journey, in the month of June, 1836. in spite of the time and trouble it would necessarily cost me, in order to put an end to my uncertainty.  After traversing the province of Leiva in different directions, without meeting with the object I was in search of, and after advancing as far as the neighborhood of Moniquira, by following the route from Gachantiva to this place, across a beautiful gently sloping plain under cultivation, I discovered a large stone, which, when seen some distance off, did not at first appear as if wrought by the hand of man  On approaching it, I found it was a sort of column, four and two-sixths varas in length by three and one-half in diameter  It seemed to me that such stones, although rudely wrought, must have served as columns.  On examining the locality, I found, scattered here and there, other stones similar to the first  and at last, thirteen stones of the largest size, ranged as in a circle about fifty varas in circumference  It appeared to me that they must have proceeded from some temple or palace, extending back to a remote period.  Some of these columns have a flattened shape, like a fish , each has notches at its extremities, which show clearly what means were employed for making fast to them and drawing them from the quarry to the site which they now occupy

" But now, when I began to despair of meeting with the ruins of an edifice, which was the main object of my journey, some Indians from a hut pointed out to me a spot some four hundred varas distant from the thirteen last mentioned columns  I immediately proceeded thither, and great indeed was my joy at beholding ruins !  I found cylindrical columns, exceedingly well wrought, fixed in the ground, and occupying a surface forty-five varas long by twenty-two broad. These ruins extend, in the direction of their length, from east to west , some arranged in a straight line running in the same direction, with this peculiarity, that the columns are so near together that their distance from each other does not exceed half a vara.  Their circumference also is not over half a vara (*sic*)  As to their length, it could not be determined, these remains being so much damaged, that the highest of them is not more than one and a-half varas above ground; others are scarcely visible, the ranges to which they belong being interrupted. The diameter of these columns is precisely alike, they resemble each other exactly, and are so well turned into a cylindrical shape, that they seemed to me of better workmanship than those now made use of at Bogota, they form, by their light-ness and elegance, a striking contrast with the thirteen enormous fragments men-tioned above

" It is impossible to affirm that the edifice in question was only forty-five varas long and twenty-two broad; because, in this space, the columns touch each other. Over the whole extent of the place, which covers a considerable surface, there are scattered numerous fragments of columns, as also of other stones, which appear to have been wrought on one of their faces   At a distance of one hundred varas, I also found a spot covered with brambles and a considerable number of stones, which, from a cursory examination, I concluded to have been wrought. The columns which remain sunk in the ground are about twenty-nine in number.

" In all that I saw, I observed no trace of mortar, lime, or any other cement By taking up some of these columns, some may perhaps be found

" The examination of these vestiges made a deep impression upon me, and I became convinced that the territory which contains them, and which is about two miles in extent, must have been occupied by a large city, and as I conclude, by a nation much more ancient than the Muyscas.

" The ignorance which has always reigned in the province of Tunja, explains the little attention shown to monuments so interesting, and so worthy of being studied.   The inhabitants of the country have alone been acquainted with them up to the present time, and although not comparable in importance and grandeur to those which have been discovered in Guatemala and Yucatan, they nevertheless attest the existence of ancient populations already far advanced in civilization "

Monuments analogous to those here described are found on the shores of Lake Titicaca, in Peru   Their origin is lost in obscurity, and they are supposed, by M. D'Orbigny, who has carefully investigated and given the world drawings of them, to have been the work of a race anterior to the Incas, denoting, perhaps, a more advanced civilization than the monuments of Palenque   They have been described by a number of the early writers, commencing with Pedro de Ceica, one of the followers of Pizarro   M D'Orbigny speaks of them as follows   " These monuments consist of a mound raised nearly a hundred feet, surrounded with pillars, of temples from six to twelve hundred feet in length, opening precisely toward the east, and adorned with colossal angular columns, of porticoes of a single stone, covered with reliefs of skilful execution, though of rude design, dis-playing symbolical representations of the sun, and the condor, his messenger; of basaltic statues loaded with bas-reliefs, in which the design of the carved head is half Egyptian, and lastly, of the interior of a palace formed of enormous blocks of rock completely hewn, whose dimensions are often twenty-one feet in length, twelve in breadth, and six in thickness.   In the temples and palaces, the portals are not inclined, as among those of the Incas, but perpendicular, and their vast dimensions, and the imposing masses of which they are composed, surpass in beauty and grandeur all that were afterwards built by the sovereigns of Cuzco "— (*L'Homme Américain*, Tome I., p. 323 )

Structures like those, the ruins of which are here described, on the eastern continent, were almost invariably of religious origin, and dedicated to sacred purposes And as the priestly and civil offices in early and patriarchal times were usually conjoined, it not unfrequently happened that the rude temples were places of judicature     They had also sometimes a monumental significance , that is to say, were erected by some chieftain or powerful individual at places which had been signalized by some important event,—a delivery from danger, or a victory, in accordance with a vow, or as a grateful acknowledgment to overruling powers     Not long after the delivery of the Law at Mount Sinai (says Kitto), the people entered into a solemn covenant with God     On this occasion Moses built an altar of earth at the bottom of the mountain, and erected around it twelve stones, corresponding to the twelve tribes —(*Exod* xxiv 4 )     This rude open temple was the type of the great temple afterwards erected at Jerusalem , and the principles involved were, in both cases, the same     An example of the erection of stones as sacred memorials, is afforded in the account of the passage of the Jordan at Gilgal     The object is specifically declared ·  "That this may be a sign among you , that when your children ask, in time to come, saying, What mean ye by these stones ?     Then ye shall answer them     The waters of Jordan were cut off, and these stones are for a perpetual memorial to the Israelites "     The term Gilgal implies a circle or wheel, and indicates the probable manner in which the stones of memorial were arranged.

As we have said, sacred places, the residences of the priests, etc , were anciently also places of deliberation and judicature, where nearly every affair of public importance was transacted     Gilgal seems to have been devoted to all of these purposes.   The first " Messenger " or prophet which we read of in the Bible, as being sent on a special mission, came from Gilgal (*Judg* ii 1), a circumstance which seems to imply that it was a station where priests or prophets resided to perform specific duties.   And it is remarkable that the places where Samuel held his courts of judicature, in his annual circuits from his residence at Ramah, were places of sacred stones.   ' He went from year to year in circuit to Bethel [the place of the sacred stone set up by Jacob], and Gilgal, and Mizpeh, and judged Israel in all these places "—(1 *Sam* xii 16 )   Mizpeh was the name of the place of the stones set up by Jacob and Laban.   It was almost equal with Gilgal as a place of public transactions.   Here the tribes met at the call of the Levite, to deliberate on the war against Benjamin (*Judg* xx 1 ); and here Samuel convoked the solemn national assembly of repentant Israel —(1 *Sam* vii 5–12 )   It was so well known as a place of public gathering, that the Philistines no sooner heard of the assembling, than they marched against it   Here, too, Samuel called the people together to elect a king.—(1 *Sam.* x 17 )

There seems to have been an altar at Gilgal , for that burnt-offerings and other sacrifices were made there, is manifest from Samuel's direction to Saul     " Go down before me to Gilgal, and behold I will come down to thee, to offer burnt-offerings, and to sacrifice sacrifices of peace-offerings "—(1 *Sam* x. 8 )   Here

Saul was inaugurated as king on a subsequent occasion  And after Saul's victory over the Ammonites, "Samuel said to the people, Let us go down to Gilgal, and renew the kingdom there  And all the people went to Gilgal, and there they made Saul king before Jehovah in Gilgal, and they sacrificed peace-offerings before Jehovah, and there Saul and all the men of Israel rejoiced greatly."—(1 *Sam.* xi. 14, 15)  Here Saul afterwards gathered the people to war against the Philistines, and, after waiting for Samuel, himself offered sacrifices —(1 *Sam.* xiii. 4, 7, 12, 15)  It was under pretence of sacrificing them to Jehovah in Gilgal, that Saul spared the choice cattle of the Amalekites  And it was "before Jehovah in Gilgal," that Samuel hewed Agag in pieces. This place also seems to have been the customary residence of the prophet Elijah, which confirms the suggestion that there was some establishment of the prophets here.—(2 *Kings* ii 1)  In the later prophets there are many denunciations of the corruptions of which Gilgal ultimately became the seat.—(*Amos* iv 4, v 5, *Hosea* iv 15, ix 12; xii 11.)  It is sometimes coupled in condemnation with Bethel, another place of sacred stones, which shows that these places had become devoted to idolatrous purposes.

Another instance of the erection of stones is afforded in the account of the great solemnity at Ebal and Gerizim  In this case, "great stones" were set up, covered with inscriptions from the word of the Law, and with them was raised the primitive altar of unhewn stones

The resort to their places of unhewn stones, amongst the Hebrews, indicates the ideas which seem universally to have been connected with such monuments. It is probable that their religious use formed the primary idea in their construction, and that their civil use was secondary, or rather, involved in the other, and it also seems likely that after the religious notions connected with structures passed away, they long continued to be appropriated to civil purposes

Homer more than once alludes to councils as being held within or near circles of stones  The remarkable passage in the Iliad (xviii, l. 585), may be mentioned It is thus translated by Mr. King  "The herald at length appeased the tumult ; and the elders sat at rough hewn stones, within a sacred circle "  So, too, the council, summoned by Alcinous to confer upon the affair of Ulysses, sat at rough hewn stones—(*Odyss* viii 5)

Abundant facts may be produced showing the use of stone circles at various occasions, as of inaugurations and councils, as late as the fourteenth century, in the north of Germany, Sweden, Denmark, and the Western Islands  And Pinkerton (*Des of Empire*, 1802) says, "the Icelandic writers tell us that such circles were called *domh-ringr*, that is literally, *doom-rings*, or circles of judgment, being the solemn places where courts were held for various purposes"  And Olaus Magnus (1550) mentions that the practice of crowning kings at such places was continued in his day  A circle of stones called *Morasten*, near Upsal, Sweden, was the spot appropriated, from immemorial time, for that purpose.—(*Hist of the Goths*, pp 12, 13.)  Sir R C Hoare observes of the stone circles and similar monuments of the British islands, that there is abundant evidence that "the circle, the enclosure, and the mound, such as we see at Abury, Marden, and Stonehenge, were connected first with the Druidical and afterwards with the Bardic systems, and made use of for the joint purposes of religion and judicature." Cæsar, writing of the Druids, is understood to allude to their sacred structures in the following passage "Once a year the Druids assemble at a consecrated place. Such as have suits depending, flock thither from all parts, and submit implicitly to their decrees" —(*De Bello Gallico*, Lib VI) The Bardic successors, who preserved and transmitted in writing many of the ideas and usages of their predecessors, speak of their sacred mounts and circles in distinct terms Meagant, who wrote in the seventh century, says that they had their sacred mount where the judges assembled to decide the causes of the people.—(*Davies' Myth. of the Druids*, p 6) In a poem by Cynddela, we find, "Bards were constituted the judges of excellence, and bards will praise thee, *even Druids of the circle*, of four dialects, coming from the four regions; *a bard of the steep mount* will celebrate thee" In another passage he exclaims, "It is my right to be master of song, being in a direct line of the true tribe, *a bard of the enclosure*"

These illustrations might be extended through nearly all the early nations of the world, upon both continents. They strikingly confirm the identity in the early practices and primitive notions of mankind.

---

## ADDITIONAL MONUMENTS IN NEW YORK

ONONDAGA COUNTY

SINCE the foregoing pages were printed, a work on the early history of what is popularly called the "Onondaga Country," has been published by Mr. J V H. Clark, of Manlius, Onondaga county. Mr. Clark's attention having been specially directed to the subject, he has collected, with great industry, a large amount of information respecting the antiquities of that interesting region, which are embodied in his work, and from this are condensed the subjoined facts, additional to those heretofore presented

In reference to some aboriginal remains in the town of Elbridge, which are probably those to which Mr Clinton alluded, as occuring in the same township, Mr. Clark observes ·

"Upon lot 81, N E. part, on land now occupied by Mr John Munro (previously the Judge Munro farm), was formerly a fort, situated on high ground. In 1793, the ditch and embankment were easily to be traced Large trees stood upon the wall and in the ditch The work was square, except that the line of embankment toward the west curved slightly outward. The area was about an acre and a

22

quarter   The walls were about two feet high; the gateway opened toward the west, and was twelve feet wide. It was situated on a beautiful eminence, nearly surrounded by ravines."

"About half a mile N W of this work," continues Mr Clark, "on what is called the Purdy lot, was another work, of larger dimensions, containing about four and a half acres of ground. It is situated upon one of the most considerable elevations of the town, and is nearly or quite square, with gateways opening to the east and west. The embankment was originally about three feet high, and an oak tree, two feet in diameter, was standing upon it. On the south side were numerous holes, about two feet deep and six feet apart. Large quantities of broken pottery and fresh water shells are still to be found  An oaken chest was discovered here, somewhere about the year 1800, which contained a quantity of silk goods. The folds and colors were easily distinguishable, but the fabric crumbled on exposure. Some copper coins, it is said, were found with the silks.

"On lot 84, on the farm now owned by Mr. Caleb Brown, about forty rods south of the road, was formerly a circular work, of upwards of three acres' area. The embankment was about two feet high, the ditch exterior and four or five feet deep  There was a wide gateway upon the west side, and a smaller one on the northeast, opening toward a spring, some rods distant. In digging near the western gateway, fragments of timber, bearing marks of edge tools, were found, and in an excavation called a well fourteen feet deep, a quantity of charred Indian corn was discovered. Upon the site of Mr Brown's house and garden, was also an ancient circular work, enclosing about an acre of ground. Within it were cinders, charcoal, etc., as if it had been the site of a blacksmith's shop."

Mr. Clark describes another ancient work. "situated on a hill, about a mile and a half south of Delphi, in this township, on lot No 100  It has an area of about eight acres, and occupies an elevated piece of ground, surrounded by a ravine made by two small streams which pass around it and unite on the north  It had a large gateway upon the south, and a smaller one on the north  Before the first

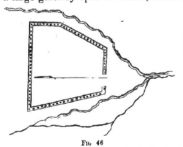

was a kind of mound  The defences consisted of a ditch and pickets. At every place where a picket stood, a slight depression is still distinctly visible. In one corner were evident marks of a blacksmith's shop, including various smith's tools, a bed of cinders, and a deposit of charcoal  Beneath one of these piles was found, *en cache,* a quantity of charred Indian corn, and squash and pumpkin seeds. A short distance to the south of the work is

Fig. 46

an extensive cemetery, in which the bodies were buried in rows"  Quantities of the implements and trinkets introduced among the Indians, at the period of the 'first European intercourse, are found with the skeletons  The palisades were set in the bottom of the ditch, which, when first known, was six feet deep. About a mile west from this are the remains of another work of similar character; and about a mile north of Delphi, on a farm owned by a Mr. Sheldon, is still another    Around a number of these works, the corn hills of the Indians could be traced for a long period after the occupation of the country by the whites.   Medals, crosses, gun-barrels, knives, axes—in short, every variety of article introduced by the Europeans after the discovery, are to be found here in abundance

Perhaps the most interesting work of which any traces yet remain in Pompey township, is the one of which Mr. Clark gives the accompanying plan, and which occurs on lot No 3, on land owned by Mr Isaac Keeler

Mr Clark describes this work as follows " It had been enclosed with palisades of cedar, and contained some ten acres of ground.   The plan was a parallelogram, divided by two rows of palisades, running east and west, and crossing in the centre   The space between the rows was about twelve feet.   At the N W. corner was an isolated bastion and an embrasure.   At the period of the first cultivation of the land, many stumps of the palisades, which had been burned off even with the ground, were ploughed up.   Within the southern division of the fort were several mounds, the principal one of which was four feet high, rising on a base of about fifteen feet in diameter, composed chiefly of ashes, in which were found many beads of the size of bullets, and a great variety of trinkets made of red pipe-stone   Several hundred pounds of old iron, consisting of axes,

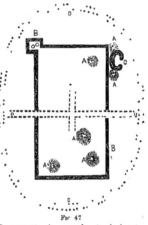

Fig 47

B, parapet—A, mounds—C, look out—
D, palisades

gun-barrels, files, knives, etc., etc , were also found in the same place.   The smaller mounds contained charred corn, many bushels of which were ploughed up   At a distance of about thirty rods north of the work was a ditch, nearly forty rods long, and varying from three to six feet in depth.   It seems to have been entirely disconnected from the work in question   The situation of this ancient fort is on an elevation of land rising gradually for about a mile in every direction; and, at the time of its occupancy, several hundred acres of land must have been cleared around it.   Fragments of pottery, pipes, flint arrow-heads, stone hatchets, etc , etc , are abundantly found on this spot.   In many places, both within and exterior to the work, were found pits for hiding corn and other articles, *en cache* "   Some small mounds containing human bones are found on the lands of Mr. S. A Keene, in this vicinity

A relic of some interest, and which has given rise to no inconsiderable speculation, is a stone bearing an inscription. found in this township in 1820, by Mr. Philo Cleveland   It is about fourteen inches long, by twelve broad, and eight thick, granitic, and bearing upon one side a rude representation of a tree, entwined by an equally rude representation of a serpent, with some letters and a date, as shown in the cut.

There seems to be little doubt that the stone was found as represented, and that it is a genuine remnant of antiquity   Some have supposed it to attest that Ponce de Leon, Narvaez, or some other Spanish adventurer, penetrated thus far to the northward, during the period of Spanish adventure in Florida.   The stone is now in the museum of the Albany Institute.

FIG. 48

Mr. Clark presents the following plan of a stockade work, surveyed by Judge Geddes, and probably the very one referred to by Mr. Marshall, on page 31 of this memoir

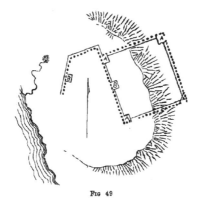

FIG 49

It is situated on the shores of Onondaga Lake, between Brown's pump-works and Liverpool.  A fine spring of water rises near it, and quantities of relics, of various kinds, have been found within it.

There are yet traces of an old palisaded work in the township of Cazenovia, Madison county, about two miles north of Delphi, of which Mr Clark gives the accompanying plan, Fig 50.

It will be observed that it essentially corresponds with those in Onondaga county, already described. It has an area of about five acres, and numerous graves of the Indians are to be found both within and without the walls, in the vicinity.

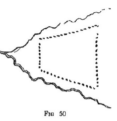

Fig 50

ST LAWRENCE COUNTY

In addition to the ancient remains found in St Lawrence county, and described in the foregoing pages, we have the subjoined notices of others, contained in a communication made to the Board of Regents of the University of New York, by F. B. Hough, M D, of St. Lawrence, and published in their annual Report for 1850, pp. 101, 110.

"In the town of Macomb, St Lawrence county, are found three trench enclosures, and numerous places where broken fragments of rude pottery, ornaments of steatite, and beds of charcoal and ashes, indicate the sites of Indian villages. It may be proper to state that this region was not inhabited at the time of its first settlement by the whites

"One of these ruins is on the farm of William P. Houghton, near the bank of Birch creek, and is the one which has furnished the greatest quantity of relics Beads of steatite, pipes and broken utensils of earthenware. the bones of fish and wild animals, shells, etc, occur, mixed with ashes and bits of charcoal, throughout the soil, within and without the limits of the trench, and have been collected and carried off in large quantities. Cultivation has nearly obliterated every trace of the

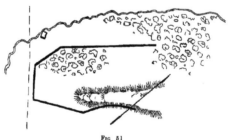

Fig 51

enclosure, but by the aid of several persons who were acquainted with the locality when first discovered, the accompanying plan has been drawn, which is believed to represent the situation and extent of this work, before the land was tilled

"The ground formerly occupied by the trench, is at present the site of an orchard, and used as a mill yard. Reference to this work is made in several

Gazetteers and "Historical Collections," as occuring on the farm of Capt. Washburn, in Gouverneur, (the former owner of the land, before the erection of the township of Macomb,) and in these it is erroneously stated that rude remains of sculpture occur within the enclosure. No traces of sculpture (except the beads, pipes, and other articles) have ever been found here

"About half a mile northeast of this place, is the trace of another enclosure, but so obliterated by cultivation, that it could not be surveyed with any degree of certainty  It occurs on the farms of Josiah Sweet and William Houghton, the greater portion being upon the farm of the latter  It is situated on a small stream, the outlet of a tamarack swamp, formerly a beaver meadow, is of an irregular oval figure, and can be traced with tolerable accuracy about one hundred and sixty paces, which is nearly half of the original circumference.  It longest direction was N N E and S. S.W.  Numerous fire-beds occur within the enclosure; and in one instance, a quantity of ashes and charcoal was found five feet below the surface  In a field a few rods distant, large quantities of broken pottery, and traces of an Indian village, are found  About three fourths of a mile from the enclosure first

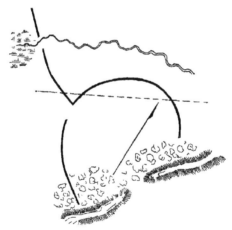

Fig 52.

described, there occurs another trench, of semi-circular form, and in a far more perfect state of preservation than either of the others.  This is on the farm of Robert Wilson, and about twenty-five rods south of "Wilson's Lead Mine."

"For the topography and extent of this trench, reference is made to the accompanying plan, Fig. 52.

"As the land around this has never been ploughed, it has not furnished any relics of interest

"In the town of Massena, St. Lawrence county, is an ancient enclosure, on the farm of Josiah C Bridges, about half a mile southwest of the bridge over the

Racket river  It is on a considerable eminence, about half way between the Racket and Grasse rivers, and three miles from the mouth of the latter   The hill may be fifty feet higher than either river, the ancient work is on the southern declivity of the hill, near the top, and the outer ditch may enclose perhaps an acre. It is nearly square, with the corners projecting beyond the line of the sides ; from which it may perhaps be inferred that it was a defensive work, and belonged to a different period from the circular works above described.  The bank, when first discovered, was surrounded by a ditch about three feet wide, and between one and two feet deep   In the ditch were the remains of old pine trees, some of which must have been at least five hundred years old   Within the enclosure were two elevations, about fifteen feet square, and two feet above the level of the surrounding ground.  The location commands a prospect of the country around, in every direction, to a considerable distance

' In Potsdam, St Lawrence county, there existed, on the first settlement of the country, a work similar to the one last described, but which is now nearly obliterated by the plough  It was on the west side of Racket river, about half way from Potsdam village to Norfolk.  Like the other, it was situated near the top of an elevation, conspicuous from all the surrounding country.  Like it, also, it was quadrilateral , its size was nearly the same, and the vicinity of both furnishes numerous remains of rude pottery, stone axes, flint arrows, and various ornaments wrought in steatite   The location in Potsdam is about eighteen miles distant to the southwest from that in Massena ; and there is little doubt but that one might be seen from the other, if the the intervening timber were cut away

" The foregoing are the only remains of ancient art which the writer has been able to learn of in St Lawrence county, after making the most diligent inquiries "

ESSEX COUNTY

The following passages are extracted from a private letter addressed to the author, by P W Ellsworth, M D., of Hartford, Connecticut : " In the summer of 1848, while passing through the town of Keene, Essex County, New York, my attention was arrested by what was instantly recognised as a mound, identical in form with those found at the West.  No notes were taken at the time, and in giving you an account of it, I must trust entirely to memory , but there is little danger of error, as Dr. A. Smith, at this moment at my side, was then with me.  We did not go upon the tumulus, but had a distinct view of it from the road, a few rods distant. It was situated near a little stream, in a large, level meadow, which was surrounded on every side by high ground   It was about fifteen or twenty feet high, with a proportionate base, and rose rapidly, with a graceful curve, from the plain, forming a regular cone  Upon inquiry, I ascertained it was considered to be of Indian origin ; that it had been partially excavated by money-diggers, but found to contain nothing beyond human bones  It attracted my special attention, from the circumstance that I supposed no monuments of the kind occurred to the eastward of the Alleghanies "

It has already been observed that very few entire vessels of aboriginal pottery

have been recovered in the State of New York. Their general form is, however, sufficiently evident from the fragments which cover the site of every ancient town. Figure 53 is a sketch of a vessel or vase found in 1811, in Township No 10, Chenango County. It was buried in the earth, in an inverted position. The capacity was about three quarts. The original drawing was published by Dr. Hosack, in the "New York Medical and Philosophical Register" for 1812. The form, as will be seen by reference to the first volume of these Contributions, p 189, is that which seems to have been common to all the rude tribes within the boundaries of the Northern and Eastern States. A few of the aboriginal vases had bat bottoms, but most were oval or rounded The groove around them was designed to receive a withe, whereby they could be suspended over the fire.

Fig 53

---

## USE OF COPPER BY THE AMERICAN ABORIGINES

In the paragraphs relating to St Lawrence county, mention is made of a singular aboriginal deposite or burial, on the Canadian shore of the St. Lawrence River, near Brockville  Here were found a number of skeletons and a variety of relics, among which were a number of copper implements.  They were buried fourteen feet below the surface of the ground.  Two of the copper articles were clearly designed as spear-heads. they were pointed, double-edged, and originally capable of some service  One was a foot in length  A couple of copper knives accompanied these, and also an implement which seems to have been designed as a gouge.—(*Ancient Monuments of Mississippi Valley*, p 201.)  Some implements entirely corresponding with these have been found in Isle Royal, and at other places in and around Lake Superior.  Whether or not these are relics of the existing Indian tribes, it is not undertaken to say, although it seems highly probable that they are  That the Indians of New England, New York, and Virginia, to a limited extent, possessed copper ornaments and implements at the time of the Discovery, is undoubted, but it is not to be supposed for an instant that they obtained it by smelting from the ores  They unquestionably procured it from the now well known native deposites around Lake Superior.

Raleigh observed copper ornaments among the Indians on the coast of the Carolinas, and Verazzano mentions articles, probably ornamental, of wrought copper, among the natives which he visited in a higher latitude, "which were more esteemed than gold." Granville speaks of copper among the Indians of Virginia, which was said to have been obtained among the *Chawanooks* (Shawanoes?) "It was of the color of our copper, but softer" He endeavored to visit the place where it was represented to be found; but after a toilsome journey of some days into the interior, the search was abandoned This was a grievous disappointment at that time, when the minds of men were filled with visions of vast mineral wealth, and when the value of the New World was thought to consist in its mines Granville thus concludes his account of his fruitless expedition. "I have set down this voyage somewhat particularly, to the end that it may appear unto you (as true it is) that there wanted no good will, from the first to the last of us, to have perfected the discovery of this mine, for that the discovery of a good mine, by the goodness of God or a passage to the South Sea, or some way to it, and nothing else, can bring our country in request to be inhabited by our people "—(*Granville's Voy*, 1585, in *Pinkerton*, Vol. XII p 580 ) Heriot says, "In two towns 150 miles from the main, are found divers small plates of copper, that are made, we are told by the inhabitants, by people who dwell farther in the country, where, they say, are mountains and rivers which yield white grains of metal, which are deemed to be silver For the confirmation whereof, at the time of our first arrival in the country, I saw two small pieces of silver, grossly beaten, about the weight of a *tester*, [an old coin about the weight of a sixpence sterling,] hanging in the ears of a Wiroance The aforesaid copper we found to contain silver "—(*Heriot's Voy*, 1586, in *Pink*, Vol. XII, p 594 ) Robert Juet, in his account of Hudson's discovery of the river which bears his name. asserts that the savages "had red copper tobacco pipes, and other things of copper, which they did wear about their necks." He makes mention, in another place, of "yellow copper," as distinct from what he terms "red copper." Both Behring and Kotzebue found copper implements in use among the Indians of the Northwest Coast.—(*Behring's First Voy.*, p 85; *Kotzebue, Voy*, Vol I., p. 227 ) McKenzie mentions copper as being in common use among some of the extreme Northern tribes, on the borders of the Arctic Sea. "They point their arrows and spears with it, and work it up into personal ornaments, such as collars, ear-rings, and bracelets, which they wear on their wrists, arms, and legs. They have it in great abundance, and hold it in high estimation "—(*Second Journey*, p. 333 ) Owing to the difficulty of reducing iron from the ore, an acquaintance with that metal has usually been preceded by a knowledge of copper, silver, and gold "These three metals," says Robertson, "are found in their perfect state in the clefts of rocks, in the sides of mountains, or in the channels of rivers They were accordingly first known and applied to use. But the gross and stubborn ore of iron, the most serviceable of all metals, and to which man is most indebted, must twice feel the force of fire, and go through two laborious processes, before it becomes fit for use " Says Lucretius

" *Sed prius æris erat, quam ferri cognitus usus* '

23

It was the difficulty of obtaining iron from the ores, or the possession of the art of so tempering or hardening copper as to make it answer most of the purposes to which steel is now applied, one or both, that perpetuated the use of bronze instruments in Egypt, as well as in Greece and Rome, long after those nations became acquainted with the former metal.

It may be regarded as certain, that the American aborigines, at the period of the Discovery, were in ignorance of the uses of iron  It is true Vespucius mentions a tribe of natives near the mouth of the La Plata, in South America, who possessed iron points to their arrows  It was probably obtained from native masses in that vicinity  The inhabitants of Madagascar obtain a part of their iron from such sources *  A late traveller in Chile observes  "It appears that the Indians of Chile had, at the time of their discovery, in some very rare instances, iron blades to their lances ; which led to the erroneous supposition that they were so far advanced in metallurgy as to be able to reduce and refine that metal from the ores  Our surprise will cease upon recollecting that this valuable metal already existed naturally in South America, in the very extensive deposits of native iron at *Santiago del Estero*, which has proved to be of meteoric origin, and differing from that at Zacatecas and Durango in Mexico, described by Humboldt, in the absence of earthy matter, and in not being, like them, in round masses, but in a horizontal bed of considerable extent and variable thickness, now for the most part covered with drifting sand, and resting on a bed of the same material "—(*Mier's Travels in Chile, etc*, Vol. II, p 464 ) Copper, on the other hand, seems to have been very abundant, and much used for implements, among all the semi-civilized nations of the continent  Columbus, when at Cape Honduras, was visited by a trading canoe of Indians  Amongst the various articles of merchandise which constituted their cargo, were " small hatchets, made of copper, to hew wood, small bells and plates, crucibles to melt copper,

---

* *Lieut B C Flagg, Trans Am Association, 6th Meeting*, p 40  It is unnecessary to remark, that all accounts of the discovery of iron in the mounds, or under such circumstances as to imply a date prior to the Discovery, are sufficiently vague and unsatisfactory  The fragment of an iron wedge, found in a rock near Salem, Washington County, Ohio, and which has been alluded to by several writers upon American antiquities, does not probably possess an antiquity of more than fifty years  It is now in the possession of Dr S P Hildreth, of Marietta , and its history, stripped of all that is not well authenticated, is simply that it was found fastened in the cleft of a rock, and no one could tell how it came there!  The author of the paper on American antiquities, in the first volume of the Archæologia Americana, states that, in a mound at Circleville Ohio, was found amongst other articles "a plate of iron which had become an oxyde , but before it was disturbed by the spade, resembled a plate of cast iron  (*Archæol Am* , Vol I , p 178 )  It is obviously no easy matter to detect iron when fully oxydized in the earth , and when we are obliged to base our conclusions respecting the use of that metal, by an evidently rude people, upon such remains, if any there be, the strictest examination should be given them , appearances alone should be disregarded, and conclusions after all, drawn with extreme caution  Whether it is likely the requisite discrimination and judgment were exercised in this case, it is not undertaken to say  But few masses of native iron, and these of small size and meteoric origin, have been found in this country , consequently the presence of iron to any extent amongst the mound-builders, can be accounted for only on the assumption that they understood the difficult art of reducing it from the ores, which involves a degree of knowledge, and an advance in the arts of civilization, not attained by the Mexicans nor by the Peruvians, and not sustained by the authenticated remains of the mounds

etc."—(*Herrara*, Vol. I., p. 260.) When the Spaniards first entered the province of Tuspan, they found the Indians in possession of an abundance of copper axes, which, in their greediness, they mistook for gold, and were much mortified upon discovering their mistake. "Each Indian," says Bernal Diaz, "had, besides his ornaments of gold, a copper axe, which was very highly polished, with the handle curiously carved, as if to serve equally for an ornament as for the field of battle. We first thought these axes were made of an inferior kind of gold; we therefore commenced taking them in exchange, and in the space of two days had collected more than six hundred; with which we were no less rejoiced, as long as we were ignorant of their real value, than the Indians with our glass beads." In the list of articles exacted as an annual tribute from the various departments of the Mexican empire, as represented by the Mexican paintings, were "one hundred and sixty axes of copper" from the southern divisions.

Fig. 54 is copied from the tribute tables, and illustrates the form of the axes required to be paid to the emperor. This seems to have been the usual form, which, however, was sometimes slightly modified, so as to give them a broader cutting edge. The following example, Figs. 55 and 56, are drawings of originals obtained by Du Paix, and published among the plates of his antiquarian tour. They are engraved of one fourth their actual size.

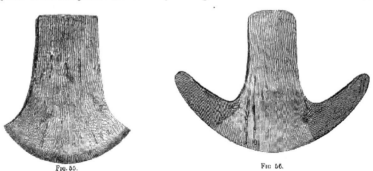

Fig. 55.        Fig. 56.

They were part of a deposit of two hundred and seventy-six, of like character, found buried in two large earthen vases, in the vicinity of Oxaca, and are of alloyed copper, and cast. "Such," says Du Paix, "are much sought by the silversmiths, on account of their fine alloy."

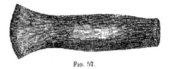

Fig. 57.

Fig. 57 is a chisel, of similar composition, found in the vicinity of Mexico, and also figured by Du Paix. It is engraved *one fourth* of the original size.

The methods in which these axes were used are well shown in the subjoined cuts, faithfully copied from the Mexican paintings, Figs 58 and 59   They require

Fig 58                    Fig 59                    Fig 60

no explanation beyond what is furnished by Clavigero, who says ·  " The Mexicans made use of an axe to cut trees, which was also made of copper, and was of the same form as those of modern times, except that we put the handle in an eye of the axe, while they put the axe in an eye of the handle"   Fig 60 is copied from the Mendoza Paintings, and represents a carpenter using one of these axes, or one very similar, adjusted, probably, so as to answer the purpose of an adze.

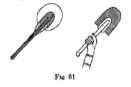

Fig 61

In the Mexican battle paintings, we occasionally observe weapons, the blades of which were of copper, as is shown by their green color, and which were used something after the manner of the battle-axe.   Examples are here given, Fig. 81.

But although copper was used for such purposes, it does not appear that it entirely substituted itself for stone, for stone axes, and weapons formed by inserting blades of obsidian or *itzli* in solid pieces of wood, were common as late as the period of the Spanish conquest.   The instrument this formed was called *mahquahuitl*, and was much dreaded by the Spaniards, who told wonderful stories of their efficiency, affirming that a single stroke was sufficient to cut a man through the middle, or decapitate

Fig 62                    Fig 63                    Fig 64

a horse   Figs 62 and 63 are examples from the paintings, and Fig 64 is copied from the monuments at Chichen Itza, in Yucatan   The latter represents an axe, or rather, weapon of war, made by inserting blades of obsidian in a handle of wood, as above described.   It will be seen by reference to Vol I., p. 211, of these Contributions, that there is reason to believe that an entirely corresponding practice prevailed amongst the mound-builders.   The device is an extremely simple one, and seems to have been common to many rude nations

The copper axes of ancient Egypt closely resembled those above described, both in form and the mode of attachment to the handle   The accompanying illustration, Fig 65, reduced from one of Visconti's plates, represents one of unique

Fig 65

and ornamental workmanship   It will be observed that it is also lashed to the handle with thongs: differing from the primitive American axe, only in the manner of insertion   In this instance the broad end of the tool is sunk in the wood

The Mexicans also used copper to point their spears and arrows, although here obsidian was often substituted   Fig 66 is a representation of a short javelin, which we find of frequent occurrence in the paintings, and which seems to have been used only in close combat.   The long javelin, or that which was thrown from the hand, is well shown in Fig 67, which exhibits the

Fig 66

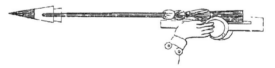

Fig 67

manner in which it was thrown, and also the *xuatlatl*, or instrument used in throwing it, and by means of which it was sent with greater accuracy and force than could otherwise be attained   The gods are almost always represented, in the mythological paintings, holding the *xuatlatl* in their hands.   It is often fancifully ornamented with tassels and feathers

The Peruvians used copper for precisely the same purposes with the Mexicans. Says La Vega, "They make their arms, knives, carpenters' tools, large pins, hammers for their forges, and their mattocks, of copper ; for which reason they seek it in preference to gold"   And Ulloa adds, "The copper axes of the Peruvians differ very little in shape from ours ; and it appears that these were the implements with which they performed most of their works   They are of various shapes and sizes; the edge of some is more circular than others, and some have a concave edge."—(Vol I, p 483.)

The knowledge of alloying was possessed by both the Mexicans and Peruvians, whereby they were enabled to make instruments of copper of sufficient hardness to answer the purposes for which steel is now deemed essential. Their works in stone and wood, whether in dressing the huge blocks of porphyry composing some of their structures, or in sculpturing the unique statues which are found scattered over the seats of their ancient cities, were carried on entirely with such instruments, or with still ruder ones of obsidian and other hard stones

The metal used as an alloy was tin; and the various Peruvian articles subjected to an analysis, are found to contain from three to six per cent of that metal. The chisel analyzed by Humboldt contained copper 94, tin 6.—(*Res.*, Vol. I, p 260.)

Figure 68 is a reduced sketch of a copper knife found in Peru, by J H Blake, Esq, of Boston. It has about four per cent of tin  This gentleman informs me, that "The knives, gravers, and other implements found by myself in Peru, contain from three and a half to four per cent. of tin, which is sufficient to give them a very considerable degree of hardness.* The knives which I send you were found about the person of a mummy which I took from an ancient cemetery near Arico. Various household articles were found

Fig 68

with it, but these were the only ones of metal, except a medal of silver suspended around the neck. The chisels or gravers are pointed at one end, with a cutting edge at the broad part  They were found at various places in the northern part of Peru  At the ancient city of Atacama, I found several hoes of copper, shaped very much like the 'grubbing-hoes' to be found in our warehouses."

Figure 69 is a reduced sketch of an ancient Peruvian spear-head, of copper,

Fig. 69

found in a Peruvian *huaca* or tumulus, near Lima, whence it was brought by the late Dr. Marmaduke Burroughs, in 1826, and by him presented to Dr S G Morton, of Philadelphia, in whose possession it now is  It is somewhat flattened, and regularly four-sided from the point to within a third of the distance from the larger end, where it becomes cylindrical  This part is hollow, for the reception of the handle.  The metal is not hardened, and is now covered with a green oxyde  The

* The Indians of Chile, previous to the discovery by the Spaniards, made use of a kind of *bronze metal*, found native in the country, which is an alloy of copper zinc, and antimony, called *campañil* by the Spaniards  From this they formed their cutting instruments —(*Mier s Trav*, Vol II, p 464.)

length of the weapon is seventeen inches, and the diameter, at the larger end, one
inch and one-tenth

Figure 70 is a full-size engraving of one of the arrow-points discovered with a
skeleton, near Fall River, Massachusetts, in the year 1831   With this skeleton
were found a corroded plate of brass, supposed to have constituted a breastplate,

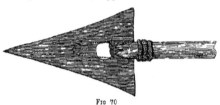

Fig 70

and a number of rude tubes of the same metal, composing a sort of belt or cinc-
ture   The arrow-points are two inches in length, and one and one-third inches broad
at the base   This skeleton attracted a good deal of attention at the time, and was
supposed to lend some sanction to the then popular theory of the early discovery
and settlement of the coast of New England by the Northmen   An analysis of the
compound metal of which the relics were composed, was made by Berzelius, under
the direction of the Royal Society of Antiquaries of Denmark   The result of the
analysis was published by that learned body, in the following comparative table

|  | Copper | Zinc | Tin | Lead | Iron |
|---|---|---|---|---|---|
| Brass from Fall River, | 70 29 | 28 03 | 0 91 | 0 74 | 0 03 |
| Old Danish, | 67 13 | 20 39 | 9 24 | 3 39 | 0 11 |
| Modern Brass, | 70 16 | 27 45 | 0 79 | 0 20 | —— |

It will be seen by the table, that the metallic relics found at  Fall River bear in
their composition a suspicious resemblance to modern brass.   They certainly differ
widely, in this respect, from any of the alloys of copper found elsewhere on the
continent   Without alluding to the rudeness of the workmanship exhibited by the
Fall River relics,—a rudeness entirely inconsistent with that stage of advancement
indicated by a knowledge of smelting and alloying the metals,—the fact that the
skeleton accompanying them was found buried, after the Indian mode, in a sitting
posture, and enveloped in bark, places in a very strong light the probability that
the burial was made subsequent to the first settlement of New England, in 1625,
and that the relics were of native manufacture, from sheets or plates of brass
obtained from the early colonists   This probability is further sustained, by the
circumstance that a portion of the wood attached to the arrows was still preserved,
as was also a large proportion of the bark envelope of the skeleton, at the time of
its discovery ,  which could hardly be the case, if its interment had been made as
early as the tenth century, which is the period assigned to the Scandinavian visits
It cannot be claimed that the preservative properties of the salts of the copper
could have more than a very local application or influence

And while upon this point, it may be mentioned that Wood, in his " New England

Prospect," published in 1634, (p. 90,) distinctly states that the Indians obtained brass of the English for their ornaments and arrow-heads, the last of which, he adds, "*they cut in the shape of a heart and triangle, and fastened in a slender piece of wood, six or eight inches long*"—in a manner, according to the description, precisely similar to that observed in the articles found with the Fall River skeleton.  If any further evidence were needed to establish the opinions already advanced, it might be found in the fact that, a few years ago, in the town of Medford, near Boston, in

Massachusetts, a skeleton was exhumed, accompanying which were found some flint arrow-heads, and some brass arrow-points, *identical* with those discovered at Fall River, together with a *knife of the English manufacture* of two hundred years ago  Fig 71 is a full-sized engraving of the arrow-point in question, which is now in the possession of the author

It has already been suggested that the shore of Lake Superior is the probable locality whence the copper used by the aborigines of, at least, the Eastern and Middle States was obtained  This

Fig 71          suggestion is rendered more than probable by the fact that abundant traces of aboriginal mining have been discovered there in the course of recent explorations.  Some of the more productive veins in the " Copper Region " seem to have been anciently worked to a considerable extent.  The vein belonging to the " Minnesota Company " exhibits evidence of having been worked for a distance of two miles   The ancient operations are indicated by depressions or open cuts on the course of the vein  Upon excavating these, ample proofs of their artificial origin are discovered, consisting of broken implements of various kinds, stone axes, hammers, etc.  Traces of fire are also frequent   Some of the excavations are found to have extended to the depth of thirty feet   In the mine of the particular company above named, covered by fifteen feet of accumulated soil, and beneath trees not less than four hundred years old, was found a mass of pure copper, weighing 11,537 lbs., from which every particle of the rock had been removed.  It had been supported by *skids*, and was surrounded by traces of the fire which had probably been used to disengage the rock     Here, too, were found various rude implements of copper

At the Copper Falls and Eagle River, as at the Vulcan and other mines, the ancient shafts are frequently discovered.  Professor W  W  Mather, the eminent geologist, in a private letter, referring to the two mines first named, says .  " On a hill, south of the Copper Falls Mine, is an excavation, several feet in depth and several rods in length, extending along the course of the river  Fragments of rock, etc., thrown out of the excavation, are piled up along its sides, the whole covered with soil, and overgrown with bushes and trees   On removing the accumulations from the excavation, stone axes of large size, made of green-stone, and shaped to receive withe handles, are found   Some large round green-stone masses, that had apparently been used for sledges, were also found.  They had round holes bored in them to the depth of several inches, which seemed to have been designed for wooden plugs, to which withe handles might be attached, so that several men could swing them with sufficient force to break the rock and the projecting masses of copper. Some of them were broken, and some of the projecting ends of rock exhibited marks of having been battered in the manner here suggested"

The great Ontonagon mass of virgin copper, now deposited at Washington, when found, exhibited marks of having had considerable portions cut from it, and the ground around it was strewed with fragments of stone axes, which had been broken in endeavors to detach portions of the mass. It is not impossible that this mass was one of those which had been brought to the surface by the ancient miners [*]

The questions naturally arise, By whom were these ancient mining operations carried on? and to what era may they be referred? Without noticing the improbable suggestion, that the various excavations which have been discovered are due to the French, (who, it is well known, were early acquainted with the mineral riches of the Northwest,) we may find a satisfactory answer to the first of these questions, if not to the last, in the character of the deposits which recent explorations have disclosed from the mounds of the West. Among the multitude of relics of art found buried upon the ancient altars, or beside the bones of the dead, articles of copper are of common occurrence. It is sometimes found in native masses, but generally worked into articles of use or ornament. I have taken from the mounds axes, well wrought from single pieces, weighing upwards of two pounds each. They are symmetrical, corresponding very nearly in shape with the Mexican and Peruvian axes. Some are double-bladed, others *gouge-shaped*, and evidently designed to be used as adzes. Beside these, chisels, graving tools, and a great variety of ornaments, bracelets, gorgets, beads, etc., etc., composed of this metal, have been discovered. Some of the ornaments are covered with silver, beaten to great thinness, and so closely *wrapped around* the copper that many persons have supposed that the ancient people understood the difficult art of plating.

Some years ago, a mass of native copper, weighing upwards of twenty pounds, was found upon the banks of the Scioto River, near Chilicothe, in Ohio. Large portions had evidently been cut from it. The discovery of these native masses, not to mention the amount of the manufactured copper, implying a large original supply, points pretty certainly to the shores of Lake Superior as the locality whence the

---

[*] Since the above was written, the subjoined additional facts have been published in the Lake Superior Journal newspaper, of the date of September 25, 1850.

"We have been shown by Charles Whittlesey, Esq., of the Ontonagon Mine, a copper arrow-head, and a piece of human skull and other bones, which have lately been found in the ancient Indian excavations on the Ontonagon River. The arrow-head is now about two inches in length, and seems to have had originally a socket, though but part of it remains. Several chisels or instruments resembling chisels, having sockets like the common carpenter's chisel, and small gads or wedges, have also been found at the Minnesota Mine.

But the greatest curiosity we have seen in the way of these articles is a stick of oak timber lately taken out of one of the ancient 'pits,' or shafts, at the Minnesota Mine, twenty-seven feet below the surface. It is a small tree, about ten feet in length, and eight or ten inches in diameter, having short limbs two feet apart, and at nearly right angles with one another, and on this account, and from its standing nearly upright, it is supposed to have been used as a ladder by the ancient miners. In this shaft, and around and over this stick, were rocks and earth, and large trees were growing over it. Many centuries must have elapsed since that ancient ladder was placed there."

24

metal was obtained    There are other circumstances, still more conclusive, and which, taken in connection with the traces of ancient mining in the mineral region, leave no room to doubt that the race of the mounds obtained their supplies of copper from that direction.  It is well known that while some of the Lake Superior copper is almost perfectly pure, a part is alloyed with silver in various proportions, and some is found having crystals of silver attached to it,—a peculiar *mechanico-chemical combination*, known to exist nowhere except in this region    This characteristic combination has been observed in some of the specimens, both worked and unworked, found in the mounds, and enables us to identify fully their primitive locality    The great industry and skill which the mound-builders displayed in the numerous and often gigantic monuments which they have left us at the West, warrant us in ascribing the ancient excavations, etc., in the mineral region to them    The Indian hunter is proverbially averse to labor, and we have no instance of the Indians undertaking works of this extent    Still, it cannot be doubted that they also obtained copper from this region    Indeed, we have direct evidence of the fact ; but it is probable that they procured it only in small quantities, when it was found exposed at the surface, or on the banks of streams    Alexander Henry, who penetrated to Lake Superior at the period of the second French war, assures us that the Indians obtained copper here, which they "made into bracelets, spoons," etc.—(*Travels*, p. 195.)  As we have seen, the early explorers on the coasts of New England, New York, Virginia, the Carolinas, and Florida, among whom we may mention Hudson, Verrazano, Raleigh, Heriot, Ribaude, De Soto, all concur in saying that the Indians had copper in small quantities among them, which they worked into pipes and ornaments    De Soto found copper hatchets among some of the tribes along the Gulf, which they professed to have obtained from "a province called *Chisca*, far toward the North."

All the copper found in the mounds appears to have been worked in a cold state, and although the axes and other instruments appear to be harder than the copper of commerce, they have been found, upon analysis, to be destitute of alloy.   The superior hardness which they possess over the unworked metal, is doubtless due to the *hammering* to which they have been subjected    Some of the sculptures in porphyry, and other hard stones found in the mounds, exhibit traces of having been *cut*, but as they now turn the edge of the best tempered knife, we are at a loss to conjecture how they were so elaborately and delicately worked.   The lack of cutting implements, among most rude people, is partially met by various contrivances, the most common of which is attrition, or rubbing or grinding on hard stones    It was thus the stone axes, etc, of the early Indians were slowly and laboriously brought into shape.   It however needs but a single glance at the mound sculptures to convince the observer that such rude means are wholly inadequate to the production of works possessing so much delicacy of execution

The Mexicans and Peruvians were wholly unacquainted with the use of iron ; and their carvings, etc., were all wrought with copper tools    They, however, contrived to harden them with an alloy of from three to seven per cent of tin. I have some of their implements in my possession, which answer a very good cutting purpose    It nevertheless seems incomprehensible how then extensive works in granite, porphyry, and other obstinate materials, could be carried on with such aids. The Egyptians, although not ignorant of iron, were compelled, by a variety of circumstances, to use copper tools, and with these most of their gigantic labors were effected. They must of necessity have had some means of hardening the metals, yet it is a singular fact, that, with the exception of a few bronze weapons of probably a comparatively late date, the chisels and other implements found in the monuments and at the quarries are *pure copper*

USE OF SILVER BY THE AMERICAN ABORIGINES —Granville, as we have seen in the quotation from his voyage on page 177, speaks of finding pieces of silver amongst the Virginia Indians, "grossly beaten," and used for purposes of ornament. Having shown that the copper found amongst the Indian tribes of the north was probably obtained from the native deposits around Lake Superior, we have little difficulty in accounting for the presence among them of small quantities of silver, derived from the same locality, where it also exists in a native form. That the silver in use amongst the mound-builders was principally if not wholly obtained there, seems incontestible. In no instance does it appear to have been smelted.

A variety of silver ornaments were discovered some years ago in one of the mounds at Marietta, Ohio, under very singular circumstances, and in a remarkable connection. The circumstances have been detailed by the accurate pen of Dr S. P HILDRETH, in a communication to the President of the American Antiquarian Society, dated "Marietta, Nov 3, 1819"

"In removing the earth composing an ancient mound in the streets of Marietta, on the margin of the plain, near the fortifications, several curious articles were discovered. They appear to have been buried with the body of the person to whose memory the mound was erected

"Lying immediately over, or on the forehead of the body, were found three large circular bosses or ornaments for a sword-belt or a buckler. they are composed of copper overlaid with a thick plate of silver. The fronts are slightly convex, with a depression like a cup in the centre, and measure two inches and a quarter across the face of each. On the back side, opposite the depressed portion, is a copper rivet or nail, around which are two separate plates, by which they were fastened to the leather. Two small pieces of the leather were found lying between the plates of one of these bosses, they resemble the skin of a mummy, and seem to have been preserved by the salts of copper. The copper plates are nearly reduced to an oxyde, or rust. The silver looks quite black, but is not much corroded, and in rubbing is quite brilliant. Two of these are yet entire, the third one is so much wasted that it dropped in pieces in removing it from the earth. Around the rivets of one of them is a small quantity of flax or hemp, in a tolerable state of preservation. Near the side of the body was found a plate of silver, which appears to have been the upper part of a sword-scabbard, it is six inches in length and two inches in breadth, and weighs one ounce. It has no ornaments or figures, but has three longitudinal ridges, which probably corresponded with the edges or ridges of the sword, it seems to have been fastened to the scabbard by three or four rivets, the holes of which remain in the silver

"Two or three broken pieces of a copper tube were also found, *filled with iron rust*. These pieces, from their appearance, composed the lower end of the scabbard, near the point of the sword. No signs of the sword itself were discovered, except the appearance of rust above mentioned. Near the feet was found a piece of copper weighing three ounces [now in the Museum of the Antiquarian Society of Worcester]. From its shape it appears to have been used as a *plumb*, or for an ornament, as near one of the ends is a circular crease or groove, for tying a thread. it is round, two inches and a half in length, one inch in diameter at the centre, and half an inch at each end. It is composed of small pieces of native copper pounded together, and in the cracks between the pieces are stuck several pieces of silver, one nearly the size of a half-dime. A piece of red ochre or paint, and a piece of iron ore [*hematite*] which had the appearance of having been partially vitrified [*polished ?*], were also found

"The body of the person here buried was laid upon the surface of the ground, with his face upwards, and his feet pointing to the southwest  From the appearance of several pieces of charcoal and bits of partially burned fossil coal, and the black color of the earth, it would seem that the funeral obsequies had been celebrated by fire  and while the ashes were yet hot and smoking, a circle of these flat stones had been laid around and over the body  The circular covering was about eight feet in diameter , and the stones yet look black, as if stained by fire and smoke  This circle of stones seems to have been the nucleus over which the mound was formed, as immediately over them is heaped the common earth of the adjacent plain  At the time of opening it i, the height was 6 feet, and diameter between 30 and 40   It has every appearance of being as old as any in the neighborhood, and was, at the first settlement of Marietta, covered with large trees  It seems to have been made for this single personage, as the remains of one skeleton only were discovered   The bones were much decayed, and many of them crumbled to dust on exposure to the air "

Engravings of the silver-plated discs and also of the embossed silver plate sup-

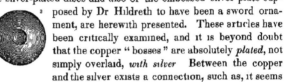

posed by Dr Hildreth to have been a sword orna- ment, are herewith presented.  These articles have been critically examined, and it is beyond doubt that the copper " bosses " are absolutely *plated*, not simply overlaid, *with silver*   Between the copper and the silver exists a connection, such as, it seems to me, could only be produced by heat; and if it is admitted that these are genuine remains of the mound-builders, it must, at the same time, be admitted that they possessed the difficult art of

FIG 72       plating one metal upon another.   There is but one alternative, viz , that they had occasional or constant intercourse with a people advanced in the arts  from whom these articles were obtained   Again, if Dr Hildreth is not mistaken, *oxydized iron*, or steel, was also discovered in connection with the above remains , from which also follows, as a necessity upon the previous assumption, the extraordinary conclusion that the *mound-builders were acquainted with the use of iron*,—the conclusion being, of course, subject to the improbable alternative already mentioned,

Leading, therefore, as they do, to such extraordinary conclusions, it is of the utmost importance that every fact and circumstance connected with these remains should be narrowly examined   If there is a reasonable way of accounting for their presence, under the circumstances above described, without involving us in these conclusions, unsustained as they are by collateral facts, we are justified upon every recognised rule of evidence in adopting it as the nearest approximation to the truth

The existing tribes of Indians, it has been demonstrated, recently and remotely, often buried in the mounds, placing the arms and ornaments, in short, whatever was valued by the possessor while living, in the grave with him at his death.   It has been shown that in some instances they opened the mounds to the depth of six or seven feet, and buried at or below their bases,—(*Ancient Monuments of the Mississippi Valley*, pp 146, 147, 149.)   It has been shown, also, that partial burial by fire was occasionally practised by them, or by races succeeding the builders of the mounds.   That it was a common custom among the Indians to cover their dead with stones, is also well known   The occurence of these remains in the position above described, does not, therefore, necessarily establish that they be- longed to the race of the mounds.

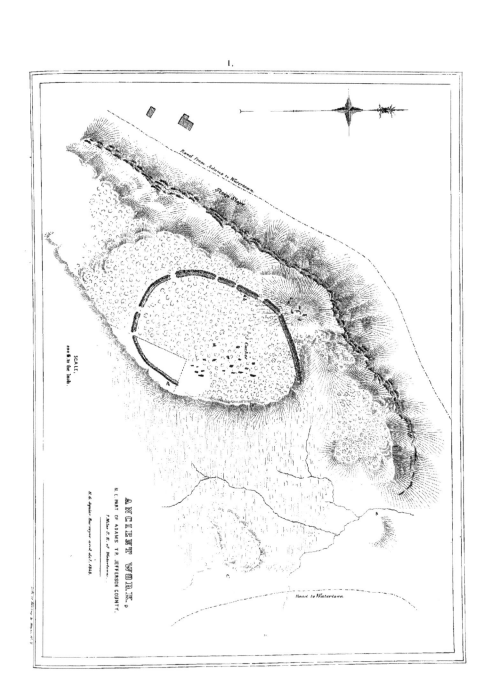

ANCIENT WORK.

N.E. PART OF ADAMS T.P. JEFFERSON COUNTY.

3 Miles S.E. of Watertown.

E.G. Squier Surveyor and del: 1848.

SCALE.
200 ft to the inch.

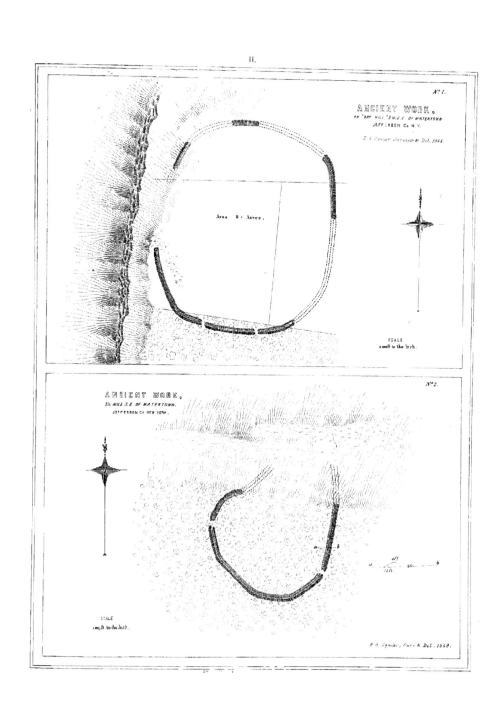

No. 1.

ANCIENT WORK,
on "DRY HILL" 3 M.S.E. OF WATERTOWN
JEFFERSON Co N.Y.

E. G. Squier, Surveyor &c Dec. 1848.

Area 8 · Acres.

SCALE
x c=ft to the Inch.

ANCIENT WORK,
3¼ MILE S.E. OF WATERTOWN,
JEFFERSON Co NEW YORK.

No. 2.

SCALE
100, ft. to the Inch.

E. G. Squier, Surv. &c Dec. 1848.

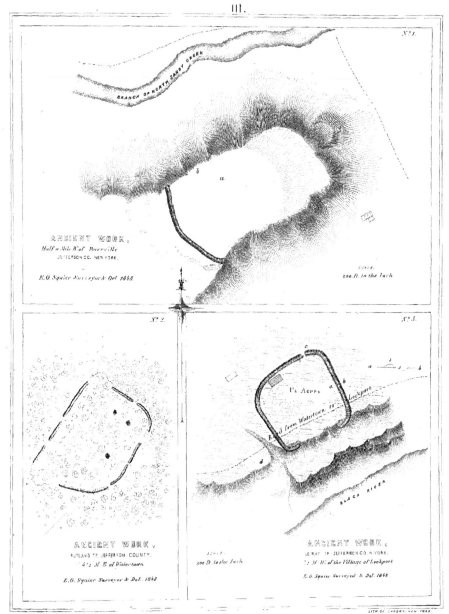

No. 1.

BRANCH OF NORTH SANDY CREEK

ANCIENT WORK,
Half a Mile W. of Burrville
JEFFERSON CO. NEW YORK.

E. G. Squier Surveyor & Del. 1848.

SCALE.
200 ft. to the Inch.

No. 2.

ANCIENT WORK,
RUTLAND TP. JEFFERSON COUNTY.
4½ M. E of Watertown.

E. G. Squier Surveyor & Del. 1848.

No. 3.

1¼ Acres

Lockport

Road from Watertown. 10.

ANCIENT WORK,
LE RAY TP. JEFFERSON CO. N. YORK.
½ M. W. of the Village of Lockport.

E. G. Squier Surveyed & Del. 1848.

SCALE.
200 ft. to the Inch.

BLACK RIVER.

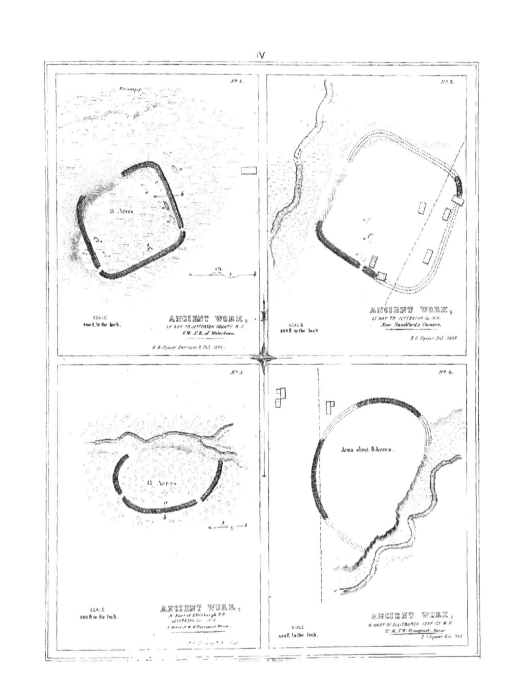

Nº 1.

Swampy

11 Acres

a 5 b

SCALE
200 ft. to the Inch.

ANCIENT WORK,
LE RAY TP. JEFFERSON COUNTY N.Y.
6 M. N.E. of Watertown.

E.G. Squier Surveyer & Del. 1848.

Nº 2.

ANCIENT WORK,
LE RAY TP. JEFFERSON Co. N.Y.
Near Sandford's Corners.

SCALE
200 ft to the Inch

E.G. Squier Del. 1848.

Nº 3.

11 Acres

a 5 b

SCALE
200 ft to the Inch.

ANCIENT WORK,
N. Part of Ellisburgh TP.
JEFFERSON Co. N.Y.
3 Miles N.W. of Pierrepont Manor.

Nº 4.

Area about 8 Acres.

SCALE
200 ft. to the Inch.

ANCIENT WORK,
N. PART OF ELLISBURGH JEFF Co. N.Y.
3 M. N.W. Pierrepont Manor.

E.G. Squier Del. 1848.

V.

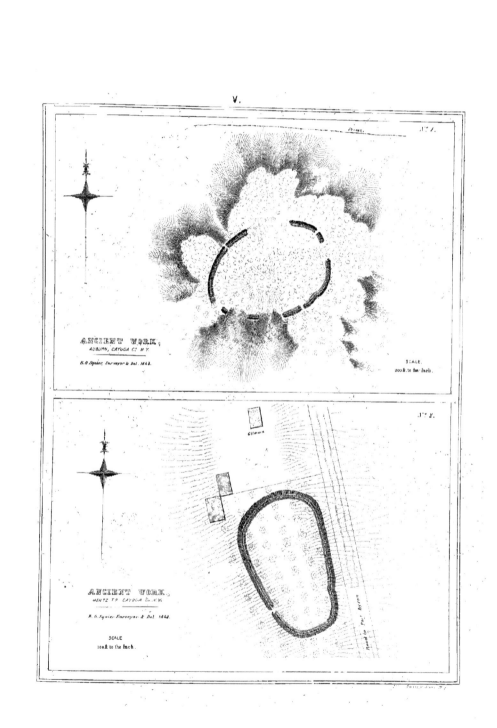

N.º I.

ANCIENT WORK,
AUBURN, CAYUGA C.º N.Y.

E. G. Squier, Surveyor & Del. 1848.

SCALE.
200 ft. to the Inch.

N.º V.

Gilman

ANCIENT WORK,
MENTZ T.P. CAYUGA C.º N.Y.

E. G. Squier, Surveyor & Del. 1848.

SCALE
100 ft. to the Inch.

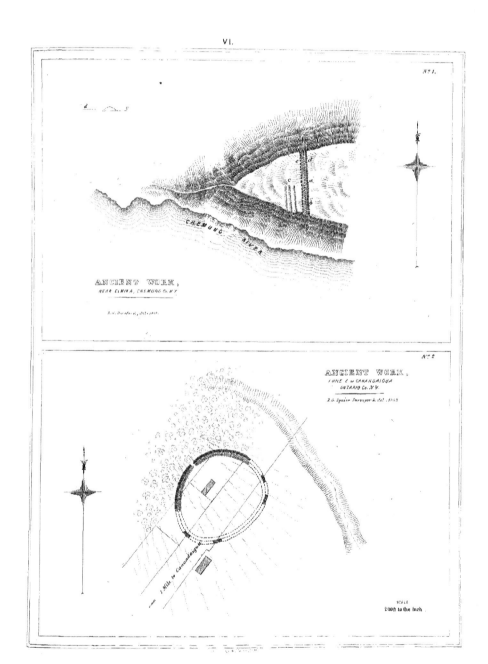

N.º 1.

ANCIENT WORK,
NEAR ELMIRA, CHEMUNG Co. N.Y.

N.º 2

ANCIENT WORK,
1 MILE E. OF CANANDAIGUA
ONTARIO Co. N.Y.

E. G. Squier Surveyor & del. 1848.

SCALE
200 ft to the inch.

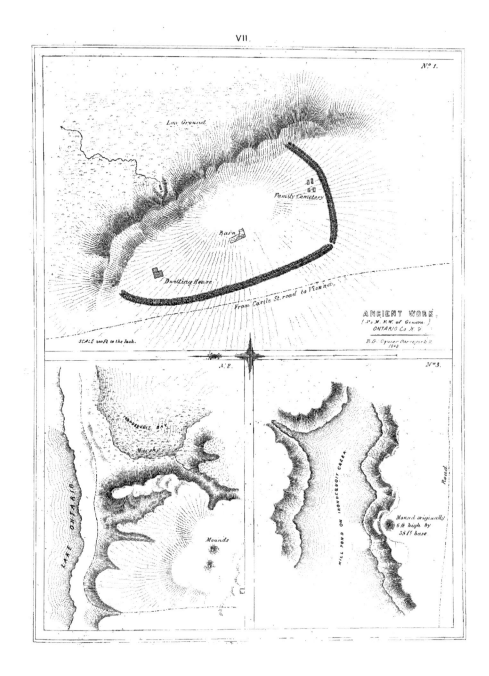

Nº 1.

Low Ground

Family Cemetery

Barn

Dwelling House

From Castle St. road to Vienna.

ANCIENT WORK,
( P¹. W. N.W. of Geneva )
ONTARIO Co. N. Y.

E. G. Squier Surveyor & P.
1848

SCALE 100 ft to the Inch.

Nº 2.

IRONDEQUOIT BAY

Marsh

LAKE ONTARIO

Mounds

Nº 3.

MILL POND ON IRONDEQUOIT CREEK.

Road.

Mound originally
6 ft high by
35 ft base.

IX.

ANCIENT WORK,
New Buffalo, Erie Co. N.Y.

E. G. Squier Surveyor & Del. 1848.

Quarry

Mission House

Road

Area about 4 Acres

Graves

Gentle Slope

Swamp Ground

REFERENCE
a. Grave of Red Jacket
b. " Mary Jemison
c. Depression, natural.

SCALE
200 ft to the Inch

N°. 2

Little Buffalo Creek
1½ of Mile nearly

ANCIENT WORK,
LANCASTER TP. ERIE CO. NEW YORK.

E. G. Squier Surveyor & Del. 1848.

SCALE
200 ft. to the Inch.

N°. 3

REFERENCE
a Withered pine tree
18 ft. in Circumference
8 ft. from the rock

ANCIENT WORK,
Same Township

E. G. Squier 23 Del. 1848.

SCALE
200 ft. to the Inch.

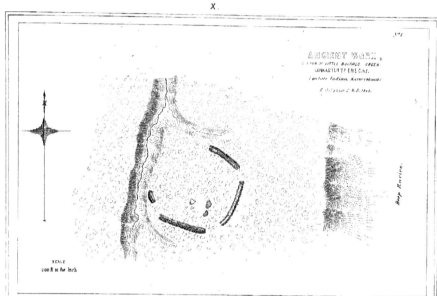

ANCIENT WORK,
ON LITTLE BUFFALO CREEK
LANCASTER TP ERIE C. N.Y.
(on late Indian Reservation.)
E. G. Squier & E. D. 1848.

Deep Ravine.

SCALE
200 ft to the Inch

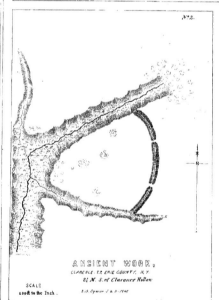

ANCIENT WORK,
CLARENCE, TP. ERIE COUNTY,  N. Y.
2½ M. S. of Clarence Hollow
E. G. Squier S & D. 1848.

SCALE
200 ft to the Inch.

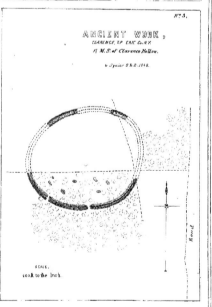

ANCIENT WORK,
CLARENCE, TP. ERIE Co. N.Y.
1½ M. S. of Clarence Hollow.

to Squier S & D. 1848.

Road

SCALE,
100 ft to the Inch.

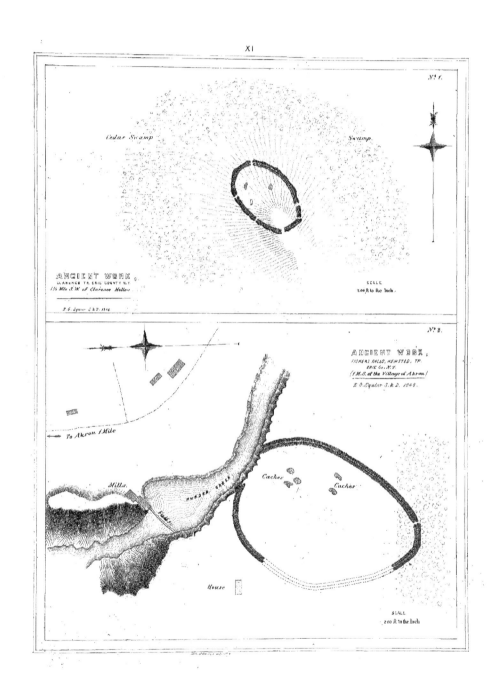

## XI

N.º 1.

*Cedar Swamp*                    *Swamp.*

ANCIENT WORK,
CLARENCE TP. ERIE COUNTY N.Y.
1¼ Mile S.W. of Clarence Hollow

SCALE
200 ft to the Inch

E.G. Squier S.&D. 1848

N.º 2.

ANCIENT WORK,
FISHERS FALLS, NEWSTED, TP.
ERIE Co., N.Y.
(1 M.S. of the Village of Akron)

E.G. Squier S.&D. 1848.

← To Akron 1 Mile

*Mills.*

MURDER CREEK

*Caches*          *Caches*

*House*

SCALE
200 ft to the Inch

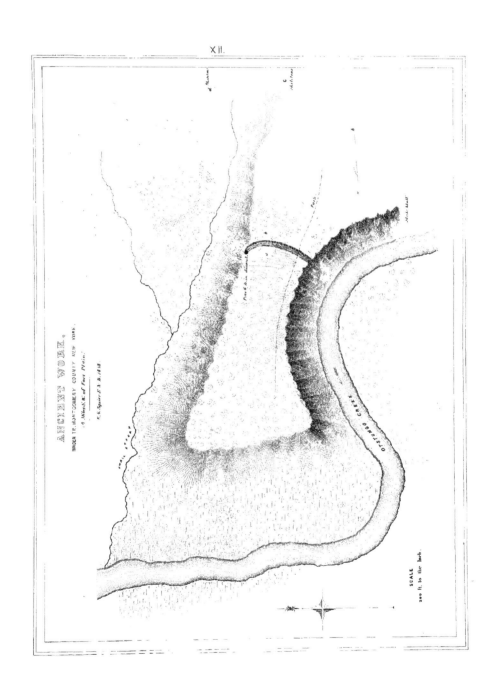

## XII

ANCIENT WORK.

MINDEN TP. MONTGOMERY COUNTY NEW YORK.

(A 1/4 mile N.W. of Fort Plain.)

E. G. Squier & E. H. Davis

OTSTUNGO CREEK

SCALE
200 ft. to the Inch

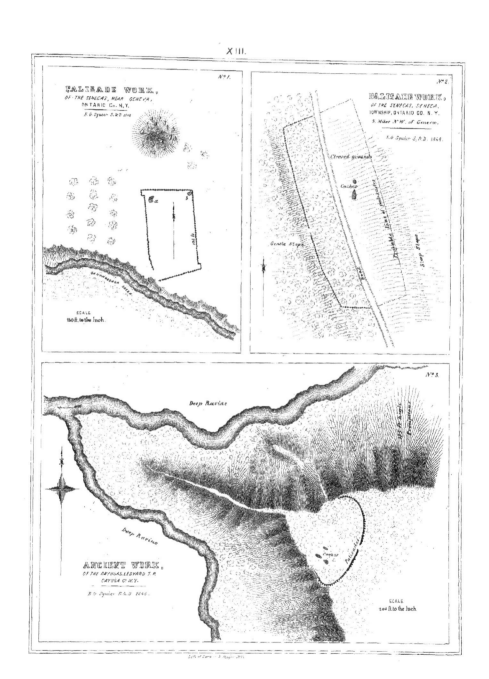

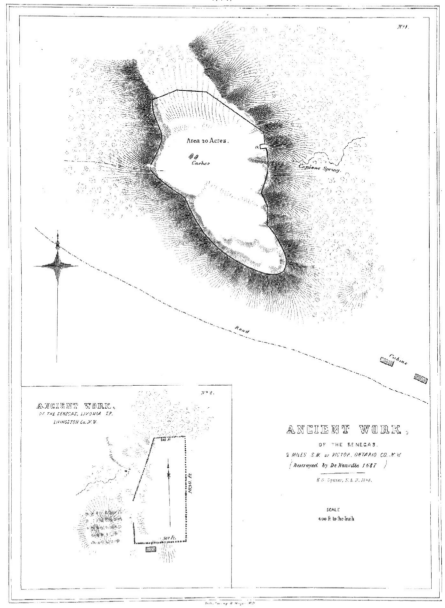

## XIII

No 1.

Area 20 Acres.

Caches

Copious Spring

Road

Cabins

No 2.

ANCIENT WORK,
OF THE SENECAS, LIVONIA T.P.
LIVINGSTON Co. N.Y.

780 Ft.

901 Ft.

ANCIENT WORK,
OF THE SENECAS,
2 MILES S.W. or VICTOR, ONTARIO CO. N.Y.
(Destroyed by De Nonville 1687)

E. G. Squier, N.H.D. 1848.

SCALE
400 ft to the Inch